INSIGHT ON THE
MIDDLE EAST WAR

INSIGHT ON THE
MIDDLE

EAST WAR

by the
**INSIGHT
TEAM**
of the
Sunday Times

André Deutsch

First published 1974 by
André Deutsch Limited
105 Great Russell Street London WC1
Copyright © 1974 by
Times Newspapers Limited
Printed Photolitho in Great Britain by
Ebenezer Baylis & Son Ltd, The Trinity Press,
Worcester, and London
Paperback ISBN 0 233 96567 X
Hardback ISBN 0 233 96566 1

CONTENTS

PROLOGUE
A bunker by the canal, 9

SECTION I
'No peace, no war' – a failure of diplomacy
The uncloseable gap, 20; Sadat decides on war, 29;
Why Israel didn't guess, 36; The secret preparations,
44; Mrs Meir decides to wait, 54

SECTION II
Week one: the victory that Egypt threw away
The Y-Day onslaught, 62; The citizen army musters, 73;
The Syrian tide rolls on, 77; 'Not our sort of war', 101;
Ismail versus Shazli, 111; Sharon versus Gonen, 120;
The rejected victory, 131

SECTION III
Week two: Israel's big gamble just comes off
The big tank battle, 140; The economics of caution,
149; Battle of Chinese Farm, 159; Enter the oil
weapon, 177

SECTION IV
Week three: the superpowers call it quits
Kissinger cobbles up a truce, 186; The battle of the
ceasefire, 196; Washington's nuclear alert, 202; Plight
of the Third Army, 213

SECTION V
'A question that has nothing to do with you'
The forgotten Palestinians, 222; The problems of
peace, 230

APPENDICES
The tank battle, 239; The missile war, 248

Acknowledgements

This book derives from the extensive coverage of the Arab–Israeli war in the *Sunday Times*, London, during October, 1973. Research into the causes and conduct of the war, however, continued for some time after the ceasefire and the text has been completely rewritten and greatly expanded.

Insight reporters in the Middle East were Peter Kellner in Cairo and Philip Jacobson and Peter Pringle in Tel Aviv. Two former Insight editors, Bruce Page and Lewis Chester, and the present Insight editor John Barry combined to write and edit the book. Research in London was by Parin Janmohamed and Marjorie Wallace. The project was coordinated by Ron Hall.

We depended heavily on the skill and experience of Eric Marsden, the resident *Sunday Times* correspondent in Israel, and many other *Sunday Times* reporters and correspondents made valuable contributions, including: Stephen Aris (New York), John Bonar (Amman), Henry Brandon (Washington), William Dullforce (Cairo), Paul Eddy (Tel Aviv), David Holden (London), Martin Meredith (Cairo and Beirut), Brian Moynahan (Beirut and Damascus), Tony Rocca (Cairo), William Shawcross (New York) and Edmund Stephens (Moscow).

The graphics and maps are by Peter Sullivan, Duncan Mil and John Grimwade, under the art direction of Edwin Taylor. The photographs are mostly by Kelvin Brodie, Bryan Wharton, Frank Herrmann, Sally Soames and Romano Cagnoni, who worked often under dangerous conditions near the front lines.

Special arrangements were made with leading news organizations for particular aspects of the coverage: the BBC monitoring service, Caversham (which provided texts of Middle East radio broadcasts); *Al Ahram*, Cairo (whose distinguished editor, Mohamed Heikal, conducted revealing interviews with General Ismail and Henry Kissinger); *Ma'ariv*, Tel Aviv (which first published a vivid tape recording of the opening of the war, edited in Hebrew by Aaron Dolav); *Ha'aretz*, Tel Aviv (whose authoritative military correspondent Zeev Schiff provided us with valuable commentaries while the war was in progress); the staff of *An Nahar*, Beirut; *Arab Report and Record*; and the *New*

York Times News Service. We used much documentary material compiled by the Department of Defense, Washington. We also drew on news agency material from Reuters, AFP, and AP. Other important sources were the *Jerusalem Post* (which published graphic accounts from the survivors of battle) and *Al Akhbar*, Cairo (which published an important interview with General Shazli, by its editor, Moussa Sabri).

Technical advice was provided by Edward Luttwak whose authoritative study of the Israeli army will be published by Allen Lane later this year, and by Edgar O'Ballance, author of *The Sinai Campaign, 1956*, *The Third Arab–Israeli War*, and other works of contemporary military history. Geoffrey Pardoe, Managing Director of General Technology Systems Ltd, advised on missiles. And Richard Ogorkiewicz of Imperial College, London, author of *Design and Development of Fighting Vehicles*, advised on tank warfare. The responsibility for accuracy, however, remains entirely our own.

We wish also to thank Elizabeth Collard, Rupert Pengelley of *International Defense Review* and Leon Charney, all of whom gave useful help. And also we would wish to thank the many diplomats, government officials and military men who gave us their time, but because of their jobs must remain anonymous. Our printers, Ebenezer Baylis and Son, cheerfully accomodated the Insight Team for two days in their Worcester premises, in order to produce the book in record time.

Finally, and with great sorrow, we must mention our *Sunday Times* colleague, Nicholas Tomalin, who was killed while covering the war on the Golan front. He was one of Britain's most distinguished journalists, and his superb war reporting was only one of his many talents. Before his car was hit by a Syrian missile on October 17, he had filed reports that had guided us with remarkable clarity through the confused events of the first days of fighting. This book is dedicated to him.

London, December 1973

Prologue:
A bunker by the canal

Avi Yaffe had just emerged from the shower and was hanging his clothes out to dry on the barbed wire when the first shells began to fly. A flight of MIGs screamed overhead, and exploding canisters on either side of the canal began to belch clouds of dark green smoke. Through the smokescreen it was just possible to make out commando boats manoeuvring into the water. Avi returned hastily to his post. The fourth Arab–Israeli war had begun. He was signalman in an Israeli bunker beside the Suez Canal. Coming over the water towards him was one of the main thrusts of the Egyptian army.

Avi – short for Abraham – had kissed goodbye to his wife Dassy ust two weeks earlier, leaving her in charge of the recording studio he runs in Jerusalem. As with all able-bodied Israelis of military age, he has to spend thirty-three days each year on duty as an army reservist. This time his unit had been posted to the Bar-Lev line, the string of Israeli forts along the canal, taking over from conscripts who had gone on leave for Jewish New Year and Yom Kippur.

For five days before the attack, Avi's unit – their fort was in the central sector, almost opposite Ismailia – had been aware of unusual activity on the Egyptian bank. On October 1, a convoy of missile trucks had been seen entering Ismailia. The roar of an armoured column could sometimes be heard behind the high sand dunes. Groups of Egyptian officers conferred by the waterfront and a resplendent Lieutenant-General was once seen making a long examination of the scene through the telescopes of a lookout post. Later in the week, a party of Egyptian sappers had arrived to drive stakes in the ground near the water's edge, while bulldozers levelled the approaches. But none of this had created much surprise: elsewhere along the bank the Egyptians had been careful to keep up appearances of normality. Unarmed soldiers sat, as usual, on the bank, dangling their feet in the cool water. Tractors continued their monotonous work of piling up defensive sand dykes. And the regular gardener turned up each day to water the gardens of the long-abandoned villas near Ismailia.

It was around noon on Saturday, October 6, that Avi's unit

became aware of more serious signs of trouble. The soldiers in the forward observation positions reported back that their opposite numbers on the Egyptian side had withdrawn from their posts. The tractors had stopped working and a suspicious silence had fallen over the Egyptian bank. About noon, too, a message from headquarters came via Avi's communications centre: arrange to evacuate two smaller forts to the south. The message was passed to Avi's commander, known to his men as 'Meyerke' (a diminutive of his name Meir), a reservist from a kibbutz near Jerusalem. The evacuated men rolled up in an armoured personnel carrier, bringing the complement of Avi's fort to thirty-three. Minutes later, the first Egyptian shelling began. The time was 2.00 pm.

Avi, with a sense of detachment not uncommon amongst people in extreme danger, now became not only a participant in the drama that followed, but a remarkable observer of it. He had as usual brought along a heap of electronic equipment from his recording studio, including test-gear for better servicing of his army radio sets and a high quality tape recorder plus spools of tape. He had been using the tape machine mainly for playing music to entertain his fellow soldiers during their tedious tour of duty. As the Egyptian assault began, Avi automatically switched his machine to 'record' and reeled out a microphone. For sixty nerve-wracking hours, while Avi and his fellows were trapped in their bunker, the tape recorder picked up snatches of conversation and radio messages, with an occasional commentary that Avi spoke into the microphone. The resultant tapes, which Avi preserved through a near-miraculous rescue, vividly convey the courage and confusion of men in battle.

First there is a long series of reports from the men in the forward observation posts:

'Egyptians are putting in boats directly below us . . . they're crossing now . . . full of crowds of infantry . . . landing with anti-tank missiles . . . a few odd tanks rushing at Egyptians . . . artillery fire . . . shells falling close, closer, fire getting nearer. Armoured troop carriers crossing . . . lots of them jumping on the bank and running forward with missiles . . . six helicopters – Egyptian commandos – flying over.

'T-54 tank is opposite. . . . It's shooting at us. More boats crossing, wave after wave . . . they're fanning out in our area . . . they're putting up a commando flag . . . Egyptians are laying a bridge . . . automatic trailer is lowering floats . . . huge convoys, lots of armour . . . tanks, halftracks, trucks with missiles, lines of jeeps and batteries of artillery.'

The forward spotters are complaining – why isn't the Israeli air force in action? Planes could make mincemeat of such a traffic jam. A battery of mortars from a wood across the canal ranges in and the yard of the fort becomes pockmarked with craters. The Israelis reply with all their weapons, shooting at the massed crossing and the artillery batteries. Shells fall on the fort, gushing yellow choking smoke. The men are afraid: they consult the fort's doctor (in civilian life a hospital intern from Kfar Saba) who reassures them it is not poison gas. The men prepare small arms expecting hand-to-hand combat.

But the assault on the fort does not come. The shelling is ranging deeper and deeper into Sinai, and at 5.30 pm there is a complete pause. The men begin to realize they have been bypassed by the attacking troops. They are now totally cut off.

By radio, Avi continues to monitor the battle as tanks go into action on the road behind the fort parallel to the canal. The tank unit commander asks a mobile artillery commander for information on activities at the crossing point.

ARTILLERY COMMANDER: Everything quiet there now. Artillery is a few hundred metres from the junction. I'd like you to join up with us – I don't want to move until you've joined us.

A warning goes to the tank commander about infantry with anti-tank missiles: Take care not to get hit . . . take cover . . . I want you to save all your strength for a general counterattack.

The tank commander radios the fort to ask Meyerke if he would like a platoon of armoured infantry.

MEYERKE: Armoured infantry! Sure!

But after a pause the tank commander replies: Armoured infantry can't do anything there. There's an unbelievable fog, can't see a thing. I'm in radio contact with self-propelled artillery that's absorbing missile fire. I'm withdrawing them back a bit so they can change their positions.

In the bunker an exchange between Meyerke and his deputy commander, Yehoshua, known as 'Shuki' . . .

MEYERKE: Are those tanks over there?

SHUKI: There's no fire on us at the moment. (He makes a spitting sound – tfu, tfu – for luck.)

MEYERKE: Shuki, get hold of a piece of wood real quick and make touch-wood.

Before nightfall, ten miles inside Sinai to the south-east, they see Egyptian paratroops dropping from transport planes. The battle continues by moonlight and at last Israeli planes fly over and drop bombs.

MEYERKE (to Shuki): Why didn't they do that at five, or at four?

One of the forward lookouts, known as 'Marciano', is injured in the neck by a ricochet. 'Not serious. He can make it to command bunker himself.' But on the radio comes news that in the fort to the north the commanding officer is seriously wounded and two men killed: they keep calling for help.

Base camp has troubles too. A MIG bombing raid has killed several soldiers and the girl secretary of the commander; Egyptian helicopters are setting down infantry nearby. But an attempt is made to relieve the northern fort: an Egyptian ambush prevents it.

The artillery commander comes through on Avi's radio to ask if the artillery is hitting well.

SHUKI: Negative. Tell him to range 200 southwards.

Headquarters (on the radio): What's new with you?

SHUKI (in a voice of unflappable calm): Nothing special here, Headquarters. There's fire around us. We've seen one more boat cross the canal. Aside from that, there are people around us.

H.Q.: You asked for artillery.

SHUKI: Yes, we asked.

DOCTOR: Bloody hell! Don't allow Shuki to send situation reports. For him everything is always fine, even now.

AVI: We've lots of Egyptians around us.

MEYERKE: Hello Headquarters. I don't know what's happening with you. The guns are firing far from target. They're hitting a dead area. I can't see but it's far from target. It's nowhere near the right direction.

The HQ and artillery attempt to range guns in more effectively. Meyerke still can't see the hits. Calls for help continue to arrive from the northern fort.

AVI (offering a water flask to the doctor): Here, take water. Have three sips to make up for what you've lost sweating. I'm after you. Holy Allah! All this war. Who invented it?

DOCTOR: Craziness! Fighting! Getting killed!

AVI: And what do we get out of all this business? Instead of getting leave we'll have to stay till the end of the reserve tour.

MEDICAL ORDERLY: After the war they'll let you go home.

AVI: After this business is over, our fort will be in the rear. That's clear. We'll sit in the rear because the boys will be in Cairo, right? Then we won't be in the first line, we'll be in the rear.

MEDIC: You're laughing now but in a few days our army will really be across the line.

AVI: I've never had this sort of thing before. The situation has always been that the enemy is a kilometer from me, 200 metres from me, no distance at all. But enemy from all sides? By the way, we'll soon be able to dial home. What day is it now? Sunday? We can call home from three to four in the morning. I'm dying to call home. I'd just want one call home. They don't know what's happening here.

MEDIC: They're more worried than we are.

AVI: I'm not worried so much for myself. ,

On the radio from a tank unit: I've been hit. My machine got hit. I'm going down to check damage. We've had a report that they've identified parachutists . . . Look a little to the left of their tank area. There are parachutes there now.

AVI: Well, Egyptian parachutists. That's also something.

MEDIC: Where are *our* paratroopers?

AVI: Our paratroopers won't jump against those missiles. They have other ways of getting there. Aside from which, they're busy.

A unit of halftracks is approaching the northern fort, without support and exposed to anti-tank weapons.

HALFTRACK UNIT (on radio): We have three enemy tanks at the entrance to the northern fort. We've hit them. All three are burning now.

COMMANDER OF ARMOURED ARTILLERY UNIT (warning): Watch out! They're firing missiles at you! Change your positions and be on the lookout all the time.

The halftrack unit that tried to break through to relieve the northern fort, is forced to return for refuelling and re-munitioning. The fort keeps radioing for help, especially to evacuate the injured commander. Again, more problems with the artillery.

HQ: Hello. Say, how is it with our artillery fire? Does it need correction?

MEYERKE: I don't see any hits. Maybe they aren't shooting at all.

HQ: What do you say? Are you ranging them?

MEYERKE: Ranging? That's not our thing at all. I don't see any hits. He should hit further west. No?

AVI: Shuki, who's shooting?

SHUKI: Egyptians.

AVI: On whom?

SHUKI: On us, I think. They just stopped.

MEYERKE: Give me Shuki. Shuki, do you hear armour in the Egyptian concentration?

SHUKI: So Marciano says. (Dull noises can be heard – the roar of many Egyptian armoured vehicle motors. The whole front wakes up.)

AVI (into mike): The time is twenty to five, early Sunday morning. In the morning there'll certainly be a serious battle. There's tension in the air. (Avi hangs photographs of his three children and his wife over the communications equipment, and the doctor rakes through his wallet for pictures of his daughter.)

AVI: You know she looks like you.

DOCTOR: They say she's more like my wife.

AVI: What do you photograph on?

DOCTOR: On Kodak.

AVI: Nice colours.

(Sound of powerful explosion. Bombs fall around the fort.)

AVI: Now it's starting.

DOCTOR: Wake everyone in the bunker.

MARCIANO (radioing from an outpost): Our planes are flying over.

TANK COMMANDER (by radio): Take care of yourselves. We're putting planes down over this area.

MEYERKE: Moment, moment. North of us there is a target. Between us and the Egyptian crossing, 700 to 1,000 metres, Egyptian infantry, well dug in.

TANK COMMANDER: There are giant yellow mushrooms over your position. Is there any danger?

AVI (repeats): Two giant yellow mushrooms over our position. Is there any danger!

OUTPOST 2 OF FORT: They're shooting heavy AA into the sky on the planes that were bombing us.

SOLDIER: Proves they're *ours*, right?

MARCIANO (from his outpost): Our planes are blasting rockets on the Egyptians.

AVI: Excellent. You're a darling, Marciano. What time is it?

DOCTOR: Ten to seven in the morning.

AVI: I thought it was already twelve. (The Egyptians are apparently aware that the fort is spotting and reporting and bring down another heavy smokescreen on it.)

MEYERKE: Avi, tell the artillery we don't see any hits on the Egyptian infantry.

ARTILLERY COMMANDER: They said on the telephone that you will have to wait. It's being taken care of.

MEYERKE (impatiently): I want to know why I don't get fire on the Egyptian infantry. I want to see one hit, already.

AVI: Now you'll see a hit. A bull's eye on us!

Suddenly, two Israeli Phantoms swoop in to bomb Egyptian concentrations near the fort on the banks of the canal. Part of the bomb load goes into the canal itself and a huge quantity of water is sprayed on the fort. The men run soaked into the bunker shouting with glee.

SOLDIER: What a shower. Wow-eem! You should see what planes can do. You see four bombs fall like that and four Egyptian trucks go up in flames. Two of them went up together with one hit. There's a boat down here below – may have got here from the blast.

That is one of the rare exuberant moments in sixty-eight terrifying hours. By now, the fort had become of vital tactical importance to the Israelis: it was the last remaining spotting unit for artillery and bombing strikes in the sector of the central Egyptian crossing. Meyerke's unit could not expect to be relieved in a hurry: they were clearly too valuable to the new sector commander, Major General Ariel ('Arik') Sharon, who just at this time had arrived to try and sort things out.

The fighting had begun very differently for Arik Sharon, the man who in many Israeli eyes was to become the hero of the war. Just three months before, at the age of forty-five, he had retired from regular service to become a politician. Up to that time – during twenty-six years of intermittent warfare – he had become undoubtedly the most popular leader among the Israeli rank and file. Yet the army's upper echelon found him erratic and incautious, and it was scarcely surprising when he was passed over as a potential chief of staff. Disappointed, he decided to run for the Knesset, and he energetically set about welding together the Likud, a right-wing opposition coalition.

In retirement, Arik Sharon had remained in command of a reserve division. At 11.30 am on Friday, October 5, the day before the war began, he was summoned to Southern Command Headquarters (which he had formerly commanded) and was shown air reconnaissance pictures. There were signs of a large-scale build-up of water crossing equipment, and, Sharon afterwards claimed, 'I told my division officers, "I think there is going to be war in one or two days".' However it was not until 9.30 the following morning, barely four hours before the shooting started, that a telephone order came to his ranch near Beersheba to mobilize his division. 'My uniform was still in the back of my car,' he said, 'so I put it on and rushed to HQ.'

The order to head for the canal front came as soon as the Egyptian attack started, and shortly afterwards they were on the move. But there were no tank transport trucks available, so Sharon had to order his armoured brigades to grind across the long desert roads on their tracks. They did so – with great wear to the tanks – at a painful average of twelve miles an hour, while Sharon himself raced ahead in a civilian pick-up truck. On arrival he was given charge of the central sector of the front opposite Ismailia, and around five o'clock on Sunday morning set up his forward command post near Tasa. It was not until noon that day that the main body of his over-strength division of three armoured brigades, two brigades of paratroops, an artillery group and other specialized units began to arrive.

'The situation was very grave,' he said. 'It was impossible to understand exactly what was going on.' Just before his division became operational he picked up the field telephone to get some first-hand information.

Towards noon on Sunday the telephone in Avi's communications bunker rings. The CO is on the line.

MEYERKE: I have a force here, not just mine but all sorts of hangers on and people who got stuck here. No injured *Al-Hamdu-Lellah* (praise Allah), except a few small ricochets, but not serious.

SHARON: Are you getting knocked up?

MEYERKE: We, not directly at this moment but they're getting organized around us. Two platoons of infantry behind us. We can see armoured troop carriers going in, perhaps also tanks.

SHARON: Tell me, is there much traffic on the canal road?

MEYERKE: Well, earlier on they were moving on it, a few hours ago, a number of armoured personnel carriers that got as far as us. We began to hit them so they turned around and left soldiers, a few groups. I can't understand to this moment the logic that they should scatter soldiers along the road. And they return north, north-west, to the area where all their tanks are – the tank battalion that got it from the air force earlier.

SHARON: Were there some good hits?

MEYERKE: There were some good hits. We saw some scenes you'll probably remember from the good old days of the Six-Day War.

SHARON: Where are you from?

MEYERKE (naming his kibbutz): Nativ Halamed-Heh.

SHARON: And your men are Jerusalemites?

MEYERKE: Jerusalemites.

SHARON: Their tanks went up in flames, or what?

MEYERKE (tone of satisfaction): Yes.

SHARON: They're not attacking you and they're not doing anything?

MEYERKE: As far as I'm concerned, no. What is happening in my direction is directly on the banks of the canal. Armoured personnel carriers and tanks have approached there in my direction to a range of 700 to 800. They have dug-in infantry. When they raise their heads we shoot. And also with the 81 mm [mortar].

SHARON: Do you have ammunition?

MEYERKE: Yes. We try not to just shoot away. I've started going stingy with the 81.

SHARON: Did you have artillery support?

MEYERKE: I had, then they stopped it.

SHARON: They stopped the artillery support?

MEYERKE: Now I have it from the south.

SHARON: Tell me, opposite you, north, close to the crossing area, are there any enemy forces between you and them?

MEYERKE: I went down about five minutes ago and there weren't any of them. One moment, I'll see if number two is listening in. Shuki, Shuki, speak.

SHARON: Peace to you. Tell me . . .

SHUKI: Peace and blessing.

SHARON: . . . how many tanks do you see there?

SHUKI: Some forty, forty-five.

SHARON: On what formation? Concentrated?

SHUKI: Some are concentrated, others are standing in rows.

SHARON: Were there any tanks burned?

SHUKI: Not burned, but it seems they were damaged without burning.

SHARON: The men ran away?

SHUKI: The men all came down from them. They're around now. They have like dykes. They're on top of the dykes and in the area on the dykes. (Sharon cross-questions him on distances, but the description remains confused.)

MEYERKE: Arik, understand, they're holding a sort of flat area, do you hear? A flat area a few hundred metres long and a few hundred metres wide, and they've taken up directions facing the area from which, it seems, our armour is blocking them. . . . It seems that together with everything they have behind them, with trucks and everything, they're taking up an area of almost a kilometre long.

SHARON: Tell me, your impression in general is that – all these Egyptians, are they tired or are they swinging?

MEYERKE: I tell you. When you look at them after the air force came down on them, you remember what it was like six years ago.

SHARON: Were you a soldier then, or what?

MEYERKE: Of course I was a soldier. Look, I'm already fourth time – no, third time, a soldier in wartime. You're talking to an old man of nearly forty-one.

SHARON: Look fellows, we've only just got here. Now I'm planning to make every effort to extricate you. A little bit later we'll contact you, tell you what to do . . .

(Sharon inquires about transport at the fort, says he will get the artillery to give further instructions on spotting, and repeats his promise to extricate them – then rings off.)

Shortly after Sharon's call ends, the most serious shelling to date begins on the fort. By now, twenty-four hours after the war had begun, 150 tanks – almost a tenth of the Israeli total – have been lost in Sinai alone. A key commander is only just starting to pick up the threads. And Israel, the triumphant victor of the Six-Day War, is gravely threatened. How did it happen?

We will return later to the story of Avi, Meyerke and Shuki. But first we must look at the Arab side, the diplomatic decisions that led up to war, and the puzzling failure of the Israelis to read the signs of danger.

Section I

June 1973: President Sadat (below) visits the canal and takes a long look at the Israeli positions. He had already decided on war. Behind him is General Ismail, planning the attack of four months later.

'No peace, no war' – a failure of diplomacy

1: The uncloseable gap

The failure of Israel, the Arab states, the superpowers and the United Nations to bring peace to the Middle East goes back decades. Historically, the conflict has involved the competing claims of two peoples – the Jews and the Palestinian Arabs – to the same strip of land between the River Jordan and the Mediterranean Sea. On three occasions, in 1948–9, 1956, and 1967, Israel fought to make the Jewish state secure. Each time it won a decisive military victory; but each time it was unable to translate its victory into peace with its Arab neighbours. The Middle East stayed at the brink of war.

For Israel when, for the fourth time, open warfare began on October 6, 1973, the central issue was once again the security of the Jewish state. But for Egypt and Syria, who launched their attack after months of meticulous planning, the war was different from the previous three. This time their stated war plans contained no intention of destroying Israel; nor were the claims of the Palestinians among their main considerations. Israel's principal offence by now, so far as Egypt, Syria and Jordan were concerned, was not its existence, but its continued occupation of the Arab land it had conquered in 1967.

The June 1967 fighting had stopped in response to ceasefire demands by the United Nations Security Council. In the years that followed, most attempts to start peace negotiations also centred on the United Nations. From the start, the struggle was uphill. Early in August, Arab leaders met in Cairo, where they reportedly rejected any form of negotiations with Israel. In return, Abba Eban, Israel's Foreign Minister, said the map of the Middle East had been 'irrevocably destroyed', though he held out the hope that Israel would withdraw from most of the occupied lands following peace negotiations. A fortnight later, an Arab summit conference in Khartoum called for 'political efforts at the international and diplomatic level to eliminate the effects of the aggression' – but within the principles of 'no peace with Israel, no recognition of Israel, no negotiations with it, and insistence on the rights of the Palestinian people in their own country.'

The cornerstone of international attempts to bridge this gap was Security Council resolution 242, adopted unanimously – and therefore with both American and Soviet support – on November 22, 1967. (It was again invoked in the ceasefire resolutions at the end of the 1973 war.) It called for 'a just and lasting peace' based on two principles:

(i) Withdrawal of Israeli forces from territories occupied in the recent conflict;
(ii) Termination of all claims or states of belligerency and respect for and acknowledgement of the sovereignty, territorial integrity and political independence of every State in the area and their right to live in peace within secure and recognized boundaries free from threats or acts of force.

The Resolution also affirmed the necessity

(a) For guaranteeing freedom of navigation through international waterways in the area;
(b) For achieving a just settlement of the refugee problem;
(c) For guaranteeing the territorial inviolability and political independence of every State in the area, through measures including the establishment of demilitarized zones.

To 'promote agreement' in the Middle East, U-Thant, the UN Secretary General, was asked 'to designate a Special Representative' as mediator.

In all respects except the most important one, Resolution 242 was a triumph for behind-the-scenes UN diplomacy, and for its main sponsor, Britain's UN representative, Lord Caradon. It carefully balanced Israel's desire for security with the Arab states' demand for recovery of the occupied territories. It was acceptable to the two superpowers. And it spelt out a procedure for moving towards peace negotiations. But it failed to prevent another war.

A major problem was that Resolution 242 left certain critical issues unresolved. Its demand for Israeli withdrawal 'from territories occupied in the recent conflict' contained an important ambiguity: did it mean *all*, or merely *some*, of the occupied territories? The Soviet Union and the Arab states argued for the 'all the territories' interpretation; the United States, Britain and Israel argued that it left open the possibility of readjusting Israel's borders. In reality, the ambiguity was necessary: had the resolution been more explicit, one or other superpower would certainly have vetoed it – or at best abstained.

Most differences could, perhaps, have been resolved had peace negotiations ever started. On November 23, U Thant named Dr Gunnar Jarring as his Special Representative. Jarring was a Swedish diplomat with a finely tuned ear for delicate negotiations. He came from a neutral country with no history of partisan behaviour towards the Middle East. As ambassador to Moscow – and previously to Washington – he had developed a sophisticated understanding of both Soviet and American diplomacy.

But although Jarring succeeded in retaining the support of both these governments he made only limited progress in closing the gaps between Israel and Arab states. For a start, Syria still refused to contemplate any kind of *modus vivendi* with Israel. On December 12, the Syrian government announced that it would not work with the Jarring mission, because it was 'useless to meet Dr Jarring as long as his mission is limited to the framework of the resolution adopted by the Security Council and completely rejected by Syria.' The leaders of Israel, Jordan, Lebanon and Egypt, however, did agree to meet Jarring; but it quickly became clear to him that the start of peace talks – let alone the conclusion – was still a long way off.

The Israeli government told Jarring that the steps to peace had to take place in the following order:

1. Direct negotiations between Israel and the Arab states, leading to:
2. Peace Treaty. Followed by:
3. Israeli withdrawal to the borders agreed in negotiations.

Egypt and Jordan insisted on a different sequence:

1. Israeli withdrawal to the pre-1967 lines, before:
2. Indirect negotiations through the United Nations, leading to:
3. Peace agreement.

Israel's insistence on direct negotiations was based on the argument that the two sides could hardly live in peace in the future, if they were not prepared to speak to each other now. But the Arabs equated Israeli insistence on direct talks with a demand for *de facto* recognition of Israel before talks began. More important, Egyptian and Jordanian leaders were afraid that as their defeat had been so humiliating they would be unable to reach a fair settlement without a middleman to hold the ring.

Yet there were some signs that Egypt, at least, was beginning to depart from the intransigence of the Khartoum conference. In February 1968, Yugoslavia's President Tito reported after a visit to Cairo that President Nasser would accept UN demands for demilitarized zones, the ending of the state of war, and the freedom of Israeli shipping to use the Suez Canal.

By the end of that month, Jarring was sufficiently hopeful that peace talks might begin, to return to the Middle East carrying two draft letters he intended to send to U Thant. One referred to talks with Israel and Egypt, the other to talks with Israel and

Jordan. Otherwise they were identical. Jarring wanted the agreement of the three countries to the letters. They described the willingness of each country 'to devise arrangements, under my auspices, for the implementation' of Resolution 242; and their acceptance of Jarring's invitation to meet with him in Nicosia 'for conferences within the framework' of the resolution.

The letters were never sent. Israel eventually accepted them, but insisted that the Nicosia meetings could only be a prelude to direct talks. Egypt and Jordan dropped their previous demand for Israeli withdrawal prior to negotiations, but wanted 'a more precise declaration by Israel of its willingness to implement Resolution 242.' They also wanted the talks to take place at the UN's New York headquarters.

Jarring leaned hard on the two Arab states, and persuaded them to drop their demand for Israel's 'more precise' declaration. But they still wanted the talks to be held in New York. Israel was not prepared for a change in venue. Eventually, Jarring simply decided that the talks would take place in New York, but he did not issue any formal invitations. By this time it was clear that only desultory talks would take place. And so it turned out, with no substantial moves towards serious negotiations. For the time being, the Jarring mission was forced into hibernation.

By the spring of 1969, an enormous gulf still existed between Israel and the Arab states over the interpretation of Resolution 242. Could the superpowers bring pressure to bear on their clients to close the gaps?

Their involvement was becoming increasingly necessary, for the emergence of the Palestinian guerrilla movement was by now a potential threat to any peace initiative. The longer a settlement was delayed, the more difficult it would be to implement it. Until 1968, the guerrillas were an irritant rather than a major threat. But as they gathered momentum – and even though they have never consisted of more than a small minority of Palestinians – they became more difficult to ignore. Certainly Israel was not ignoring them: in retaliation for a guerrilla attack on an El Al airliner at Athens airport on Boxing Day 1968, Israeli commandos attacked Beirut airport. In a forty-five minute raid, thirteen aircraft – eight of them belonging to Middle East Airlines – were destroyed. The Security Council unanimously condemned Israel's 'premeditated military action,' but made no reference to the Palestinian attack which had preceded it.

For the major powers to break the diplomatic deadlock before it was too late, they first had to agree between themselves on the interpretation of Resolution 242. Starting in April 1969, the UN representatives of the Soviet Union, the United States, France and Britain met from time to time until September 1971; but no common interpretation of the resolution was ever agreed.

Israel's Prime Minister, Golda Meir, was less than enthusiastic about the four powers' intentions. In an interview with the *Sunday Times* in London in June 1969 she rejected the idea of international guarantees; 'I cannot imagine that Israel would again consent to any deal under which we would have to depend for our security on others. We are more intelligent than that. One does not have to be very sophisticated to come to the conclusion, after the bitter experience of twenty years, that the only people we can depend on for our security are ourselves.'

By this time not only the Palestinian guerrillas were beginning to cause trouble. Along the Suez Canal, a war of attrition had begun. On the east bank of the canal, Israel had started some months earlier constructing the Bar-Lev line – a series of defensive strong points to protect the Israeli forces from any Egyptian incursion across the canal. Determined to prevent construction, Egyptian troops stepped up artillery barrages on the Israeli forces; Israeli forces returned the fire. At the end of April, U Thant described the Suez Canal Zone as in 'a virtual state of active war'.

On May 1, following a series of Egyptian commando raids across the canal, President Nasser claimed that sixty per cent of the Bar-Lev line had been destroyed. The Suez Canal, he told UN officials, was no longer considered by Egypt as a ceasefire line. A few weeks later he pressed the point home by ordering air raids on Israeli troops in Sinai.

On September 9, 1969, Israel took the war of attrition west of the canal, with the first of a series of air raids south of Suez town, as cover for an assault across the Gulf of Suez by around 150 Arab-speaking Israeli soldiers in captured Russian-built tanks and personnel carriers. The force killed 150 Egyptian troops – and ferried back to Israel two of the latest Russian tanks, the T-62, which had only weeks before been supplied to Egypt for the first time. On December 27, 1969, another Israeli raid across the Gulf of Suez removed one of Russia's newest mobile radar installations, the P-2. (Apparently abashed by their own success, the Israelis later secretly handed this back.)

The Soviet Union responded. By March 1970, the *New York Times* reported, 1,500 Soviet advisers and large quantities of SAM-3 missiles had arrived in Egypt. Israel, on the other hand, was not receiving all the military aid it had sought from the United States. On March 23, President Nixon announced that Israel would not be getting the twenty-five Phantoms and one hundred Skyhawks which Mrs Meir had requested in September 1969. Israel, evidently, was only too capable of fending for itself.

To head off the drift into all-out war, US Secretary of State Willam Rogers added his name to the growing list of would-be peacemakers. (A quick list of peace plan authors would include Lyndon Johnson, Marshal Tito, General de Gaulle, and British Foreign Secretary Michael Stewart). Rogers launched his initiative on June 19, 1970.

As a first stage, Rogers asked Israel and Egypt to agree to a three-month ceasefire along the Suez Canal. Apart from creating a better atmosphere for peace negotiations to start, it would enable the canal to be cleared of the ships which had been stuck there since the 1967 war. (Each ship was left with a skeleton crew and most of its cargo. One ship had been carrying apples, by now well past prime condition.) Israel was to commit itself to withdrawal from occupied territories. Subsequently, the dormant Jarring mission and Resolution 242 were to be revived.

President Nasser arrived in Moscow on June 29, for what were evidently protracted and difficult talks with the Russians – whose acceptance of the plan, though with reservations, Rogers had obtained in advance. Twice Nasser delayed his return to Cairo; but by the time he left on July 17, he had decided to accept the plan unconditionally. Palestinians stormed through the streets of Cairo denouncing Nasser as a coward; his course now decided, Nasser quelled opposition by closing down the two Palestinian radio stations, and ordered preparations for the dredging of the canal.

Israel, like Egypt, had been initially sceptical about the Rogers plan. Golda Meir at first described the ceasefire proposal as 'a trick which would enable Egypt to prepare for a renewal of the war in a more intense form.' Within Israel several tense cabinet meetings were held, but eventually the government agreed to a ceasefire, on July 31, 1970 – at the cost of weakening the coalition government. The rightwing Gahal party, with twenty-six seats in the 120-seat Knesset, went into opposition in protest.

The short-term imperative of a ceasefire is one thing: the long haul of arriving at a political settlement is quite another. Having engineered the August 7 ceasefire, the superpowers handed back to Jarring the task of once more cranking up his peace mission. He opened discussions on August 25, but they were terminated on September 8: Israel refused to participate, in the words of the official UN report, 'so long as the ceasefire standstill agreement was not observed in its entirety.'

The violation referred to was the movement of the SAM batteries. But the Israeli withdrawal from the talks was due, in part at least, to strong domestic pressures. This point emerged more clearly when Jarring made another attempt at resuming talks in

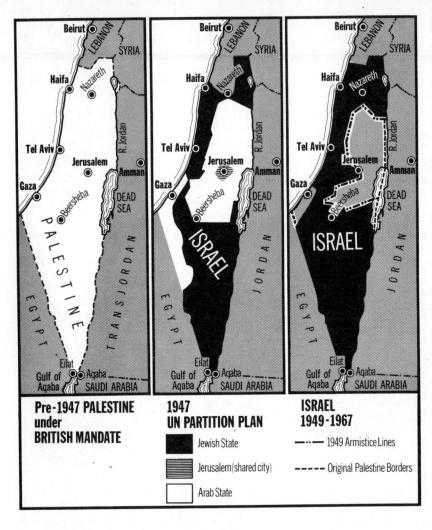

Pre-1947 PALESTINE under BRITISH MANDATE

1947 UN PARTITION PLAN

- ■ Jewish State
- ☰ Jerusalem (shared city)
- □ Arab State

ISRAEL 1949-1967

- —··— 1949 Armistice Lines
- ----- Original Palestine Borders

The changing shape of Israel

Until 1948, Palestine — a land of two million people, in which two out of three were Arabs, and one in three was Jewish — was controlled by Britain under mandate from first the League of Nations, and then the United Nations. In November 1947, the UN decided to partition the country into a Jewish State (57% of the land) and an Arab State (42%). Jerusalem was to be shared, and administered by the UN. The Jews accepted the plan, but the Arabs did not. When the British left in May 1948, Israel was born. Immediately Arab forces attempted to crush the new Jewish State — and the Israelis attempted to extend their control over more of Palestine. The Israelis were more successful: in May 1949 Israel signed an armistice with its Arab neighbours, gaining more land than the UN had intended. Jerusalem was divided between Israel and Jordan. The proposed Arab State was never formed. Up to a million Palestinians fled from Israel, and became refugees. The borders remained intact until 1967, despite the 1956 war when Israel in collusion with Britain and France invaded Sinai.

ISRAEL 1967-1973

- Pre-1967
- .... 1967 Cease-fire Lines
- Occupied Territories

Beirut

LEBANON SYRIA

Damascus

GOLAN HEIGHTS

Haifa Nazareth

Mediterranean Sea

Tel Aviv

WEST BANK

R. Jordan

Jerusalem

Amman

Gaza

Gaza Strip

DEAD SEA

Port Said

Beersheba

ISRAEL

Ismailia

SUEZ CANAL

JORDAN

Bitter Lakes

CAIRO

Suez

SINAI

EGYPT

Gulf of Suez

Eilat Aqaba

SAUDI ARABIA

Gulf of Aqaba

Sharm el Sheikh

In the Six-Day War of June, 1967, Israeli forces occupied the whole of what had been Palestine, together with the Sinai desert in Egypt, and the Golan Heights in Syria. Israel subsequently offered to withdraw from most of the occupied territories, but not Sharm el Sheikh, the Golan Heights or Jerusalem. In the absence of negotiations, Israeli forces continued to control the occupied areas.

November 1970. The Israeli representative had to stall: the matter, he said, was 'under consideration in the Israeli cabinet.

Jarring entered into his fourth year of trying to get peace talks off the ground in 1971. Discussions with Israeli, Jordanian and Egyptian representatives again made it depressingly clear that, while informally each side was beginning to hint at concessions which might have been effective three years earlier, officially nothing had changed.

If peace negotiations were impossible, perhaps Jarring could attack the core of the problem – the differences between Egypt and Israel. With Nasser's death on September 28, 1970, Anwar Sadat had become President of Egypt. He might respond to a new initiative. On February 8, 1971, Jarring wrote to both countries' leaders.

From Egypt he requested a commitment to enter into a peace agreement with Israel, to include:

    (a) termination of all claims or states of belligerency;
    (b) respect for and acknowledgement of Israel's sovereignty, territorial integrity and political independence;
    (c) respect for and acknowledgement of Israel's right to live in peace within secure and recognized boundaries;
    (d) responsibility to do all in its power to ensure that acts of belligerency or hostility do not originate from or are not committed from within Egypt against the population, citizens or property of Israel;
    (e) non-interference in Israel's domestic affairs.

From Israel, Jarring sought a commitment to withdraw its forces from Sinai to the pre-1967 lines. This was to depend on 'satisfactory arrangements' for demilitarized zones; freedom of access by Israeli ships to the Gulf of Aqaba past Sharm el Sheikh; and freedom of navigation through the Suez Canal.

Sadat replied in a week, making the commitment Jarring wanted. Egypt also undertook, as part of a peace settlement, to ensure freedom of Israeli navigation through the Suez Canal; freedom of access to the Gulf of Aqaba, with a United Nations peacekeeping force at Sharm el Sheikh; and a demilitarized zone 'astride the borders in equal distances'. Provided Israel agreed, Egypt would also accept a UN force on the borders, in which the superpowers could participate.

Eleven days later, Israel's reply arrived. It was long and detailed, and accepted many of Jarring's proposals. But on the central commitment which Jarring sought, the reply was highly discouraging: it agreed to withdrawal 'to the secure, recognized and agreed boundaries to be established in the peace agreement

. . . Israel will not withdraw to the pre-June 5, 1967 lines.' The letter made no reference to the idea of a demilitarized zone.

Jarring and U Thant were dismayed by the Israeli response. The flat refusal to withdraw to the pre-1967 line in Sinai – a late addition to Israel's initial draft reply, added to meet strong feelings in the Knesset – was, they felt, particularly unfortunate. On March 5, U Thant placed the blame for the diplomatic deadlock on Israel, and appealed to it to give the requested commitment on withdrawal at least to the pre-1967 Sinai borders.

There was no response from Israel. Two days later, on March 7, Sadat refused to extend the ceasefire, or to give any promise that shooting would not be resumed. (In practice, however, a *de facto* ceasefire held.) Jarring returned to his post as Swedish Ambassador to the Soviet Union, giving up the struggle. A year later, at the instance of the new UN Secretary General Kurt Waldheim, he made another attempt to start negotiations. Egypt reaffirmed its willingness to stand by Resolution 242 and the 1971 Jarring proposals, but Israel wanted the 1971 proposals withdrawn. 'In the event,' Waldheim reported, 'it was not possible to reactivate the mission.' It was a turning point in the road to a new war.

2: Sadat decides on war

President Sadat, by nature a somewhat repressed man given to swoops between euphoria and depression, has always been harder to fathom than the expansive Nasser. But after the war, Sadat did unburden himself with considerable frankness to one western friend. 'From the day I took office on Nasser's death, I knew I would have to fight. Nasser had known we would have to fight. It was my inheritance. But captivity by the British teaches you patience.' (From 1942 to 1945, the young Sadat, anti-British during the war for nationalist reasons, was kept under house arrest.) So Sadat had been willing to give American and United Nations plans a chance. 'I had slight hopes of Secretary of State Rogers in 1970 and 1971. But all he did was to extract more and more concessions from me and not a single response from the Israelis.' And Sadat began to realize why: 'Rogers thought we would never fight. The Israelis thought they could never be surprised. The West thought we were poor soldiers without good generals.'

Complacency indeed was a factor in Israel's refusal to withdraw totally, but so were its doubts that Egypt's leaders – whatever they told the UN – really wanted peace. Consistently, Israel demanded full peace – *sulh* in Arabic – implying reconciliation and the establishment of friendly relations. At first, Israelis pointed out, all that Nasser had been prepared to offer was an end to the state of belligerency, while Syria would offer nothing at all. Later Egypt offered a peace – *salaam* in Arabic – a live-and-let-live agreement acknowledging Israel's sovereignty, but falling short of friendly relations. To Egypt, *sulh* was premature; to Israel, *salaam* disconcertingly insufficient.

Almost every olive branch offered by the Egyptians, moreover, contained a reference to 'the restoration of the legitimate rights of the Palestinian people'. For Israel, each reference to the Palestinians was a source of anxiety; but for Egypt it was a necessary acknowledgement that any peace settlement which could not be sold to the Palestinians would be fragile indeed.

Twice in a quarter of a century, hundreds of thousands of Palestinians had been uprooted following Israeli military victories: in 1948, and 1967. By 1973, there were more than two million Palestinians, most of whom were living away from what they considered their home; 600,000 were living in refugee camps. As the years passed, and they failed to regain their land, groups of Palestinians (though only a small proportion of the total) turned to terrorism and guerrilla warfare. There had been considerable friction between Palestinian groups and Arab governments as well. A bloody crackdown on Palestinian guerrillas by Jordan in 1970 led directly to the formation of the most extreme of the major Palestinian groups, Black September – a name chosen to recall the occasion of the bloodshed. But the most spectacular acts of terrorism had been directed against Israel: notably the kidnapping and killing of Israeli athletes in September 1972 at the Munich Olympic Games. Israel could thus point to the Arabs' public tolerance of these exploits (though, privately, some leaders were embarrassed).

In turn, the Arabs were outraged by the creation of Israeli settlements in the occupied territories. Between 1967 and 1973, more than forty settlements were established, containing on average, about a hundred civilians. Most were clustered on the Golan Heights and the west bank of the Jordan, though there were also a few in the Gaza Strip and Sinai. 'These settlements', said Foreign Minister Abba Eban in December 1971, 'are being built in lands that would be part of Israel's boundaries.'

But at other times, Israeli leaders, and especially Eban, were distinctly more conciliatory. In a speech to the United Nations General Assembly in September 1971, Eban held out the hope of the Suez Canal reopening, under Egyptian control, prior to a more general peace settlement. And in September 1972, he said that he could 'not conceive that we would refuse representation' to the Palestinians at peace talks. Sadat was not persuaded.

For while Sadat steadily lost his slight faith in diplomacy, it became apparent that the pressures of 'no peace, no war' were also wrecking what unity the Arabs possessed. In August 1971, Syria had severed relations with Jordan: six months later, Egypt followed suit after a speech by King Hussein to some 500 political leaders from both sides of the Jordan River. Hussein offered to replace the Hashemite Kingdom of Jordan with a United Arab Kingdom with two equal regions. The Jordanian region would have its capital in Amman, which was also to be the federal capital; the Palestinians would have their own region, and a capital in the old city of Jerusalem.

Hussein's plan was, not surprisingly, rejected by both Israel and the Palestinians. For Israel, the plan meant giving up too much occupied territory (in particular, the old city of Jerusalem); for the Palestinians it meant gaining too little. But the Egyptians and Syrians were the most disturbed of all: the fact that Hussein had launched the plan at all meant that he was envisaging a separate peace treaty with Israel, even outside the framework of Resolution 242. Politically, Sadat had no choice but to sever relations.

But it was the corresponding internal discontent which finally brought Sadat to view in specific terms the necessity for war. On January 25, 1972 – after two days of student rioting, the first in Cairo since 1968 – Sadat assured a gathering of student, professional and union leaders that a decision to go to war against Israel had already been taken. 'It is not mere words; it is a fact,' he said. This was only a slight exaggeration, as Sadat afterwards explained. He understood the discontent: 'After six years, our men on the Suez Canal and our students wanted action. Ideas started to crystallize in my mind in early 1972.'

They gained urgency from Sadat's swift discovery that the growing detente between America and Russia had already eroded his ability to capitalize on superpower rivalry. To wage war, Egypt's first need was arms. But when Sadat went to Moscow on February 2, he came away disappointed. He saw the Communist Party leader, Leonid Brezhnev; the Russian Prime Minister, Alexei Kosygin; and their foreign and defence ministers. He asked them for new, offensive weapons. They refused. Sadat was disgusted: 'It was clear that the stalemate – no peace, no war – suited the superpowers. There was some agreement between them about the level of arms supplies.' The Russian communique after the visit pointedly reiterated its faith in Resolution 242.

Apart from any reasons of global strategy, Brezhnev was frankly sceptical of the Arabs' ability to use even the weapons they had. He was still shocked by the 1967 debacle. 'If each of your tanks had fired just one shot, the pattern of that war would have changed radically,' he told Sadat. 'But your guns were untouched.' To Sadat, however, this Russian bluntness was further evidence that the balance of Soviet policy was tilting towards detente. And his next visit to Moscow proved this.

On April 27–29, 1972 – after a strong speech criticizing Russia for not supplying the weapons he wanted – Sadat returned to see Brezhnev. 'I went to Moscow,' Sadat reminisced later, 'and I told Mr Brezhnev that we would have to fight one day. There was no alternative. He said he did not want a superpower confrontation.'

Sadat at least persuaded Brezhnev of his seriousness of purpose. The Russian communique after the visit declared that the Arabs 'have every reason to make use of other means [than diplomacy] for the return of the Arab lands seized by Israel' – a careful limiting of objective. But still Russia would not give Sadat the arms he wanted. He recalled: 'The Russians prevaricated throughout the summer and autumn of 1972. They said they were awaiting the American presidential election in November. Don't forget that when I was in Russia in April, they didn't know whether Nixon would come back, though he did go to Moscow after that – following his trip to China.'

By midsummer, Sadat knew he had to bring matters to a head: 'The Russians felt they had a presence on our soil, even if they kept discreetly out of sight.' It was a considerable presence: 4,000 to 5,000 advisers with the Egyptian forces; and 10,000 to 15,000 other personnel; some manning the fifty SAM-2 and SAM-3 missile sites; 200 pilots with groundcrew for the MIG-21, MIG-23 and Sukhoi-11 fighters; and heavy Russian contingents at four Egyptian ports and virtually in control of seven airfields. Effectively, Russia could veto any of Sadat's military plans.

This caused enough trouble for Sadat with his own officers. Many were pro-western; others were simply fed up with what they saw as Russian arrogance towards them. But that was not the problem Sadat's Prime Minister, Dr Aziz Sidqi, went to Moscow on July 13 to resolve. His talks with Brezhnev and his cohorts were expected to last three to five days. But on July 15 he flew home. And on July 17, Sadat ordered Soviet military personnel and their families – in all, 40,000 people – to leave Egypt immediately. Egyptian troops would take over the airfields and SAM sites. On July 19, Sadat explained why. Speaking to the central committee of Egypt's Arab Socialist Union – the sole and governing party – Sadat put the message politely: 'The Soviet Union is a big country which has its own international role and its own strategy. As for us, our territory is partly under occupation and, therefore, our target at both the Egyptian and the Arab levels is to remove the consequences of the aggression.' But he then hinted at the problem Sidqi had tried, in vain, to resolve. Egypt had never sought to create a confrontation between the Soviet Union and the United States, and Egypt had never expected Soviet soldiers to fight Arab wars, he said. But whatever weapons Egypt obtained from abroad, their use was a matter for decision by the Egyptian people 'without obtaining permission from any quarter whatever its importance'.

Privately, Sadat at the time said merely: 'I felt we all needed an electric shock.' His real purpose he explained after the war: 'I expelled them to give myself complete freedom of manœuvre.'

Sadat's action strengthened his position remarkably: all whispers of army disaffection were immediately stilled. At the same time, it raised the army's hopes that Sadat would do something equally decisive about Israel. In the short run, however, there was no alternative but to attempt once more to break the deadlock diplomatically. At a private meeting of the Peoples' Assembly on August 17, he stated: 'What we need now is to move with the Soviet Union, the United States, western Europe, nonaligned and Arab nations in preparation for a new initiative.'

But Sadat now had even less confidence in that expedient. And he could not afford another year of failure. He would probably fall; the Egyptian economy could not indefinitely bear the staggering military burden; it was even doubtful whether Egypt's social structure could long survive the strains of 'no peace no war'. While exploring peace, Sadat simultaneously began to prepare for war. In October 1972, he appointed as War Minister and Commander-in-Chief one of his oldest army colleagues and supporters, General Ahmed Ismail. (One of Egypt's most dashing and aggressive combat officers, Lieutenant-General Saad Shazli, was already the Chief of Staff. The conflicting careers and personalities of these two generals were to affect the coming war at a crucial moment.)

Ironically, the Russians' continuing caution was the final catalyst, as Sadat explained: 'After the November election, Mr Nixon was returned, and I had a letter from Mr Brezhnev saying that they wished to support the policy of detente and they advised me to accept the situation. They said they could not increase their normal arms supplies.' On November 14, Sadat spoke to closed meetings of the Socialist Union central committee. 'We had a meeting of our higher council,' Sadat said, 'and we rejected this. We started planning the October 6 offensive from that moment.' Thus, for the final eleven months to war, the story now has two simultaneous and parallel strands: Sadat's last, unhopeful, diplomatic initiative; and Ismail's slow, methodical and brilliant planning for war. But what sort of war?

According to a highly detailed account he gave much later to *Al Ahram*, Ismail swiftly decided that merely to repeat the 1969–1970 war of attrition would be disastrous. 'Any attempt on our part to do so would be met with a more violent reaction on Israel's part . . . greater than the political and military importance of any action we took,' he said. He concluded: 'Our strike, therefore, should be the strongest we could deal.' But what sort of strike? Here, Ismail agreed with the long-held views of his Chief of Staff: the way to beat the Israelis was not to mimic their swift-strike *blitzkrieg* tactics, but to chop them up in what Shazli called a 'meatgrinder' war.

The new year brought a further military option. On January 21, 1973, after several weeks of negotiation, Ismail was made Commander-in-Chief of the armies of the so-called Federation of Arab Republics. Since two members of this federation, Egypt and Syria, had somewhat ambivalent relations with the third, Libya, the post was seemingly honorific. But Ismail was more hopeful. 'My second idea,' he told *Al Ahram*, 'was now that our strike should be dealt jointly from two fronts.' Ismail's defence headquarters are a small compound of modest offices surrounded by a ten-foot wall on July 23 Street, in the Cairo suburb of Abbasiya. Sometime early in February, the forty-strong Egyptian planning staff housed in these offices began to prepare for the new war. The irony no doubt occurred to them that the compound is only a few hundred yards from the new Nasser mosque, tomb of the last man to take on Israel.

Sadat's final and parallel diplomatic initiative reached its peak in February 1973. It was, without exception, the most carefully planned and vigorous of all Egypt's attempts to break the deadlock. The job was entrusted to General Ismail's namesake, Hafez Ismail, who is Sadat's National Security Adviser and – though the parallel cannot be taken too far – Egypt's closest equivalent to Henry Kissinger. Hafez Ismail set off on a tour which included Moscow, London, Washington, the United Nations and Bonn. In addition, Egypt's Foreign Minister, Muhammad Zayyat, went to New Dehli and Peking. But in that itinerary, the only stops that mattered were Moscow and Washington – and Sadat already knew he could expect nothing from the Kremlin.

On February 23, Ismail met President Richard Nixon in the Oval Room of the White House. And Nixon was certainly not discouraging. He spoke of America's wish to get negotiations going; later in the day, Rogers echoed his response. Their remarks were somewhat pointed: Egypt had, on January 18, firmly rejected Rogers' advance warning of a new US initiative, which was to be based once again on 'negotiations of a Suez Canal agreement'. Cairo had objected that the plan simply allowed Israel 'to perpetuate her occupation of Sinai'. Still, Ismail later described his talks with Nixon and Rogers as 'warm, objective and fruitful'. Rogers spoke next day of a 'new warmth' in relations with Egypt.

But on February 25, Assistant Secretary of State Joseph Sisco emphasized in an interview that the US had no intention of using its position as Israel's armourer to put pressure on Israel's leaders. A few days later, on March 1, Golda Meir talked with Nixon at the White House. Afterwards, she outlined Israel's policy at the National Press Club. She reiterated that 'If President Sadat is prepared to meet with us on any level, even indirectly, I could not welcome it more.' This helpful gesture was offset somewhat by a statement that the Golan Heights and Sharm el Sheikh were still 'non-negotiable'.

While Egypt pondered Mrs Meir's position, her statement was followed within a fortnight by an announcement from the United States that it would supply Israel with forty-eight more jets. It confirmed what Sadat had expected: Nixon – re-elected and confident of Brezhnev's need for detente – was not going to lean on Israel.

At the end of March, Sadat gave an interview to Arnaud de Borchgrave of the American magazine *Newsweek* in which he repeated that negotiations had now finally failed, and that war was necessary. After contacts with the world's major powers, there was only one conclusion: 'If we don't take our case in our own hands, there will be no movement. . . . There is no sense turning the clock back. Everything I've done leads to pressures for more concessions. I was even told by Rogers that my initiative for a final peace agreement with Israel was very courageous and had transformed the situation. Every door I have opened has been slammed in my face – with American blessings.'

'I can only conclude, from what you say,' said de Borchgrave, 'that you believe a resumption of hostilities is the only way out?'

'You are quite right. Everything in this country is now being mobilized in earnest for the resumption of the battle – which is now inevitable.'

Sadat was determined to convince the West that, this time, he was not bluffing. He had 'run out of ideas' for peace, he emphasized – and, if there was not to be peace, 'this will be the nightmare to end all nightmares – and everybody will be losers.' He complained to de Borchgrave: 'Everyone has fallen asleep over the Mideast crisis. But they will soon wake up'; and made it clear that Egypt expected to have the hardware with which to fight, because the Russians were now 'providing us with everything that's possible to supply.'

For the first time Sadat was prophesying war in earnest. The irony was that virtually nobody believed him.

3: Why Israel didn't guess

Israel's bloody failure to forecast the October war has three main causes. The first is practical. For the previous four years, the Israeli intelligence services had concentrated on hitting the Palestinian guerrillas and, in particular, their exploits abroad. But Israeli manpower is scarce: to staff this effort, Israel had to withdraw – principally from Egypt and Syria – a considerable proportion of its *political* intelligence agents. The resulting dearth of political intelligence was to lead Israel into what a British diplomat later called 'a classic case of intelligence understanding the capabilities of an enemy but not his intentions'.

This obsession – the word is not too strong – with the Palestinians led also to the second and deeper cause of Israel's blindness. That was a total inability to grasp that the Arabs might wage both terrorism and conventional war. The Israeli Defence Minister, Moshe Dayan, and successive chiefs of staff all repeated their contemptuous conviction that the Arabs had been reduced to random terrorism precisely because they dared not face Israel in battle – even their cross-border raids had been stamped out. It was even the Palestinians who were responsible for the third and most ironic cause of Israel's failure. Israeli intelligence did predict war in 1973, but thought it was about to break out in May – as a result of Palestinian actions.

Blinded by the Palestinian bogey, Israel thus ignored through the summer the accelerating pace of Arab preparations. In March, Sadat began to build a common political strategy with Syria. Syria still challenged the concept of a Jewish state: the most political basic decision which Egypt and Syria had to agree was thus what the war was to be about – the existence of Israel, or merely the recovery of the occupied lands? (For Syria and Jordan, of course, had also lost territory in 1967.) A further problem was that Egypt and Syria had no diplomatic relations with Jordan: a major task would be to bring Jordan back into the Arab fold.

On April 21–22, the Arab chiefs of staff met in Cairo to examine Israel's military situation. General Ismail later formulated his conclusions: 'My appraisal was that (Israel) possessed four basic advantages: its air superiority; its technological skill; its minute and efficient training; its reliance on quick aid from the United States, such as would ensure . . . a continuous flow of supplies. This enemy had also his basic disadvantages: his lines of communication were long and extended to several fronts, which made them difficult to defend. His manpower resources do not permit of heavy losses of life. His economic conditions prevent him from accepting a long war. He is, moreover, an enemy who suffers the evils of wanton conceit.'

To 'exploit his points of weakness', the enemy must, Ismail knew, be forced to distribute counterattacks widely. But this presupposed a common Arab strategy enabling pressure on many fronts. At the April meeting, unity was still far from assured. As the Egyptian Chief of Staff, General Shazli, announced on leaving the conference: 'The presence of some political and military problems is obstructing joint action.' One of the political problems soon asserted itself forcefully. On May 2, savage fighting broke out between the Lebanese army and Palestinian guerrillas.

An Israeli action sparked it. On April 10, in Beirut, Israeli commandos in civilian clothing assassinated three noted Palestinian leaders, as well as two women bystanders. The Lebanese government promptly fell and on May 2 – basically because of bad feeling over the army's inaction during the raid – a miniature civil war broke out in Lebanon. It lasted nine days. And Israeli intelligence thought it was going to spread beyond Lebanon. Jittery over Sadat's speeches prophesying war, Israel feared that Syria was about to intervene on the guerrillas' behalf in the Lebanon. And that, Balkan-fashion, could have sucked into confrontation the other Arab states around Israel – a confrontation which would inevitably spill over into Israel itself. The Syrians certainly prepared. But the Israeli forces were put on alert – the May 7 military parade through Jerusalem to mark Israel's twenty-fifth anniversary was a good cover – and Israeli infantry manoeuvred conspicuously on the Golan Heights.

It was a false alarm. But it illuminates the problems which just four months later were to baffle the Israelis. Because, according to the Israeli Chief of Staff, Lieutenant-General David Elazar, that May alert was based upon far more convincing indications of Arab war preparations than were to be detected later in the summer. And the alert cost Israel £4·5 million which it could ill afford; this was to be a factor in Israel's reluctance to damage its economy by mobilizing the civilian reserves during the next wave of danger signals.

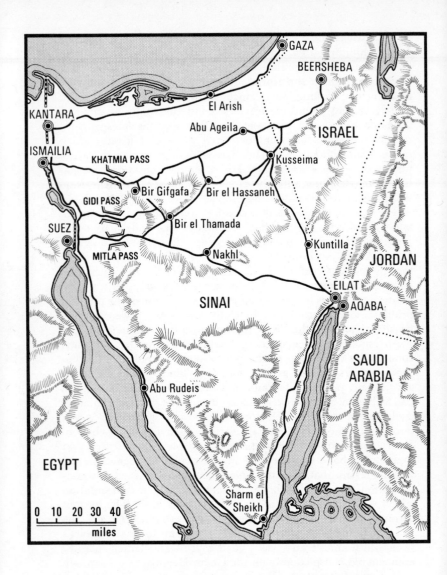

The mountains that control Sinai strategy

The keys to Sinai are the three passes: Khatmia, Gidi and Mitla. Southern Sinai is impassable mountains. The Mediterranean strip is largely soft sand seas, which so hem in the coast road through El Arish that tanks cannot manoeuvre in strength. So an assault has to capture the passes through the Central Ridge, which control the limited road network eastward to Israel's border. Since Israel captured Sinai in the Six Day War of 1967, its defensive strategy has been based on this, along with the delaying role of the Bar-Lev line of fortifications along the Suez Canal.

For Israel's ultimate guarantor, America, May was also a critical month in the run-up to war. The American intelligence community comprises several independent, overlapping and frequently warring agencies, of which the CIA is merely the best publicized. The smallest of these agencies is the State Department's own Intelligence & Research Bureau: with access to the work of the other agencies but without agents of its own, the Bureau's function is analysis. And its track record is pretty good: it was a lonely and consistent voice of pessimism over Vietnam, for instance. Surveying the May crisis – and the gathering pace of Sadat's strategy – the Bureau's analysts produced a paper giving their long range assessment of the Middle East. They predicted war in the autumn. The CIA agreed, though its dating was vaguer. Through the summer, both agencies repeated to the American Government a generalized warning: war in the Middle East was coming 'soon'.

One factor behind these assessments seems to have been the sheer weight of weaponry which the Arabs – in particular Syria – were now getting from Russia. The fresh shipments of Russia's latest T-62 tanks to Egypt and Syria need not have worried Israel. Trials of the two stolen T-62s had convinced Israel of their own Centurions' superiority. If the odds were high, that was for Israel a traditional disparity. More worrying were the new Syrian air defences. On May 3, President Asad made a twenty-four-hour trip to Moscow. He returned with a Russian promise of a complete air-defence system of SAM missiles plus another forty MIG-21 fighters. To supervise the arrangements for the SAMs, Asad returned from Moscow with the Russian air force commander, Marshal Kotakhov. And for Syria's swelling tank forces, Asad got the help of the Chief of the Czech General Staff, Karel Rusov – intriguingly, an expert in the defensive use of armour. In all, according to American estimates, Russia supplied Syria through the first half of 1973 with $185 million worth of arms – $35 million more than the shipments through the whole of 1972.

While Syria rearmed, the political negotiations over a common strategy with Egypt continued. These, so far as we can tell, were the most important meetings:

May 9: Egyptian War Minister Ismail visits Damascus briefly on his way back from Iraq.
May 19: Sadat visits Damascus for seven hours.
June 6: A Syrian military delegation, led by Defence Minister Lieutenant-General Mustafa Tlas, arrives in Cairo.
June 12: Sadat again flies to Damascus for talks with Asad.

It was at this last meeting that Sadat finally persuaded Asad of the fact that, even with its Russian equipment, Syria – its population only six million – could not hope to fight Israel except together with Egypt. Asad thus had no choice but to accept Sadat's objective and limit Syria's war aims.

At last the Cairo planning staff could set a date for war. The Director of Military Operations, Major-General Abdel Ghani Gamasy, controlling the planners, became the key figure at this point. General Ismail later described, with no false modesty, the work his men did on timing the attack: 'It was a great and scientific piece of work of the first order. When our documents are all laid out for historical study, this work will certainly earn its full share of appreciation and will enter the scientific history of wars as a model of minute precision and genuine research.'

The precise hour of the attack was in fact the subject of some dispute with Syria right up to October 2 (when Ismail himself flew to Damascus to resolve the issue). 'For several reasons', Ismail afterwards explained, 'most important of which was to have the sun in the eyes of the enemy, the Syrians preferred to begin at the first light of dawn. But for several reasons also – not only the direction of the sun, but the necessity of setting up bridges and moving tanks across the canal under cover of night – we [the Egyptians] preferred to act at sunset.' In the event, Ismail, as c-in-c for both fronts, comprised by bringing the time forward to the afternoon.

The preferred date of October 6 was, on the other hand, decided by the Egyptians much earlier in the planning – 'months before the war began', said Ismail. 'There was the general consideration that the situation had to be activated when Arab and world support for us was at its highest. More particularly, we needed: first, a moonlit night with the moon rising at the right time; second, a night when the water current in the canal would be suitable for crossing operations; third, a night on which our actions would be far from the enemy's expectations; and fourth a night on which the enemy himself would be unprepared. These particular considerations suggested October 6. On that day, astronomical calculations gave us the best times for moonrise and moonset. Our scientists examined the records of the old Suez Canal Company to assess the speed of the water currents and that day was found most suitable. In addition, the Israelis would not expect any action from our side during the month of Ramadan. And for their part, they would be preoccupied by a number of events, including their forthcoming General Election.' (Ismail does not say so specifically, but obviously to choose Yom Kippur, the holiest day of the Jewish calendar with Israel at a virtual

40

Hussein, Asad and Sadat at the Arab summit on September 10, at which differences were settled and the objectives of war were determined

standstill, could hardly have served his purpose better.)

October 6 also had a more atavistic appeal for the Arabs. In 1973 it would be the tenth day of Ramadan. On that day in the year 623, the Prophet Mohamed began preparations for the Battle of Badr, which led ten days later to his triumphant entry into Mecca – and the start of the spreading of Islam. It was a portent not to be missed. The military assault was codenamed 'Operation Badr'. And in another codeword chosen by Ismail, October 6 became 'Y-DAY'. (Y stands for *Yom*, meaning 'day' in both Arabic and Hebrew.)

While military planning was that far advanced, however, Sadat had still to succeed in the other aim of his political strategy: the wooing of King Hussein. It was not easy: there is some evidence that an early approach to Hussein – by way of Saudi Arabia's King Faisal, who throughout was the key, though secret, inter-mediary – was rebuffed. On May 13, Hussein sent a secret memorandum to his army officers. 'It is clear today,' he wrote, 'that the Arab nations are preparing for a new war. . . . The battle would be premature.' Hussein's differences with Egypt and Syria were political; but his reluctance to join a new war with Israel had sound military reasons, as we shall see later.

But Sadat persevered: the strategic value of imposing on Israel

41

a war on three fronts was worth rebuffs. And Jordan was prepared to resume diplomatic links. Again, the sequence of the
more important contacts between the Arab capitals indicates the
progress made:

> *June 18:* Abdel Rifai, Hussein's special envoy – and an
> uncle of his Prime Minister – arrives in Cairo.
> *June 30:* Rifai went on to Damascus. His purpose, he made
> clear, was to restore diplomatic relations with both states.
> *July 19:* Rifai is back in Cairo, with a message from Hussein.

More secret were meetings which Jordan's Prime Minister,
Zaid Rifai, had around this time: two with Sadat, one with
Asad. The reason for the secrecy was that those early negotiations
by his uncle were not going well. Again, Faisal of Saudi Arabia
was crucial. On July 28, the Jordanian Prime Minister went to
talk to him for twelve hours. That was the start of the serious
resolution of Jordan's political differences with Egypt and Syria.
On August 6 – while in Damascus Egypt's Chief of Staff,
Shazli, was refining military tactics with Syria – an envoy from
Sadat arrived in the Jordanian capital, Amman, and left four
days later with Hussein's envoy, Abdel Rifai, to see Asad.

The way was now clear for the culminating summit meeting.
Now too, military talks with Jordan could begin. On August 29,
Syrian Defence Minister Tlas arrived in Amman.

When King Hussein and President Asad arrived in Cairo on
September 10 for their summit with Sadat, most of the diplomatic and military differences had been ironed out. Jordan had
been brought back into the alliance. Syria had agreed to limited
war aims. And Sadat now had the arms he required. From April,
Egyptian leaders were again acknowledging that Russia was
building up Egypt's armed forces once more. Egypt, like Syria,
got tanks, missiles, aircraft, Russia's latest bridging equipment –
and seventy to eighty technicians for its forces.

The basic war aim, ratified by the Cairo summit, was a final
solution to the twenty-five-year confrontation with Israel. This
was to be achieved by sparking a crisis into which the superpowers would inevitably be drawn – and then to make *them* force
concessions from Israel. For this reason, Sadat called this broader
political strategy 'Operation Spark'.

Militarily, the objectives were the recapture of those parts
of Syria, Egypt and Jordan occupied by Israel. Even this was to
be achieved in two phases, however. For while Syria might be
able to regain its limited losses on Golan, Sadat had no intention
of letting his army loose through the back of beyond in Sinai.
And Hussein was in no position to tackle Israel at all. Egypt's

objective was thus the retaking of a slice of Sinai along the east bank of the Suez Canal. Hussein's task was to pose merely the threat of a third front for Israel – so tying up Israeli forces, and preventing a flank attack through Jordan into southern Syria. The rest of Sinai and the west bank of the Jordan would come as Israeli concessions.

For the military strategy agreed was brutally simple: Israel would be subjected to a war of attrition – the 'meatgrinder'. If the superpowers failed, the Arabs would continue for weeks, even months, until Israel, through sheer exhaustion of money and lives, had to settle.

This strategy, of course, said nothing about the cause theoretically dearest to the Arab heart: the rights of nearly two million Palestinians or descendants of Palestinians dispossessed at the foundation of Israel. And, indeed, even while the summit was in progress, the Palestinians' radio station in Baghdad condemned the 'series of basic retreats by certain Arab regimes. . . .' From the Palestinians' viewpoint, that was true enough: Egypt and Syria now accepted the existence of Israel. But the stakes Sadat was playing for were too high to be left to guerrillas. Besides, the three leaders might reasonably argue that their strategy was likelier to win something for the Palestinians than anything the Palestinians could do themselves. (In the event, of course, the leaders did not bother to argue. Asad simply closed down the Palestinians' Damascus radio station; and Hussein tried to appease them by releasing prisoners.)

Still, it was a successful – even momentous – summit. So far as we can tell, however, when it ended on September 12 with a formal resumption of diplomatic relations between the three countries, the final decision on whether to go ahead with the war was left to Sadat. Certainly, Asad and Hussein were not told the precise date of Y-day. According to Ismail that secret was still known only to Sadat and his own staff at that point. And Sadat still wanted to leave his final options open. Next day, September 13, Israel settled the question.

Israel may not have intended to pick a fight with Syria. The Israeli Chief of Staff insisted afterwards that the battle 'was not initiated by us', and that may well have been true. But what were four Israeli fighters doing cruising along over the Mediterranean, temptingly near to, if not in, Syrian airspace? Israel said it was a routine patrol. On the other hand, it was a trick the Israeli air force had tried before. Either way, the Syrians fell for it. A force of MIGs was scrambled to intercept them. What happened next is again disputed. Israel claims it had to send up reinforcements. Other accounts hold that the reinforcements were already waiting – in ambush up-sun. All that is certain is that in the ensuing melee, at least eight and possibly thirteen Syrians were shot down, for the loss of one Israeli plane.

If it was an Israeli ploy – just to remind the Arabs of Israeli power in the wake of the Cairo summit – it backfired appallingly. Because excellent sources in Cairo claim that it was after this battle that Asad phoned Sadat to urge that the time had come for action. Sadat agreed. He summoned his most senior military men: War Minister General Ahmed Ismail; Chief of Staff Lieutenant-General Saad Shazli; Director of Military Operations Major-General Abdel Ghani Gamasy; Director of Armaments and Organization Major-General Omar Gohar; Commander of Air Defence Major-General Mohamed Ali Fahmy; Air Force Commander Air Vice-Marshal Mohamed Mubarak; and the Commander of the Engineers Corps and the man who would have to construct the bridges across the canal, Major-General Aly Mohamed. To these and about another ten officers present at the meeting, Sadat gave the order to activate Operation Badr. From that moment, the countdown to war had begun. The most brilliant feature of the three weeks that followed was how completely the Arabs managed to disguise this.

4: The secret preparations

When Egyptian armour began assembling in the last week of September, few Israelis were worried. For ten years past – save in 1967, when it was otherwise engaged – the Egyptian army had held manœuvres every autumn. True, for the past two or three years, the manoeuvres and other, more frequent, exercises had seemed to concentrate on the canal. Even in the scattered strongpoints of the Bar-Lev line, it was hard enough for the Israelis to remain efficient; and they had air-conditioning and a four- to six-week tour of duty. For the Egyptian conscript, his two *years* on the canal must have been a nightmare of tedium. So the Israelis dismissed the exercises – and the new embankments and fortifications the Egyptians had thrown up over the past nine months. They were just to keep the troops busy.

One oddity, though, Israel passed to American intelligence. Each year, the Egyptian manoeuvres got bigger. It was not Israel, however, who spotted the sinister difference this time. Around September 24, the American Central Intelligence Agency worked out that these were the first exercises in which the

Egyptian army had manœuvred in formations as big as a full division. They were also stockpiling more ammunition than ever, assembling their most extensive logistics support yet seen – and, most disquieting of all, they were hooking up a vastly more complex field communications network than mere exercises could warrant. As soon as America learned this, Israel was warned. Specifically, Washington intelligence sources now claim, Israel was asked 'at very high level' whether this was not an indication of Arab preparations for the assault expected – by some of the American intelligence community, at least – since the spring. Israel rejected the fears.

Precisely as the Egyptian war planners had calculated, Israel was distracted. To its politicians, facing an October election, the most pressing battles were those of rival manifestos. On top of that, the government faced serious domestic and international problems. In New York, a new session of the United Nations General Assembly had just opened; Israel was already aware that the new Secretary of State, Henry Kissinger, proposed to use it to move towards a settlement in the Middle East.

Diplomatically, the failure of its African policy had left Israel more isolated in the developing world than ever. More drastic still, Israel's appeal seemed to be fading even among the Diaspora. Immigration of western Jews was almost nil: for white immigrants, Israel was now almost wholly dependent upon the flow of Jews from Russia. Meanwhile, even the financial aid from western Jews was failing to reach its monthly targets – aid which Israel relied upon to balance its monstrous budget deficit. Yet the government's ability to tackle these problems was waning steadily as serious internal rifts opened under pre-election pressure. It was a bad time. Even so, Israel's blindness to what followed is hard to explain.

The first Syrian moves also seem to have begun around September 24. There was no dramatic dash for the front; steadily and methodically, tanks and artillery began to mass around the triple lines of Syrian defence constructed over the plain between Golan and Damascus. One element behind that first American alert to Israel was concern over the conjunction of the Suez manœuvres with what Washington sources claim was seen as 'something seriously suspicious about the nature of the Syrian redeployment.'

Two days later, Moshe Dayan was the first to admit concern. On September 26, the Israeli Minister of Defence inspected troops on Golan during his annual tour on the day before the Jewish New Year. 'Stationed along the Syrian border,' he told them, 'are hundreds of Syrian tanks and cannon within effective range, as well as an anti-aircraft system of a density similar to that of the Egyptians' along the Suez Canal.' Publicly at least, Dayan professed to be worried less by this build-up than by the absence on Golan of the 'buffer of natural obstacles' present on the Suez and Jordanian fronts. (Israel, of course, had overrun in 1967 the only buffer there was, the Golan Heights themselves; but Dayan's irony was presumably unintentional.) Dayan talked of strengthening further the sixteen fortified settlements which Israel had established on Golan.

In private, however, Dayan was sufficiently alarmed to do two things. That same day, he put the army on alert on both fronts. And sometime during the three days of the holiday, he reinforced the single under-strength armoured brigade stationed on Golan by bringing back the usual Golan garrison, one of the Israeli army's crack units, the 7th Armoured Brigade. (It had been pulled back to armoured HQ at Beersheba.) It was perhaps the single most crucial Israeli decision of the war – yet it was done with no publicity at all.

It was as if Israel were wishing away unwelcome news. Dayan's warning of the Syrian build-up was barely reported. (There were no papers on the three days, September 27–29.) When news of the alert did leak after the holiday, it was soothed away as 'standard practice during Israel's festive season' – with the added reassurance that tourists were still allowed on Golan. Nobody mentioned that on September 27, the day after Dayan's Golan visit, the Americans launched from Vandenburg Air Base, California, a SAMOS reconnaissance satellite on an orbit over the Middle East. The American intelligence community thought that something needed watching.

Next day, Sadat himself provided another clue. September 28 was the third anniversary of Nasser's death. His successor took advantage of the occasion to release from jail several politically deviant journalists and students. And Sadat ended his speech announcing the amnesty with a strange, foreboding passage. 'Brothers and sisters,' he said, 'perhaps you have noticed there is a subject which I have not broached. This is the subject of battle. I have done this deliberately. We know our goal and we are determined to attain it. We shall spare no efforts or sacrifices to fulfil our objective. I promise nothing. I shall not discuss any details. However, I only say that the liberation of the land, as I have told you, is the first and main task facing us. God willing, we shall achieve this task. We shall realize it and we shall attain it. This is the will of our people. This is the will of our nation. It is even the will of God.' Rarely had Sadat, in a major speech, discussed war in such a low-key, almost subdued, manner.

What happened next was – perhaps – a stroke of bad luck. That same day, two Arab gunmen identifying themselves merely as

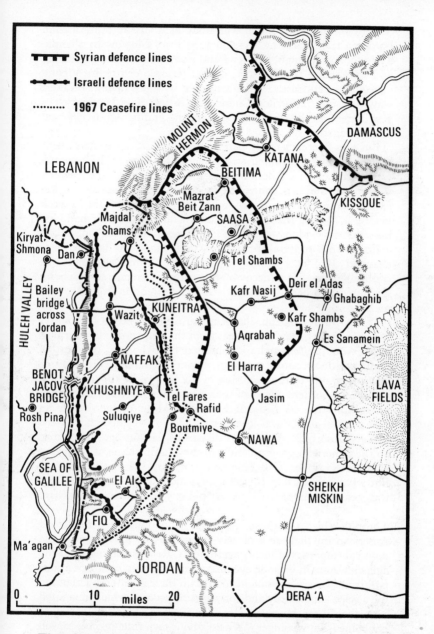

The danger Israel faced on Golan

For Israel, Golan's danger was that it lacked natural defences but was only 17 miles deep from the 1967 lines to Benot Jacov crossing. Three other roads led down the cliffs into Israel. To guard them Israel had strengthened Syria's old lines, while its strongpoint on Mount Hermon overlooked the whole plateau. Eastward, Syria had now built three new defence lines to guard Damascus. The only natural barrier to an Israeli advance across the plain was the Saasa lava ridge astride the Damascus road.

'Eagles of the Palestine Revolution' held up at the Austrian border a train carrying Russian Jews from Moscow to Vienna. They took as hostages five Jews and an Austrian customs official, and demanded that Austria close a transit centre in Vienna called Schonau Castle, which was used by Russian Jews on their way to Israel. Austria's Chancellor Bruno Kreisky, himself a Jew, agreed to the demand – and let the gunmen go free. Israel was outraged.

But was Schonau really bad luck, or was it – as some Israelis now suspect – a cunning stroke of misdirection? The gunmen were members of a Palestinian organization called Sai'qa, which is based in Syria, is controlled by the Syrian authorities to the extent that even Syrian army officers are members. Only a week before Schonau, the Sai'qa leader, Zuhair Muhsen, had dismissed such exploits as 'adolescent actions requiring no special courage and undertaken for fame and glory.' What, or who, changed Muhsen's mind? Egypt's War Minister Ismail was certainly proud of his 'decoy plan' – certain elements of which, he said later, had been 'intended to distract attention from what we meant to do'.

If it was misdirection, the Schonau raid succeeded brilliantly. It is no exaggeration to say that from that day until the morning before war itself, Israel was obsessed by Schonau: demonstrations, petitions, public meetings, banner headlines and pages of newsprint – all to the exclusion of the far graver threat massing on Israel's borders. News of such developments was tucked into paragraphs buried beneath Schonau. More dangerously, the Israeli government and its military and intelligence chiefs were equally absorbed. Which was disastrous, because on September 30 the American government – in the plump shape of Secretary of State Kissinger – became concerned by the Arab build-up. But what he was told by the American intelligence community was heavily influenced by the opinions of Israeli intelligence.

Through this run-up to war, the adequacy of Israeli and American intelligence is clearly critical to any assessment of the political responses of their governments. Reconstructing what the agencies thought is made even harder in this case because various politicians have since sought to explain their inaction by blaming the advice – inevitably and conveniently secret – which emanated from their intelligence services. The starkest accusation of failure has come from Kissinger: 'We asked our own intelligence, as well as Israeli intelligence, on three separate occasions during the week prior to the outbreak of hostilities, to give us their assessment of what might happen. There was the unanimous view that hostilities were unlikely to the point of there being no chance of it happening.' The reality was considerably more complex.

Technically, the intelligence was excellent. To monitor Egyptian preparations, for instance, Israel had its own highly sophisticated listening devices in Sinai – American gear manned by ex-members of America's National Security Agency, working on swiftly-supplied Israeli passports for double their American salaries. This supplemented America's own electronic espionage establishment, the National Security Agency, which listens from a highly-secret base in southern Iran to radio traffic throughout the Middle East. And if the SAM defences had curtailed Israel's ability to mount photographic reconnaissance flights, the American SAMOS satellite was filling that gap by the end of September. 'Nobody made any mistake about the facts,' Kissinger has said.

But after the facts comes their interpretation, and as Kissinger also said: 'Facts are easier to come by than intentions.' The Israeli failure was to divine Arab strategy. This has been denied. One of Israel's most distinguished soldiers, Lieutenant-General Haim Bar-Lev – ex-Chief of Staff, cabinet minister at the outbreak of war and architect of the Bar-Lev line – has claimed 'no lack of knowledge' of Arab intentions. Another source close to the military establishment asserted that 'Israel knew even the time of the attack.' But a senior Israeli intelligence officer has told us privately that all Israel concluded was that an Arab attack was possible 'sometime soon'. 'We were caught on the hop,' he said.

Background briefings given to foreign correspondents in Israel during the ten days before war provide a clue to the basic ingredient in this miscalculation. Senior Israeli political figures stressed their belief that the Arab leaders were not ready for war. The Arabs might 'miscalculate' and launch an attack, one such briefing admitted. But if so, they would doubtless be defeated. Israel, the briefing concluded with supreme over-confidence, was 'not interested in war' – the Arabs, the implication ran, therefore would not be.

By a somewhat more empirical path, the American intelligence community reached the same conclusion. On September 30, at Kissinger's request, the CIA and the State Department's own Research & Intelligence Bureau (INR) sent the Secretary of State their evaluations of the Arab build-up. Neither was as blithe as Kissinger has alleged. The INR found the moves 'inconclusive'. But it was principally after surveying the *political* scene that the INR analysts, while not 'optimistic' that there would be no war, concluded that it was 'dubious' whether one would begin soon.

The CIA's assessment was much the same. The build-up was viewed as 'very ominous'. But the Israeli confidence about Arab intentions was seen as decisive. The INR was also influenced by the views of Israeli intelligence. 'Our error was to accept Israeli reassurances about Arab intentions,' we were told. But in judging Arab intentions, the INR also looked closer to home: to the United Nations, where a new session of the General Assembly had just opened.

To the Arab and Israeli foreign ministers assembled for this opening, Kissinger – with the hubris of a man about to accept the Nobel peace prize for 'settling' Vietnam – announced that America was now keen to assist 'practical progress' towards a Middle East settlement. A lunch he had given for Arab envoys on September 25 was declared to have been his first diplomatic move. (He had, in fact, already put pressure on Israel.) And in private talks in New York through the end of September, Kissinger did get somewhere. 'The Arabs seemed more relaxed and self-confident than I have seen them for a long time,' a senior UN official privy to these talks said later. The Israeli and Arab foreign ministers secretly agreed that sometime in November – the date to be fixed after the Israeli elections – they would meet under Kissinger's auspices to thrash out 'a course of procedures' leading to substantive negotiations.

The intelligence analysts were fooled. 'The Arabs' interest in diplomacy seemed so great that though there was plenty of evidence of military movements we were misled,' a Washington intelligence man said. 'We had the right factors, but we didn't weigh their priorities correctly.' Reading the intelligence assessments, Kissinger also thought the Arabs would give his particular brand of diplomacy a chance. And since Sadat's intention had originally been to back both military and diplomatic initiatives, *perhaps* the most powerful of Kissinger's Arab contacts, the Egyptian Foreign Minister Muhammad Zayyat, was desperately eager for last-minute progress – knowing in general terms what lay in store if he failed? Whatever the motives, however, the effect was that, as the evidence of crisis mounted, Kissinger was – in the pithy phrase of a Washington columnist – 'unusually ready to duck'.

That day, September 30, as American intelligence uneasily decided that war was unlikely, Egypt's War Minister Ismail sent a warning signal to his Syrian opposite number, Tlas. The Syrians had still not been told the exact date of Y-DAY. Now, Ismail warned Tlas that the assault was likely at any time: it would be signalled, he said, by the single codeword 'BADR'.

In the early hours of Monday, October 1, Syrian tanks and heavy artillery began to move up from their rear positions to deploy opposite the Israeli outposts. Already installed to protect

them were the missiles Dayan had warned about, now inter-
locked into a formidable air-defence system the length of the
Golan front. There were also the observations from the watching
troops along the canal (among them Avi Yaffe and his comrades
opposite Ismailia). It was Y minus 5: the final countdown to
war had begun.

Israel was unruffled. From their observation post high on the
7,000-foot ridge of Mount Hermon, Israeli troops could scan
eastward as far as Damascus and peer down on the Syrian
armour marshalling unhurriedly across the rocky plain below.
The Syrians brilliantly exploited this: they mobilized in *defensive*
formation. The Syrian tanks were positioned 'hull down', dug in
to resist an assault rather than to mount one. Their medium
artillery was placed back, to cover not Israeli but Syrian territory – again apparently signifying defensive action. As Dayan
admitted later, Israel was fooled.

Even some units which Syria had previously stationed on the
Jordanian frontier had by now been moved to Golan. This 'bolstering of forces', as the ritual Israeli 'informed sources' tactfully
phrased it, was merely a gesture of goodwill towards the Jordanians in the wake of the detente between the two countries. No
Syrian 'initiative' was expected. Next day, October 2 – Y minus
4 – Syria called up its reserves. And over the following twenty-
four hours, United Nations observers on the Suez Canal saw
Egyptian officers on the bank, openly instructing their troops.
At last, down through the ranks of the Egyptian forces – from
army commander to divisions, brigades, finally to battalian
level – the order was now passed: Operation Badr was on. It was Y
minus 3.

That Wednesday, October 3, the Israeli cabinet gathered in
Jerusalem for its only meeting in the week before Yom Kippur.
It was devoted to Schonau. Mrs Meir had just returned from
Strasbourg – where she had torn up a speech to the Council of
Europe on Israel's disputes with the Arabs and instead talked
impromptu for two-and-a-half hours on Schonau. She had then
flown home via Vienna, in an abortive attempt to persuade
Chancellor Kreisky to change his mind. The Israeli cabinet had
to decide what to do now. The ominous indications of an Arab
build-up were never mentioned: their extent remained a secret
known only to a tight handful of Mrs Meir's closest colleagues.

In Cairo, with appropriate symmetry, the Egyptian cabinet
also had its only meeting that week on Wednesday – an inno-
cuous discussion of the proposed Egypt–Libya merger. In Egypt,
too, the momentous military news was kept from most of the
cabinet. It is now pretty clear, in fact, that – apart from the
military planning staffs, chiefs of staff and defence ministers of

Egypt, Syria and possibly Jordan – barely half a dozen people throughout the Arab world knew of the plan. The list probably read: Sadat, Asad, Hussein, President Boumedienne of Algeria and King Faisal of Saudi Arabia – the latter having apparently been told on a secret visit by Sadat. But not even Asad, let alone Hussein, Boumedienne or Faisal knew the precise timing of Y-DAY.

Moreover, when American intelligence had found the Arab manœuvres 'inconclusive', they had not realized how detailed was Egypt's deception strategy. 'In every war, there are two plans,' Ismail said later, 'one an operations plan, the other a decoy plan. I believe we succeeded in planning our decoy plan at a strategic and at a mobilization level – and we fixed its timings to parallel the operations plan and its timings and movements.' The CIA might have found the exercises more conclusive, for instance, had they known that Ismail was sending out a brigade in the morning but only bringing back a battalion, a third of the men, at night – 'to give the enemy the impression that the force had been on training duty and had come back after finishing it,' Ismail explained. Two-thirds of the men, in fact, remained in battle position. The Cairo paper, *Al Ahram*, announced that officers could take leave to perform the Moslem *Omrah* (little pilgrimage).

'I also made a point,' Ismail said, 'of delaying our crossing equipment as much as possible. Taking out such equipment from its depots at an earlier date would have been enough to alert the enemy to our intentions. We had even made special crates for some of this equipment so that nobody could detect that the huge trucks carrying them were engineers corps trucks. And when this equipment did finally come to the canal, by night, it was at once put into pits which had been specially dug for the purpose.' Shazli was surprised they succeeded so well: 'The last three days were especially difficult, but we did not expect the enemy to be taken in as easily as he was.'

But the most effective Egyptian camouflage was, like the Syrians', a brilliant stroke of misdirection. Egypt, it was said, feared an *Israeli* strike in retaliation for Schonau. Egypt wished to be ready: hence the preparations. The alibi was plausible. It may even have been true. There is some evidence that the Israeli Chief of Staff, David Elazar, only four days before the war was indeed occupied in planning a reprisal raid on Libya.

On Thursday, October 4 – Y minus two – the American intelligence agencies had their last chance. Their main forum, the US Intelligence Board, met just south of Washington in the CIA headquarters at Langley, Virginia, to discuss one question:

would there be war? Since the September 30 papers, Kissinger had almost daily asked the State Department's own INR specific points: the progress of the build-up and the like. And Kissinger's assistant secretary, Joseph Sisco, with not only day-to-day responsibility for Middle East affairs but also bureaucratic control of INR, had been briefed more than once by its staff – these informal views he had presumably retailed to Kissinger. But no other formal assessments had been drafted by INR or CIA. On Thursday morning, Kissinger asked INR for another full-scale assessment.

As the agencies pooled their thoughts at the final Board meeting, however, they made little progress. Russia had just launched from its pads near Archangel a COSMOS reconnaissance satellite to orbit, like America's SAMOS, over the Middle East. So they were worried too. (Had the meeting known that this was only the first of six satellites Russia would launch in the next three weeks, they might have drawn a different conclusion. A satellite launch takes several days of preparation: Russia was getting ready for something altogether bigger than the American analysts imagined.) But while the Washington meeting was worried, Israeli intelligence was still convinced of its reading of Arab intentions. And, apart from the high regard in which their intelligence is held in Washington, the meeting seems to have felt that by virtue of the Israelis' position – they, after all, faced the highest penalties for failure – their opinions carried special weight.

The mounting Arab military preparations were obviously the major topic. But here, significantly, the group closest to the Israelis – the Pentagon's Defense Intelligence Agency – still disputed even the threatening nature of these. (The three top men in the agency's Middle East branch have since been transferred.) Late that afternoon, INR staff reported back to Kissinger. The intelligence agencies' unanimous view was that war was 'unlikely'. The separate INR assessment Kissinger had ordered was never finished; it was still in draft when, to the ruin of several careers, fighting broke out.

Given the six-hour time-lag between Washington and the Middle East, in fact, the Intelligence Board's reassurance was delivered to Kissinger at approximately the moment when Thursday turned to Friday in the Middle East – and the imminence of war was further confirmed. Late on Thursday night in Cairo, road blocks were set up round the pleasant suburb of Zamalek, the Nile island which is the favoured home of foreign diplomats. In convoys of official cars, the families of Egypt's Russian advisers drove to the airport and began to evacuate. (According to western diplomats in Cairo, their departure was flurried – as if it were a last-minute decision.) The Russian airlift out of Damascus began a few hours later. Meanwhile, through the early hours of Friday morning, the Syrian armour redeployed – into offensive formation. And the Syrian heavy artillery, previously grouped around northern Golan, now ranged south – to cover the whole Israeli line. It was Y minus one.

5: Mrs Meir decides to wait

The last thirty hours to war are the most critical and the most mysterious period so far as Israel is concerned: critical because decisions the Israeli government made or did not make then conditioned its army's responses through the first five days of war; mysterious because strangely little has emerged about those decisions. As we write, major questions remain unanswered: it may be a long time before the pressures of Israeli politics bring all the facts to light.

The army tried to prepare. The troops had been on alert since Dayan's warning on Golan. Now, at 11.00 am, Elazar put them on 'the highest state of military preparedness', as he called it – cancelling leave and warning that a call-up of reservists was possible. (The air force reserves had in fact been called up, quietly, the day before.)

Some senior reservists were alerted. The briefing of Arik Sharon – summoned from his Beersheba ranch to Southern Command headquarters – was fairly typical. But there were bad hiccups: commanders as senior as brigadiers were somehow never warned. Much further down the line, though, old sweats like tank sergeants got to know what was afoot. It was a tank sergeant, in fact, who produced – remarkably, in the *Jerusalem Post* on the second day of war – the most explosive allegation about that hectic Friday. 'We were told before Yom Kippur started that we could expect something big,' he said. 'They explained to us that it was a political problem and we would just wait for the attack . . . ' While the Israeli army prepared, just what was the government doing?

The extraordinary answer is apparently that Mrs Meir and her ministers did nothing until Friday evening. One military source in Israel has hinted to us that there was indeed an informal meeting of ministers on Friday morning, and that only after this was the army's alert heightened. And Shimon Peres, Israeli

Minister of Transport, has said: 'We held a Cabinet meeting on Friday to discuss the situation and it was the shortest discussion I can remember. We were entirely unanimous in our decision not to mobilize . . .'. All other political sources now claim, however, that the critical meeting was not until Friday evening.

In the Israeli cabinet, as in any other, the doctrine of collective responsibility ignores the practical fact that some ministers are more equal than others. Mrs Meir's 'kitchen cabinet' – as Israel has nicknamed this inner group of ministers – varies in composition. But at 5.30 pm that evening – as dusk fell and throughout Israel the Kol Nidrei service signalled the start of Yom Kippur, the holiest day of the Jewish year – four ministers met in Mrs Meir's office in the Government compound in Tel Aviv: Mrs Meir herself; the Deputy Premier Yigal Allon; Defence Minister Moshe Dayan; and the Minister without Portfolio, Israel Galili, a man almost unknown outside Israel but one of Mrs Meir's closest political confidants. Either immediately or soon after the meeting started, the four were joined by the ex-Chief of Staff, Haim Bar-Lev, then Minister of Commerce, and the current Chief of Staff, David Elazar.

The key question was whether to disrupt the hallowed calm of Yom Kippur by calling up the reserves. A decision was taken against this. The official version is that nobody dissented. The truth is that Elazar was overruled – and was furious. Had the reserves been called up 'twenty-four or forty-eight hours earlier', Elazar said on November 11, the war would have 'undoubtedly looked different'. He added the explosive point that casualties would also have been fewer. But, he said, the decision was taken at 'the highest political-military level'. 'We will never know whether the war would have broken out had we called up the reserves,' he concluded.

In the decision, Dayan's role seems to have been critical. Mrs Meir hinted as much on Israel television on November 16: 'When somebody who was authorized to propose mobilization came, I agreed at once.' The authorized person was the Minister of Defence. Dayan later sought to defend himself, in front of a tense meeting of officers on November 14, by saying that on Friday he did not think there would be war – 'I was not the only one to think so, and I did not hear anyone say that war was about to break out that day.'

This seems to be correct. Remarkably, the meeting was still less worried by the Arab build-up itself than by the Russian advisers' departure – and even this, they thought, had its hopeful aspect. 'It was clear that the Russians had no intention of taking part in what was to happen,' one source close to the meeting told us. 'This was an encouragement and a worry at the same time.'

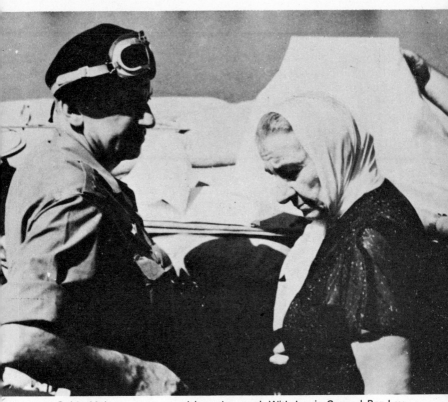
Golda Meir on a pre-war visit to the canal. With her is General Bar-Lev creator of Israel's canal-side defensive line

(It should also be recorded, however, that in Washington various CIA personnel were woken at home that Friday with news of the Russian evacuation: they dismissed its significance.)

At 4.00 am on Saturday, this complacency was shattered. Elazar, commuting between Mrs Meir's office and the Israeli war room, learned that Israeli and American monitors had now picked up the unmistakable radio traffic patterns of final Arab preparations for war. The Israeli general staff concluded that war was 'imminent and inevitable.' Elazar now proposed that the Israel air force mount a pre-emptive strike at 13.00 hours that day.

Mrs Meir vetoed the plan – and fear of America's reaction was her dominating reason. 'How many friends would we have left if we did that?' she asked Elazar. Her Chief of Staff, and perhaps Bar-Lev, argued back emotionally. 'Every time we decide to take into account the opinions of others, we have to pay for it in blood,' one Israeli source quotes them as saying. But the 1967 pre-

In the elaborate underground command centre from which Egypt ran the war: Sadat with Generals Shazli (left) and Ismail (right)

emptive strike had caught the Egyptian air force lined up on its airfields. A strike this time would have been against a prepared adversary, protected by a lethal missile screen. At best, the Israelis could have disrupted Arab preparations for a few hours – in return for dreadful losses. The argument was clinched by the American ambassador to Israel, Kenneth Keating. At 6.00 am he was woken and summoned to a meeting with Mrs Meir.

Both the American and Israeli governments have kept very quiet about what followed. But it looks as if a simple but deadly threat was relayed to Mrs Meir by Keating – probably acting under instructions from Kissinger. Evidence from military and political sources in both Israel and America suggests that Keating warned that if Israel struck first, America would feel unable to supply fresh equipment. It was said diplomatically – 'If Israel refrained from a pre-emptive strike, allowing the Arabs to provide irrefutable proof that they were the aggressors, *then* America would feel morally obliged to help,' was how one source described it. The threat was the same.

Behind this *démarche*, two strands of American thinking are apparent. The first was simply that America was sceptical about Arab intentions. As one Israeli source, describing those last hours, blandly put it: 'Not everybody agreed with Israel's assessment of the situation.' America was the only party whose agreement mattered. Secondly, the US hoped that if it was clear that this time, the Arabs were the aggressors, world opinion would prevent a shut-down of Arab oil to Israel's allies.

In the last analysis, therefore, Mrs Meir was confident that the United States would not allow Israel to perish, but was deeply uncertain whether America – particularly with its foreign affairs in the hands of Kissinger – would supply Israel with arms to defend what were, after all, captured lands. Unless, as Keating pointed out, the Arabs were indubitably the aggressors.

This led to the last, most private, reason for Mrs Meir's decision against a pre-emptive strike. Strategically, Israel had always defended its retention of 1967's gains with the plea that they gave, for the first time, defence in depth. A fighting retreat in the face of an Arab assault across the 1967 ceasefire lines would demonstate unarguably that Israel had been right to hold on to the land.

Weighing all these factors, Mrs Meir's 'kitchen cabinet' decided to take a risk. Elazar had of course been given permission to mobilize the reserves. (The first orders went out around 7.00 am.) But, meanwhile, perhaps the Arabs' story was true: perhaps they were preparing for war in fear of an Israeli strike. Mrs Meir would reassure them. Ambassador Keating was given an urgent message for Kissinger. Would he please tell the Arabs that Israel was not, contrary to their fears, planning a strike, so they had nothing to worry about.

When, finally, the Israeli cabinet were convened at around 11.00 am – to be told not only that mobilization was already under way, but that the inner circle of ministers had for days been aware of a potential military crisis – they were too stunned, as well as too late, to comment or criticize. It was this dawn decision which Mrs Meir hinted at on Israeli television on November 16, when she said: 'I think that so far as everything that happened – including the need for equipment and the obtaining of equipment – had the situation not been clear beyond the shadow of a doubt regarding who began hostilities, I doubt whether the vital equipment received in the course of time would have flowed in as it did, as it still continues to do . . .'.

Kissinger got Mrs Meir's message around Friday midnight in New York. If Mrs Meir hoped he would save matters, though, she was disappointed. As he said later: 'We were informed . . . that Israel did not intend to attack herself, but that did not indicate to us necessarily that an Arab attack was imminent.' He added plaintively: 'Nor was the possibility of hostilities raised in any of the discussions with either of the parties that took place at the United Nations during the past week.' According to the State Department, the Pentagon *had* decided by midnight that war was now probable – Kissinger cannot have been told. So, confident of his own abilities and reassured by outdated intelligence, Kissinger passed on the Israeli message without particular concern. He then retired to bed in his 35th floor suite in New York's Waldorf Towers, looking forward to a weekend of party-going in Manhattan. In Israel, it was 7.00 am Saturday, and over Sinai it was already light. It was Y-DAY.

For most of the civilian population of Israel, the realization that this was to be no ordinary Day of Atonement came at 7.00 am when a Phantom roared low over Jerusalem heading north to survey the Golan. (Other flights headed across to scan Suez.) At the Wailing Wall, relic of the ancient temple in Jerusalem, early worshippers looked up, shocked and frightened. To break Yom Kippur in that fashion was unthinkable – unless the unthinkable were about to happen. Rumour spawned rumour throughout Israel in the hours ahead, until anxiety was like a smell seeping through the air.

Only Israel's senior military had no time to be anxious. When the Phantoms landed, their film revealed the trap about to be sprung. Frantic telephoning began around 9.00 am as the defence staff alerted the many senior regular officers who had still not been told the news. Although Israel's highly efficient mobilization routine was already under way, it has to work by stages: the first logistics phase preparing for the rest. And this first phase works on the basis of one man calling ten, ten calling a hundred, and so on. In the general call-up, that is augmented by broadcast messages. There is thus no way of bringing any proportion of these reserves into battle in under twenty-four hours. Israel was trapped without its citizen army.

Section II

Below: Jubilant Egyptian Third Army troops cross the canal. This improvised bridge, south of the Bitter Lakes, was one of the last to be established, after snags with Russian bridge-building equipment.

Week one: The victory that Egypt threw away

1: The Y-Day onslaught

The first casualties in the fourth Arab–Israeli war were not, so far as we can trace, any of Avi's fellow Israelis along the Bar-Lev line stunned by the sudden Egyptian assault across the Suez Canal. They were Arab villagers, among them a mother and child. And they were casualties of the coordinated Syrian assault on Israel launched over the Golan plain just two minutes before the attack by Egypt began.

At 1.58 pm on the afternoon of Saturday, October 6, five Syrian MIG-17 fighters skimmed into attack low over the Israeli positions on the northernmost sector of the Golan lines. It was cool and cloudy, and the Israeli tanks were unmanned, their crews chatting beside them, the more religious reciting the Yom Kippur afternoon prayer. As the fighters opened up with cannon and rockets and the crews leaped into their tanks and hurriedly revved up, it crossed their minds that this was not a particularly impressive first strike by Syria. But at the northern end of their strafing run, the MIGs, their cannon still firing, curved away over the Druze village of Majdal Shams in the Mount Hermon foothills. A young mother, who had run out of her house to stare up in surprise at the sound of gunfire, was killed by a cannon shell, which also smashed the legs of the eight-month-old baby she was carrying. Several other villagers were hurt.

As another wave of fifteen to twenty MIGs – part of the initial strike by 100 aircraft – swooped over the Israeli positions, Syrian fighter-bombers made low-level attacks on the Israeli brigade headquarters ten miles behind the front line at Naffak. Then, at precisely 2.00 pm – at the moment when, 250 miles to the southwest, Egyptian commandos were scrambling down the Suez banks to launch their rubber assault dinghies – a barrage of artillery fire crashed down from the Syrian batteries massed on the Golan plain. Now the extent of the crisis facing Israel became brutally clear. For the Syrian gunners were 'walking' the curtain of fire towards the squadrons of Israeli tanks hastily assembling at their firing stations. And through the continuous explosions flung up by the shells, the Israeli tank commanders peering over their turrets could see a rolling dust cloud, in the middle of which they faintly discerned the outlines of hundreds upon hundreds of advancing Syrian tanks.

Plumb in the middle of the Golan ceasefire strip, just north of Kuneitra, was Observation Post 'Winter', one of the string of United Nations bunkers stretching down the Golan front. Incredulously, the UN official in Winter, an Australian, watched a formation of 300 Syrian tanks roll towards him. They were four abreast, two columns each side of the road, their turret hatches open and their commanders proudly to attention. 'It wasn't like an attack,' said the awed observer later, 'it was like a parade ground demonstration.' As it approached his bunker, the column divided and, like a tide, flowed past his bunker on either side – one forking north of Kuneitra, the other south. As they approached the Israelis, it seems likely that one waiting tank commander's recollection of those minutes was echoed by all : 'I never knew there were so many tanks in all the world.'

At least 700 Syrian tanks went into action along Golan in that first wave : 300 in the thrust down towards Kuneitra, another 400 rolling in an equally daunting display from the south, up the long and utterly exposed road from Sheikh Miskin to Rafid – in all, two Syrian armoured divisions. (Estimates of their infantry support vary, but it too may have as much as 7,000 men.) Facing them were fewer than 180 Israeli tanks – two armoured brigades, one of them understrength. (See map page 79.)

What followed will surely, whatever the political consequences of the October war, become an epic in military history. For the United Nations observer – trapped for days in his bunker while the battle raged around him – saw barely a handful of those Syrian tanks return. After five days of the most desperate and unrelenting battle since the war which heralded Israel's birth, twenty-five years before, the Israeli forces had destroyed that Syrian armour and advanced eastward over the Syrians' own defence lines towards Damascus.

The Golan battle was one of the two most critical actions of the war, and it made possible the other, which was Arik Sharon's crossing of the Suez Canal in the second week to disrupt the Egyptian assaults – and ultimately, to encircle part of their army. For while the Syrian armour so urgently threatened its northern front, Israel simply had not the resources to gamble on an assault like that in Sinai.

In the first phase of the war, therefore, the stories of the two fronts are very different. In Sinai, while isolated pockets such as Avi's held out – one for as long as seven days – the Egyptians consolidated their hold over virtually the whole east bank of the canal. In practice, Israel had no choice but to let them do so. Its canal defences were overwhelmed by the weight of the Egyptian attack : two armoured and two infantry divisions crossed the canal in the initial wave. But in Sinai, geography favoured Israel.

The 125 miles of desert between the canal and the heartland of Israel present to the Israelis a simple defensive equation: give ground to gain time. So Israel's initial Sinai strategy, after the first terrible twenty-four hours while its forces struggled to recover their balance from the Egyptian blow, was to fight à rearguard action – as cheaply as possible. In this aim, their greatest allies were paradoxically the Egyptians themselves, who – seemingly startled by their own swift successes and inhibited by a battle-plan of inflexible caution – frittered these away by concentrating upon defensive tactics of their own.

On Israel's northern front, however, the geography of Golan presented its forces with none of the possibilities of Sinai. From the front line to the cliffs overlooking Israel, Golan is just seventeen miles deep: to hold it the Israelis had to fight virtually where they stood. This they did. But Golan presented other – and in the final outcome, more damaging – problems for the Syrians too. While the Suez Canal supplied the Egyptians with a natural defence upon which they could group their successful assault forces on the east bank, Golan was bare of natural features for the Syrians to exploit as fixed strategic positions. To succeed, the Syrians had to fight a war of continuing movement and unceasing assault. That was precisely the warfare at which the Israeli tank crews excelled – as Syria was once more to learn at terrible cost. But the price Israel paid in this war was also high. And the first shattering blow was the collapse of the Sinai defences.

The battle for Sinai was heralded by four crashing waves of artillery fire from 1,000 guns concealed among the dunes behind the west bank of the canal. The assault that followed was concentrated along three stretches: below Kantara in the north, around Ismailia in the centre and, south of the Bitter Lakes, from Shalufa to El Kubri (see map, page 66). Amazingly, it achieved almost total surprise. The Israeli Chief of Staff, Elazar, later ascribed this unreadiness to 'a serious failure in observing the order for full battle alert at some of the lower echelons.' Nobody seems to have told the men on the front line of the imminence of war.

Manning the Bar-Lev line were reservists of the 116th Brigade, called the Jerusalem Brigade from its part in the storming of the city in 1967. Most were middle-aged businessmen. The brigade had been sent up to relieve the regular garrison. But even the 116th was not at full strength: many of its 800 men had been given leave for Yom Kippur. Mrs Meir said later that on October 6, fewer than 600 men were manning the Bar-Lev line.

When the assault came, many were, like Avi, washing their clothes – presumably taking advantage of Yom Kippur's break from more martial chores. Others were at prayer. One, Private Unsdorfer, was in a squad so religious that the majority assumed the sudden barrage was some transient local incident and, dashing to their battle stations, continued their service. 'We said our Minha prayers in our positions,' Unsdorfer recalled. 'And when we recited the Shma – "Hear, O Israel" – everybody, even the non-observant, joined in with great fervour.' Indeed, they might have. For as 8,000 Egyptian infantry slithered down the sandy banks and scudded over the water in rubber dinghies, the Israelis made their first terrible discovery. The secret weapon of the Bar-Lev line was a device to transform the canal into a moat of fire. But now the Israelis could not make it function. They did not know that, the night before, Egyptian commandos had sabotaged it.

The device was simple. Beneath each Bar-Lev strongpoint was a series of underground oil storage tanks, pipes interconnecting them and finally leading to wide nozzles down by the water's edge. A switch in each strongpoint started pumps to spray the oil over the surface of the canal in a thin film – which a thermite bomb would then ignite. The blaze would have incinerated any Egyptian assault force.

The Egyptians knew this. Reconnaissance patrols slipped across the canal, and discovered the pipes. 'Our first problem,' the Egyptian Chief of Staff, Shazli, said later, 'was to cope with the prospect of the canal turning into an inferno as soon as the crossing started. Experiments we made showed that attempting to extinguish such blazes would require at least half an hour, even supposing no further inflammable material was thrown in.'

The Egyptians thought of blowing up the tanks, but dropped the idea. 'Reconnaissance showed that the enemy stored the material sufficiently underground as a protection against artillery fire.' The Egyptian solution was simple. The system was most vulnerable, they decided, at its canal outlets. 'Our plan,' Shazli revealed, 'was to send teams to block these pipes with cement.' War Minister Ismail adds that the commando groups slipped over on Friday night.

Only at one place on Saturday morning did the Israelis discover the sabotage. 'And they brought an engineer to repair it,' Ismail said. Shazli adds that he was the engineer who had designed the system 'and he testified during interrogation that he had arrived in the area only the day before on an inspection trip.' He was, certainly, one of the first prisoners of war. As Ismail triumphantly put it: 'He was still at his job when he suddenly found our soldiers over his head.' (Israel has since claimed that the pipes were dummies. The fire weapon, they say, was tried in 1970, found 'ineffective' and so – in seeming contradiction –

65

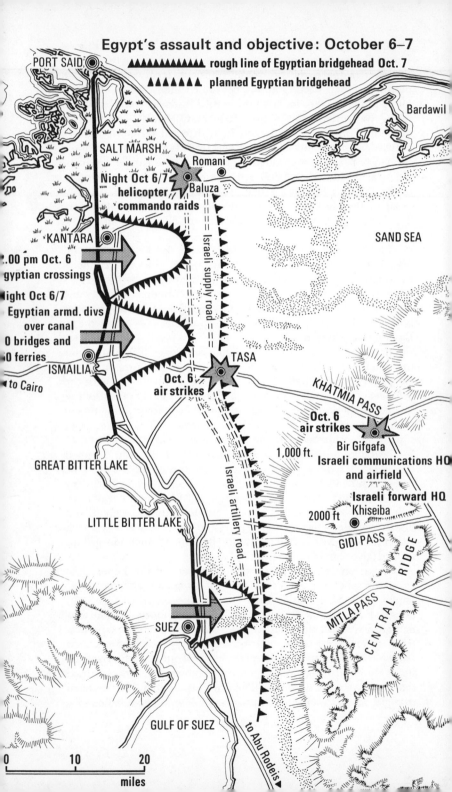

Egypt's assault and objective: October 6–7

▲▲▲▲▲▲▲▲▲▲ rough line of Egyptian bridgehead Oct. 7

▲▲▲▲▲▲▲ planned Egyptian bridgehead

PORT SAID

SALT MARSH

Romani

Baluza

Night Oct 6/7 helicopter commando raids

Bardawil

SAND SEA

KANTARA

Israeli supply road

.00 pm Oct. 6
gyptian crossings

ight Oct 6/7
Egyptian armd. divs
over canal
0 bridges and
0 ferries

ISMAILIA

to Cairo

TASA

Oct. 6 air strikes

KHATMIA PASS

Oct. 6 air strikes

1,000 ft.

Bir Gifgafa
Israeli communications HQ and airfield

Israeli forward HQ
Khiseiba

GREAT BITTER LAKE

Israeli artillery road

LITTLE BITTER LAKE

2000 ft

GIDI PASS

CENTRAL RIDGE

MITLA PASS

SUEZ

GULF OF SUEZ

to Abu Rodeis ▶

0   10   20

miles

was installed, but at only one point, in 1971.)

That was not the only shock the Egyptian assault brought. After the disaster, the soothing Israeli alibi was that the Bar-Lev line was only intended as a 'tripwire' – 'simply a forward screen to delay the Egyptian advance,' said the ambassador to Britain, Michael Comay. The truth – as proud Israeli officers had told journalists on tours of Sinai before the war – was that the Bar-Lev line and its associated defences had been reckoned impregnable. The reason was one of timing, as the Egyptian Chief of Staff, Shazli, explained later in fascinating detail. 'The Suez Canal is a unique water barrier,' he said, 'due to the steepness of the banks and their irregularity, which prevent amphibious vehicles from descending into or ascending out of the canal without a way being prepared – a feature shared only by the Panama Canal. In addition, the enemy had piled up a sand embankment thirty to sixty feet high, as well as his defences of the Bar-Lev line . . . '

Facing those obstacles, Dayan had predicted any Egyptian attack across the canal would be finished in twenty-four hours. Shazli saw why Dayan believed that. 'Dayan made his statement, I believe,' he said, 'on the basis of calculations that our engineers would need twenty-four hours to establish bridges and that heavy equipment [such as a substantial Egyptian tank force] could not be got across the canal inside forty-eight hours – allowing enough time for the arrival at the front of the Israeli armoured reserves.' In six swift and brilliant hours on October 6, Egypt showed how ingenuity plus modern weapons could destroy that Israeli strategy.

To the puzzlement of the Israelis in the Bar-Lev bunkers, almost every man who came scrambling up the rope and bamboo ladders over the Israeli canal banks, was carrying unusually-shaped equipment. Some had tubes over their shoulders; others were carrying canvas-covered 'suitcases' either in their hands or strapped to their backs. (According to Shazli, they were each laden with sixty to seventy-five pounds of equipment.) These first troops did not try to capture the bunkers themselves – that was the task of the second wave. Instead, while sappers at once reinforced the blocking of the oil nozzles, the main task of the first assault was to destroy the Israeli tanks and artillery dug-in just behind the Bar-Lev line.

The tubes were the launchers of an advanced Russian-built bazooka called RPG-7 (literally, Rocket Propelled Grenade). But the suitcases contained a considerably more sophisticated device: a Russian anti-tank guided-missile codenamed 'Sagger' – directed all the way to its target by signals the soldier firing it transmitted down hair-fine wires unreeling behind the missile in flight (see appendix). Abdul Alati was one of the first Egyptian troops across. He was twenty-three, and before he joined the army in 1969 he had been a student at an agricultural school. Now he was in charge of an anti-tank missile unit. According to his account later in the Cairo newspaper *Al Gomhouria*, his unit destroyed eight Israeli M-60 tanks on the Bar-Lev line within ten minutes. 'The tanks accelerated to their maximum speed to avoid our rockets,' Abdul said. 'But we could hit them in their weakest spots as long as they remained in range. Every Egyptian missile was worth an Israeli tank.'

The Israeli tanks and artillery were already under a barrage from Egyptian tanks firing from sand ramps on the west bank of the canal. Now, too late, the Israelis realized the point of all that Egyptian building activity – not just to keep troops busy but, as Ismail later revealed, to raise fortifications 'capable of detecting enemy positions and controlling the eastern bank as well as the western.' The combination of this artillery barrage with the missile attack by the first assault was deadly: within minutes, the bulk of the Israeli guns were silenced.

One twenty-two-year-old sergeant, a red-haired tank gunner, was a typical Israeli casualty. He was in the lead tank as his unit frantically drove towards the canal. About half a mile from the water's edge, a rocket fired from an Egyptian tank perched on the opposite ramparts killed his tank commander in the turret and slightly wounded him. He escaped, to take the place of a badly wounded man in another tank. This tank, too, was then hit by three rockets simultaneously. Terribly burned, the sergeant managed to crawl out as the ammunition began to explode.

At 2.07 pm, Cairo Radio announced: 'Communique 5: Our forces have succeeded in overrunning the Suez Canal in several sectors, seized enemy strongpoints in these sectors, and the Egyptian flag has been raised on the east bank of the canal. . . .' (The first four communiques had dealt with the outbreak of fighting, embroidering a specious claim that Israel had started it.) In fact a whole forest of flags were being raised on the canal bank: each unit had been issued with one to raise when its crossing was accomplished.

Methodically, the Egyptian missile-troops now set about their second task. What Shazli called 'small buggies, which the soldiers could use to carry awkward or heavier equipment' had by now been ferried across the canal. While the second wave – crossing under heavy fire – began the assault on the Bar-Lev bunkers with grenades, smoke, sub-machineguns and savage hand-to-hand fighting, the missile-troops loaded aboard the buggies and fanned into the desert for up to nine or ten miles. There they dug in, reassembled their anti-tank missiles – and produced the third, and most sophisticated, of all their new infantry weapons: the portable Russian anti-aircraft missile, SAM-7. The task of the missile infantry was now, said Shazli, 'to hold their ground against counterattack by tanks and aircraft for a period of from twelve to twenty-four hours while we got our tanks and heavy weapons across'.

This was the phase Dayan was relying on to delay the Egyptians enough to enable Israel's reserves to intervene. But the Egyptian corps of engineers, under Major-General Aly Mohamed, cut Dayan's timing by more than half. Shazli explained how: 'The problem was the sand barrier. To make a single hole about twenty feet across in this barrier [the minimum to get tanks through easily] would, we calculated, mean removing about 1,500 cubic yards of sand. And we needed to open sixty such holes on the east bank – 90,000 cubic yards of sand. You must also remember that we ourselves had built a sand embankment over the past six years to guard against a surprise enemy attack. This doubled our problem.

'Our first idea was to use explosives,' Shazli said. Ismail adds the detail: 'In the course of our experiments for breaking down these barriers we had tried guns of all calibres but we did not get what we hoped for.' Shazli continued: 'We stuck to explosives until mid-1971, when a young officer in the engineers suggested that we use water under great pressure. This proved to be a superior method, making it possible for us to open holes in a period of three to five hours.' This was a staggering advance: Shazli does not say, but with bulldozers or explosives it would have taken twice as long. But until the fire hoses – fed from pumps floated on pontoons to the middle of the canal – actually began to rip away their sand ramparts, Israel had never taken into account this simple device. Ismail revealed: 'We did not bring up the equipment necessary for this until the last moment, so that our secret weapon could remain strictly guarded.'

As the hoses bored away the ramparts, Shazli explained, 'we had, meanwhile, to trim the banks with explosives and other methods [presumably bulldozer tanks] to make possible the fastening of the bridges'. And here too the Egyptian engineers – with the help of the Russian knowhow – destroyed Israeli calculations. Oldfashioned military bridge-laying is a cumbersome process of bringing alloy pontoons to the bank, floating them into the water, and then marshalling them into a long line with the aid of barges. By rule of thumb, that sort of bridge can be laid at the rate of four feet a minute: to bridge the canal that way would have taken the Egyptians at least two hours. But the Russians, facing several rivers should they ever decide to invade Europe, have a new device. The crossing of the Suez Canal was the first time it had ever been used in combat. The PMP bridge, as it is called, is a series of box-shaped pontoons, each carried on a tracked vehicle. Hydraulic arms on the vehicle lower the pontoon into the water. A second vehicle then drives out on this to lower another pontoon which is clipped to the first, and so on. As the few Israelis still surviving in their bunkers reported: 'It grew across the water like an extending arm.' The PMP can be laid at almost fifteen feet a minute, so the engineers could bridge the canal in just under half an hour. Egypt was heading for a military triumph.

The Egyptian 'Operations Command Centre' is buried deep underground in the desert outside Cairo. This is an eyewitness account: 'A military jeep goes up and down the rugged land. A halt before a sand dune. An opening in the sand dune. At the end, a heavy steel door, like the door of a huge safe. Behind it a long passage. Then staircases going down and down. Another steel door and another long corridor, at the end of which stands a third steel door. Behind it, all of a sudden, the place becomes vastly wide: meeting rooms, operations rooms, communication centres, corridors, map rooms, offices ... ''.

To this centre, War Minister Ismail had come immediately on his return on October 2 from settling with the Syrians the 2.00 pm timing of Operation Badr. He did not see daylight again for fourteen days. Ismail's office was small, on its door the sign MINISTER OF WAR AND GENERAL COMMANDER. In the corridor opposite his office was a door leading to the main operations room.

The eyewitness, Mohamed Heikal, editor of *Al Ahram*, was stunned: 'A big hall it was ... bright lights ... the vivid colours of maps ... maps not merely colours but showing movements too. Around the room stood groups representing the commands of each branch of the armed forces. Behind each group stood its maps and in front its communications links with every front. In the main body of the hall stood a dais for the general command personnel: the Minister of War and Commander in Chief [Ismail]; the Chief of Staff [Shazli]; and the Director of Operations [Major-General Abdel Ghani Gamasy]. Facing the dais, on the opposite wall, were the main maps showing the situation as a whole. Drawn on large glass panels running the width of the entire hall, they displayed: the situation on land – the situation in the air – the situation at sea – the situation on the Syrian front. Minute by minute, as the situations changed, fresh coloured touches would be added to the maps. All the time, the sound of communications machines [telex and telephone] clattering and ringing. Voices in hasty discussion. The issuing of orders fraught with important consequences for Egypt ... ''.

It was a magnificent centre for conducting a set-piece battle – and during the meticulously pre-planned crossing of the canal it

Egyptians march from their canal bridge into Sinai. The gaps in the massive
sand ramparts were blasted by water cannon

worked superbly. It was only in the later, more fluid stages of the war that the disadvantages of this hierarchical, over-centralized, Dr Strangelove command structure began to appear.

'You should have seen this room on Y-day,' Ismail said. 'You would have felt then that this room symbolized not only this age but the entire history of Egypt . . . . We were all at our seats. The whole sequence of operations we had planned was displayed in front of us. As messages came from the front, we could see the operations progressing before our eyes: such-and-such a task has started, such-and-such a task has been fulfilled . . . . From two o'clock the scene in this room was exciting to the limit. The work was carried on with more precision than anybody could have imagined – efficiently and daringly. There were moments when feelings were shaken to the core, but we did not allow ourselves to be swept by emotion . . . . Our nerves had to remain cool and intact. Any confusion at headquarters would unbalance the entire operation.'

President Sadat was also in the command centre as Operation Badr unfolded. 'For the first three hours,' he said, 'I was under terrific tension, frozen. We didn't know what the Israelis had in store. What new weapons did they have? But after three hours it was clear that the Israelis had not mobilized and had been totally surprised. Our troops made their crossing over the steep canal sides . . . '.

Laying its bridges for the northern assaults around Ismailia and Kantara, Egypt's Second Army was on schedule. But, in the south, the Third Army hit trouble. The Israeli sand barrier was much deeper than they had expected and the terrain forbade the use of Russian PMP pontoons. By 5.00 pm the Third Army was stuck. Ismail took drastic action: 'I sent the commander of the engineers himself (Major-General Aly Mohamed) to positions on the bridgehead of the Third Army and instructed him to have the job completed at any cost. The job was completed, although his deputy commander was killed over on one of the bridges.' An Israeli air strike hit him. The Third Army's tanks, meanwhile, had to cross at Ismailia, and scurry forty miles south through Israeli-held Sinai to cover these bridging operations.

Even without that crisis, the engineers' achievement would have been extraordinary. 'In a period of between six and nine hours,' according to Shazli, 'our engineering corps carved out sixty holes, established ten bridges and set up fifty ferries.' This was not as many bridges as Ismail had wanted – he did not think ten gave him enough insurance against damage from Israeli air or artillery bombardment – but by dusk on Saturday, it was clear that the missile infantry were holding off the first Israeli counter-attacks. 'Dayan really miscalculated the ability of infantry to fight off tanks and low-flying aircraft and to hold on to territory for long periods without heavy equipment,' Shazli remarked later. The way was clear for the crossing of the Egyptian armour.

This phase, too, had been meticulously prepared. Shazli again: 'Signal cables had been strung across the canal from the very first moments of the assault. Different colours were used to indicate each unit's route, and our forces had been trained in these details before the operation.' Under cover of darkness, Egyptian tanks and missiles began to pour across the canal. By midnight Saturday, after ten hours of war, Egypt had assembled on the east bank of the Suez Canal 500 tanks and a forward missile defence system. 'The whole operation,' Shazli said, 'was a magnificent symphony played by tens of thousands of men.' In less grandiose terms, it was the high point of Egypt's military achievement in the war.

2: The citizen army musters

For Israelis at home, the nightmare began with an air raid warning just after 2.00 pm. As sirens wailed over every city and settlement, people halted, quickly looked up at the clear blue sky, then ran to the nearest radio set. Israeli radio does not broadcast on Yom Kippur, but at 2.40 pm the Home Service broke its silence: 'The IDF (Israeli Defence Forces) spokesman says that at about 1400 today Egyptian and Syrian forces launched an attack in Sinai and the Golan Heights. Our forces are taking action against the attackers. Because of Syrian aircraft activity in the Golan Heights sector, sirens can be heard all over the country. These are genuine sirens. . . . Orders have been given for the partial mobilization of reserves . . . necessary emergency orders . . . in view of the state of emergency, everyone who has no need to move on the roads, should refrain from doing so . . .'. Then there was classical music, with a promise of further bulletins every fifteen minutes. All morning, there had been rumour, anxiety; everyone knew someone who knew someone who had been just called up (the first logistics phase). News, any news, was almost a relief. Nobody in Israel will ever forget the hours which followed.

Shalom, a twenty-five-year-old studying for a PhD at the Hebrew University in Jerusalem, was visiting friends with his fiancée, Sara. 'A neighbour ran down the stairs, shouting "It's war". Almost immediately, before we could react, the air raid sirens started. We went down into the street. There were lots of people around but nobody knew what was happening. I think like me they were stunned, couldn't believe it . . .'. Shalom went home. He was a lieutenant in the reserves, and knew he would be called.

Israeli reserves are mobilised in two ways. Couriers come to their homes, or the codewords for their units are broadcast over the radio. Shuki, a twenty-three-year-old training to be an architect in Tel Aviv, recalled: 'I was in the centre of town with friends when the sirens went. I ran all the way home, about a mile and a half. I arrived just in time to hear my unit's call-up sign broadcast.'

In the residential quarters of Israel's cities, military jeeps growled to a halt and couriers got out to scan house numbers. Frequently, neighbours directed them to the local synagogue. All over Israel, services were interrupted as men in military uniform appeared at the door with lists in their hands. In the synagogue of Beit Hakerem, a suburb of Jerusalem, the sexton called for silence to read the list of names handed him. One of the names was that of his own son. In the Sephardi Synagogue in Jerusalem, a young man rose from his place when his name was shouted from the door. His father, sitting next to him, embraced him, refused to let him go. The rabbi unclasped the father's arms and tried to comfort the weeping man. 'His place is not here today,' he said. Young men set off hitch-hiking to their bases, leaving their fathers to clear the junk from the air-raid shelters. Shuki in Tel Aviv was frantic to obey his call-up: 'But my mother was bustling around preparing food for me to take and she wouldn't let me go until it was ready. There was enough food for a small army.'

Motley attempts at uniforms flourished: a major in full service dress except for pink suede boots; an artillery sergeant in a T-shirt proclaiming 'Let's Go Mets', the fans' chant for a New York baseball team. Everyone tried to cobble up a facsimile of uniform: the army outfitters were notorious – it was said they only had one size of trousers. Nobody wanted to go into battle in that sort of discomfort.

Family men took their wives and children to stay with relatives. The farewells were carefully phrased – not goodbye, but 'lehitraot', *au revoir*. Those not called up were impatient. Many drove to their units without being asked. Others were like Shuki's father: 'He is also a reservist but his codeword had not yet come over the radio. I think he was upset that I was going to war before him. He telephoned one of the officers in his unit but was told to wait at home until he got the call. He drove me to the main road where I thought I could hitch a lift.'

Outside the country, Israelis and Jews besieged El Al ticket desks at airports. But the El Al fleet was grounded in Israel for Yom Kippur and, anyway, Lod Airport had just been closed until further notice. (When, next day, flights did restart, reservists had priority, then doctors, then journalists and television crews.) Perhaps the most remarkable call-up was that of a man charged with forgery, who had skipped bail and fled from Israel earlier in the year. He was a lieutenant in the reserves and overcome by patriotism – and possibly reasoning that if convicted, he would certainly get a reduced sentence in consequence – he flew back to Israel. The immigration authorities arrested him at once, but the magistrate was so impressed that he accepted the man's own surety and sent him to join his unit – to stand trial, if he lived, when the war was over.

As Israel drove to war through the gathering dusk that Saturday afternoon, it looked like some 'transport through the ages' tableau: commandeered private cars; ageing buses; bread vans; removal lorries; the large open pantechnicons known as Tnuva trucks, after the dairy organisation which runs them. Men drove themselves to the front: one of the *Sunday Times* reporters on Golan later saw an abandoned Dormobile with a 'cello in the back – its owner was playing in a symphony concert away from home and drove straight to his unit. The roads began to jam with traffic. The Arab service stations in east Jerusalem – open as usual on Yom Kippur – did a roaring trade. By the roadside, soldiers were thumbing lifts – the more devout still wearing their prayer caps and shawls and clutching packets of sandwiches to eat when the fast of Yom Kippur ended, though the rabbis had hastily blessed food and transport for the war effort.

Ambulances began clearing the hospitals, ferrying the non-critical cases back to their homes. Doctors rushed to report to emergency military medical units. The civil defence authorities warned everyone to stick tape across their windows and observe blackout precautions. By dusk, pavement cafes had reopened and knots of customers sat and talked in the gathering darkness.

As the blasts of the ram's horn *shofar* signalled the end of Yom Kippur, groups of young teenagers and old people still worshipping at the Wailing Wall broke into a *hora* dance. A police loud-hailer halted them. 'Please disperse immediately to your homes. Happy New Year and good health to you and your families,' said the officer. Suddenly, the streets were deserted of young men. 'A war has begun,' said the rabbi at Katamon; 'let us pray for our soldiers, may God give them courage and protect them.'

At that moment, Israel's reservists were battling with their own army more than with the Arabs. Despite the supposed ten-day alert, mobilization was chaos. Twenty per cent of Israel's tanks were being serviced. Many other tanks in the vehicle parks at armoured corps headquarters at Beersheba had their gun barrels coated in grease to preserve them against the desert grit. Stocks of shells were low – and what there were frequently could not be brought to the tanks in time. Some reservists finally drove into combat with only a half-load of ammunition. Even when the tanks were loaded up, there were few transporters to carry them to the front. Most of those were under repair too. As for Israel's boast – 'nobody in this army walks' – one unit had to drive across Sinai in a milk float. Only the Air Force, providentially, was geared for action.

By 6.15 pm, Israel's leaders knew the war was going badly. But Mrs Meir, speaking on radio and television, hid the magnitude of the mess and glossed over the shambles of unpreparedness: 'Citizens of Israel, at around 1400 today the armies of Egypt and Syria launched an offensive against Israel. . . . The IDF is fighting back and repulsing the attack. The enemy has suffered serious losses. . . . They hoped to surprise the citizens of Israel on the Day of Atonement while many were praying in the synagogues. . . . But we were not surprised. . . . A few days ago the Israeli intelligence service learned that the armies of Egypt and Syria were deployed for a coordinated attack. . . . Our forces were deployed as necessary to meet the danger. We have no doubt about our victory but we consider the resumption of the Egyptian–Syrian aggression as tantamount to an act of madness . . .'.

Nor did she appear to question what the war was about: 'Citizens of Israel; this is not the first time that we are facing the test of a war imposed on us. We must all be prepared for every burden and sacrifice demanded for the defence of our very existence, freedom and independence. . . . The victory of the IDF is the guarantee for life and peace.'

Israeli morale was further bolstered by Moshe Dayan who, single eye glaring into the cameras, radiated aggressive confidence: 'In the Golan Heights, perhaps a number of Syrian tanks penetrated across our line and perhaps they have achieved here and there some occupation, but no significant occupation. . . . Although we had a number of losses and hits here and there, the situation in the Golan Heights is relatively satisfactory, more or less, in my opinion. In Sinai, on the canal, there were many more Egyptian forces, and the problem there is different altogether. . . . This is a large area. . . . There is no chance whatsoever of protecting every metre. . . . Since they began the war they succeeded in crossing the canal. . . . We are prepared for such a situation tomorrow . . .'.

But it was his final peroration which was to do most damage to his reputation. 'We should know that this is a war and we are prepared for the transition period, which is relatively short and then to rely on our forces . . . so that the Egyptian action of crossing the canal and north of the canal will end as a very, very dangerous adventure for them. . . . We had losses but, relatively speaking, this was more or less what we estimated to be [likely in] the first day of fighting – which will end with victory in the coming few days. Thank you.'

Dayan and Mrs Meir must have known how desperate the situation was by that point. The Egyptians held the initiative in Sinai and were in a position to dominate the battlefield by morning. In Golan, the scale of the Syrian assault had staggered them.

3: The Syrian tide rolls on

As they crushed through the high wire fences of the ceasefire line, the first Syrian tanks did not pause by the bunkers, where unbelieving Israeli infantry clutched their inadequate weapons. The opening artillery barrage was soon drowned by the roar and screech of the tanks' engines and tracks. Days later one Israeli officer still recalled the onslaught in shocked tones: 'They flowed in like water, finding their way wherever they had the chance.'

The coordinated Syrian armoured thrusts struck across the Golan lines at two separate places – one thrust spearing south-westwards along the Kuneitra road; the other scything north-west from Rafid towards Khusniye (see map page 79). Then both thrusts divided. The attack on Kuneitra separated into the classic pincer movement which so impressed the UN observer in Observation Post Winter. The other attack separated even more sharply: 200 tanks wheeled southwards along the Golan border, where cliffs drop away steeply down to the river Yarmouk; the other 200 continued straight on through Khusniye towards Naffak. For both main thrusts, Naffak was a key objective. It was the headquarters of the two defending Israeli brigades. It also controlled the main route from Golan into Israel.

The terrain of Golan, as it slopes to the Damascus plain, is flat, grey and barren – a basalt plateau littered with rocks of lava ranging in size from tennis balls to huge boulders. The desolate landscape is punctuated by conical hills, a few hundred feet high – still recognizable but long extinct volcanoes. Goatherds roam the plateau from the Druze villages surrounding Mount Hermon; farming otherwise had become almost non-existent, though crumbling walls of lava rocks show the outlines of former fields. A dry wind fans steadily across.

Over the plateau, the hamlets which once housed extensive Druze communities were abandoned in 1967 and were mostly derelict. Kuneitra had survived after a fashion – the 1967 rubble adorned with barbed wire and tank traps by the Israeli military garrison. Naffak had become no more than an underground command post amid sandbagged bunkers. Only the minaret of Khusniye – its slender form, leaning slightly, a honeycomb of bullet marks – survived to remind prying tourists of the lives that 1967 destroyed.

To the north a road twists down from the foothills of Mount Hermon to the small town of Dan, at the head of the Jordan Valley. In the extreme south west of Golan, where a high tongue of fertile land ends in cliffs over Lake Tiberias (Sea of Galilee) another road winds down into Israel. And only at two more places does the rugged western edge of the Golan plateau soften enough to allow passable roads to descend. An ugly girder contraption across the River Jordan – with the incongruously beautiful name of Gesher Benot Yacov (the Bridge of the Daughters of Jacob) – carries the main road from Kuneitra and Naffak. And the fourth and last exit is a little to the north – over a Bailey bridge below Wazit (see map page 47).

The Syrian objective had to be the capture of at least two of these four crossings – and one of them had to be Benot Yacov, the main military supply route from Israel. That was clearly the joint objective of the left hand fork of the Kuneitra column and the column pressing northwest from Rafid. As the remainder of the Rafid column veered left, it became clear that the other route the Syrians were trying to take was the southerly road at the tip of Lake Tiberias.

Israel's 'fortified settlements', designed to hold the 1967 gains, collapsed rapidly. To defend Golan, Israel had improved the triple Syrian defence lines which it had overrun in 1967. The manpower to defend these was supposed to come from the sixteen fortified settlements which Israel had established on Golan. But as Rommel had written in 1942 in an essay, *The Rules of Desert Warfare*: 'Against a motorised and armoured enemy, non-motorised divisions are of value only in prepared positions. Once such positions have been pierced or outflanked . . . they become helpless victims . . . and motorised formations have to be em-

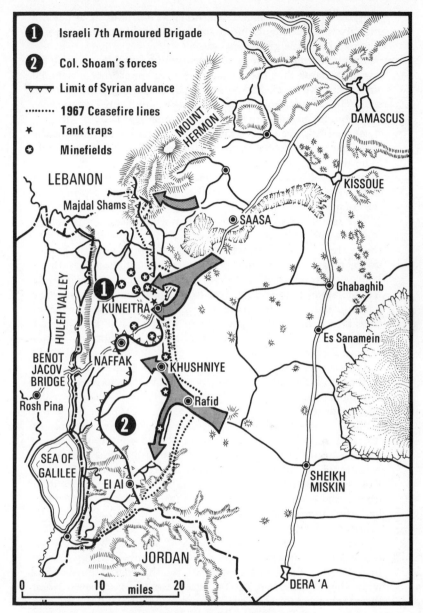

How Syria's tanks overwhelmed Israel

The Syrian thrusts were intended first to cut Golan in half down the main Kuneitra to Naffak road, and simultaneously to take the southernmost route down to Israel through El Al. To overwhelm the Israelis' 175 defending tanks, the 700 Syrian tanks in the first wave divided. Shoam's tank force was quickly scattered and destroyed, but the 7th Brigade, behind better defences, fought in formations. Syria's early airborne capture of Mount Hermon deprived the Israeli brigades of gunnery spotting, but enabled the Syrians' to range their artillery on to Israeli positions.

ployed to gain time to extricate them.' That, indeed, became a priority task for the outnumbered Israeli tanks which had to be diverted to rescue ground troops.

It was an indication of how scornfully Israel had rated the Syrian armour that the civilians on Golan were not evacuated until after the battle had begun. And, reopening old memories, many Jews once more became refugees, confronted again with situations as pitifully trivial as the old man from Giv'at kibbutz, inconsolable in the relative safety of the Jordan Valley because he had abandoned two pet goats and a parrot in a hut on Golan. 'The line of settlements contributed nothing to halt the Syrian attack. In fact, the ones which fell to the Syrians served them as solid bases for continuing their attack,' one Israeli post-mortem on the assault concluded.

The Israeli tank crews realized they were not to be reinforced immediately. 'The troops knew from the very beginning that they were to act as advance forces to stay the invasion of the Syrian army,' an Israeli communique said later. It would be at least thirty hours before any of the reserves called up that morning could trundle along the winding road from Rosh Pina down over the River Jordan and then up the steep ascent to Golan. In the meantime, two Israeli tank brigades – one of them only three-quarter strength – had to keep this overwhelming weight of Syrian armour from crashing a mere seventeen miles down into Israel.

The two brigades covered different sectors on the Golan front. In the north, defending the narrowest – and therefore, the Israeli command had reasoned, the most vulnerable – sector, was the 7th Armoured Brigade of about 100 tanks. Its commander was a brilliant Hungarian-born Israeli known to his crews simply as 'Colonel Janos'. Covering the central and southern sectors – roughly from the Kuneitra–Benot Yacov bridge down – was the brigade of no more than seventy-five tanks, under Colonel Ben Shoam. Shoam's task was to stop both thrusts of the column from Rafid – one now pressing northwest to cut the plateau in half, the other sweeping towards Tiberias.

Shoam's brigade faced horrendous odds: an average of five-to-one, and in local confrontations as great as twelve-to-one. As the Israelis opened fire, scores of Syrian tanks were hit. Others broke down, their tracks smashed by the rocky terrain. But while they could drive, the Syrians pressed on; and even when their tanks were immobolized, the crews in that first day's fighting stayed to use their tanks as fixed artillery.

A young Israeli captain named Yossi commanded seven tanks on Golan, until his throat was ripped open by a shell splinter after three hours of fighting. His account conveys the noisy horror of the scene. Through the dust cloud, he saw three Syrian tanks crashing over the ceasefire line and wheeled his squadron to face them. 'All three were hit by our first shells. I aimed at a fourth tank that appeared and after the first shot saw its turret flying into the air. We thought that was the end of the battle. But it was just the beginning. Out of the curtain of dust emerged dozens more tanks, tank-bulldozers and armoured personnel carriers. We divided the attackers among our seven tanks and picked them off one after the other . . . but before we could catch our breath, another wave moved towards us.'

Facing gunners as skilful as the Israelis, the Syrian assault was bound to be mauled. Against the first waves, the Israeli tanks could fire – as Captain Yossi did – from prepared positions, with guns ranged in to cover the likely lines of advance, each tank's field fire interlocking with its neighbour's. The Syrian lead tanks were heading into fire-traps of devastating intensity. Walking over the first few hundred yards of the assault from Rafid, a *Sunday Times* reporter counted thirteen Syrian tanks in perfect line-ahead, their guns pointing towards Israel, all blown apart by the Israeli gunners. But the two-pronged nature of that thrust finally told against Shoam's tanks. Having broken through the defences, the Syrian tanks fanned into line abreast. To avoid being outflanked and swamped, the Israeli tanks – many by now almost out of ammunition – had to abandon their prepared positions and begin a fighting retreat. As dusk fell they were losing the battle.

Against the pincer movement round Kuneitra in the north, Colonel Janos's 7th Armoured Brigade was, amazingly, faring better. One of his commanders later stressed how difficult the Golan terrain was to defend – hills, rocks, small groves of scrubby trees, low bushes and the ruins of deserted villages all obstructed the defenders' field of vision. 'You never know what's behind the next turn in the roads,' he said. 'It's not like the desert, where the whole battlefield is visible.'

But, to the Syrians, the whole battlefield was now visible. At 4.20 pm on the first day, Damascus Radio announced: 'Our forces have liberated certain positions, one of which is the Mount Hermon position.' The broadcast was slightly premature: the final victory seems only to have come on Sunday. But not for ten days would Israel admit this loss; it was a disaster for the defence of Golan, comparable to the loss of the Bar-Lev line in Sinai. Whoever controlled that observation point 7,000 feet up on the Mount Hermon ridge could scan all Golan. In a helicopter assault, Syrian commandos captured the Israeli fortress. To the tank forces on Golan, it was a catastrophic loss: Syrian artillery could now be targeted in on the Israeli tank formations far below.

With that danger allied to the odds it faced, the 7th's achieve-

A Skyhawk over Golan. The Israeli air force was decisive in blunting the Syrian attack, but a high price was paid against the SAMs.

ment was staggering. The thrust north of Kuneitra was halted in its tracks; and the division of Syrian tanks forking south of Kuneitra had been savagely depleted as dusk approached.

One of the Israeli commanders later said that the key to the achievement was coordination of three elements: tanks, infantry and aircraft. The defences in the northern sector of Golan were certainly more intricate than those protecting Shoam's brigade to the south. North of Kuneitra was a patchwork of antitank obstacles, minefields and a wide antitank canal. The Syrians had anticipated these, and the northernmost attack was spearheaded by bulldozer tanks to thrust aside the obstacles, flail tanks to beat a path through the minefields and bridging tanks to surmount the ditch. But they were easy targets for Janos's marksmen, and the triangle running from Kuneitra north to the ceasefire line was soon so choked with the smouldering wrecks of the Syrian vanguard that the Israeli tank crews' radio chat began to give the area a special name – 'the graveyard'.

Unlike Shoam's Brigade, forced to disperse his tanks to contain the widely separated Syrian thrusts, Janos managed to keep his tanks fighting in formation, covering each other with fire. He managed to contain the threat from RPGs and Sagger missiles, though the low lava walls of Golan provided excellent ambush points. Shoam's brigade, on the other hand, began to suffer heavily once it had been scattered.

From mid-afternoon, the real edge of the Syrian attack was blunted by Israel's classic weapon, the air strike. The Skyhawks played the heaviest role, with Phantoms and Mirages giving air cover. The Israelis' targeting was so precise that tank commanders could call down air strikes only a few yards from their positions. But losses were heavy. For among the defence screen which the Syrians had moved up to their Golan lines was the latest Russian mobile anti-aircraft missile, the SAM-6. In the first afternoon, Israel lost thirty Skyhawks and about ten Phantoms, mostly over Golan, and almost all to SAM-6s or the devastating flak of the mobile ZSU-23 anti-aircraft batteries (also Russian) which chewed up pilots flying at deck level in an effort to beat the SAMs. There were rarely any parachutes. The losses were so high that for a couple of hours, Elazar abandoned air-strikes, while the Air Force worked out what to do when they resumed.

Israel's pilots switched tactics. As dusk fell, the *Sunday Times* Amman correspondent, John Bonar, watched from the roof of a farmhouse in the lee of the Golan cliffs in northern Jordan as pairs of Israeli Skyhawks, silver in the half-light, skimmed in a low northward curve over Jordanian territory, hugging the contours until they rocketed up and over the Golan plateau to take the Syrian armour in the flank and then curve away west of Mount Hermon – hopefully without ever passing over the deadly SAM sites. It was partially successful: the loss rate dropped; but it was still worrying.

As night fell, the Golan plateau was a confused world of individual tank battles and ferocious hand-to-hand infantry fighting, as the Israeli defenders slowly retreated. The Israeli commander of the northern sector, Major-General Yizhak Hoffi, had now decided to place the defence of Golan in the hands of one man, Brigadier Rafael Etan. The man matched the hour.

It is recounted that after the Israeli commando raid which destroyed thirteen aircraft and damaged much besides at Beirut airport on December 28, 1968, Etan, who was in charge of the operation, strolled into the transit lounge and ordered a black coffee. As the terrified barman hastened to obey, others of Etan's men ordered drinks. Etan pulled from his pocket an Israeli ten pound note – worth about one pound sterling – signed it and put it on the counter, saying that if ever the barman got to Israel, he would pay in full for the drinks consumed that night.

Etan is a man of few words. Born on a farm in northern Israel, he is stocky, with huge hands, and is reckoned one of the best fighters in the Israeli army – even too courageous for the good of his men. Yet Etan, trained as a paratrooper, once left the army in the early 1950's and returned to the land. The story goes that in the 1956 campaign, a friend still in the army, reproached him with this. 'They are killing Jews and you are milking cows,' he is supposed to have said. Etan returned to the army – and stayed.

His actions in the Six-Day War of 1967 were 'commended', high praise in an army without medals.

Etan is no strategic genius. He survived a bullet through the head in 1967 and the army joke went that this proved he had no brains. And, taciturn, he has few close friends. His heroes are both dead: on the wall in his office – where most officers might have pictures of Mrs Meir or Dayan – Etan has a photograph of a lieutenant killed in a savage battle precipitated by Arik Sharon in the Mitla Pass in 1956, and another of a captain killed by the Palestinian guerrillas near the River Jordan during the War of Attrition.

To the battle for Golan, Etan thus brought precisely the qualities needed – courage, resource in a desperate situation, and a temperament so mulish that had he been ordered to retreat he would probably not have done so. As the first phase of the battle ebbed at nightfall, Etan set about organizing his defences for the next day. The critical question was: how soon could the reserves come?

The deployment of reserves, however, was dependent on the situation in Sinai. The early Israeli counter-attacks there had been flustered and reckless – individual tank squadrons gallantly rolling forward, only to be blown apart, sometimes by several missiles simultaneously. With professional detachment, the Egyptian Chief of Staff, Shazli, later observed that 'the element of surprise was clearly manifested in the lack of coordination and response on the part of the enemy for at least two days.' The Israelis were more bitter about it. In those early hours there was an almost total breakdown of coordination – 'not one but several Israeli armies,' one senior officer said later, 'each doing its own thing.' A lot of Israeli lives were lost unnecessarily.

The first Egyptian air strikes – 100 aircraft, according to Ismail – had hit Israel's main airfields and communications centres at Bir Gifgafa, Bir el Thamada and the forward headquarters at Tasa (though the facilities there were deeply buried and escaped intact). Until the damage to runways was repaired, Israeli counter-strikes had to operate mostly from bases back inside Israel. The Egyptians did not achieve this without loss. During the first hours of the war, President Sadat's half-brother, Adel Sadat, a 22-year-old air force captain, was shot down in his MIG over Sinai. But even the first Israeli counter-strikes hit trouble. Early targets were, obviously, the bridges being constructed over the canal, but the Egyptian infantry's portable anti-aircraft missiles were already in action. According to Shazli: 'The enemy tried extreme low-flying tactics to get at the bridges but the SAM-7 rockets proved a magnificent success in bringing

84

down the attackers.' Shazli exaggerated: the infantry-carried heat-seeking SAM-7s homed unerringly on a lot of Israeli aircraft tail pipes. But their explosive charges were too small to down many of them. It was the more formidable track-mounted SAM-6s and ZSU-23s that took the worst toll.

But the Air Force's concentration on Golan meant that the first serious counter blows to the Egyptian attack had to be by Israeli tanks. To face more than 500 Egyptian tanks assembled by the early hours of Sunday, Israel had in Sinai the 230 tanks, mostly Pattons, of the 14th Armoured Brigade, under Colonel Amnon Reshef, a burly moustachioed extrovert. But as many as a quarter of these had been stationed by the Bar-Lev line, and thus largely wiped out. By the early hours of Sunday, the Egyptian armour advancing from that shattered line was threatening to overrun Israel's second band of defence as well.

Israel had spent rather over £40 million on building the Bar-Lev line. (It is alleged that when its creator, Lieutenant General Haim Bar-Lev, then Chief of Staff, approached Mrs Meir's predecessor, Levi Eshkol, for more cash, he explained that one costly item was the piping of fresh water. Eshkol looked puzzled. 'Surely,' he asked, 'they can drink the water in the canal?') And as much again constructing roads, air strips, bases and strong-points throughout Sinai. The most important of these roads were a pair running north-south parallel to the canal – one about fifteen miles (maximum) from the canal, the other about eighteen miles. This second road ran through the headquarters at Tasa. The Israeli defence plan had always been to use the forward road for its 155mm and 175mm heavy artillery, with the road behind being used for ammunition supplies and for reserves of armour. The Egyptian advance through the early hours of Sunday disrupted any such tidy design.

As in Golan, the fighting which followed was governed by the physical geography. Southern Sinai (see map page 38) – is a lunar landscape of parched, impassable mountains. But to the north, these narrow to a central ridge which tails away in the sand seas bordering the Mediterranean. Through this ridge run three passes: the Mitla Pass in the south, the Gidi Pass in the centre, and the Khatmia Pass further north. Apart from the passes, the only other way across Sinai is by the coast road, and the Mediterranean on one side and the soft sand sea on the other virtually rule that out for tank formations.

To advance across Sinai, the Egyptians thus had to capture at least one of the passes. Their struggles to this end – and the Israelis' desperate battles to stop them – took place between the canal and that central ridge. It is a triangle of land, roughly sixty-five miles from north to south, at its widest only forty miles deep and narrowing opposite the southernmost Mitla pass to a mere twenty miles. The terrain is a complex tangle of scrub and dunes, sudden sand ridges and wide plateaux, with scattered water holes and treacherous pans of soft impassable sand. Here, on the first night of the war, the outnumbered Israeli tank crews won a remarkable victory.

From their northern and central bridgeheads, the objective of the Egyptian thrusts that night was to capture the two Israeli artillery and supply roads. Their tanks overran the artillery road in places, but the Israelis destroyed the advance before the rear supply road fell. From the southern bridgehead, the Egyptians tried to thrust the mere twenty miles to take the Mitla Pass itself. They got ten miles before the Israelis managed to stop them.

Egypt, meanwhile, was trying to disrupt the Israeli attacks from the rear. Taking advantage of the early moon-set which had been one of General Ismail's requirements for the night of Y-Day, helicopters ferried Egyptian commandos on raiding expeditions deep behind the Israeli positions – tactics reminiscent of the deep Israeli strikes in 1967. Egypt's twenty commando battalions are its toughest troops – and Chief of Staff Shazli, himself a paratrooper, took a personal pride in them: for him, they were symbols of the revival of Egyptian arms. But in combat, they were not very effective: Israeli anti-aircraft fire downed several helicopters with total loss of life. One was shot down far away from the main area of battle, near Ras Sudar, on the east bank of the Gulf of Suez. Perhaps the targets were the oil rigs of Ras Sudar themselves; perhaps the commandos were intending to swing in a southward curve to disrupt the Israeli reinforcements grinding towards the Mitla Pass.

Some commandos did get through. Sixty flew over the northern salt marsh to attack the Israelis' northern forward command post at Baluza. But the Israelis had built a floating road into the marsh, and could deploy to drive them off with heavy Egyptian loss of life. Other raiding parties, landed near Bir Gifgafa and at Sharm el Sheikh, did survive – despite confident Israeli propaganda. But they were never more than a nuisance.

By dawn on Sunday, the Egyptians – though still attacking fiercely – had not progressed in the positional war. Their bridgeheads had penetrated no further than eight to ten miles into Sinai. The Israeli 14th Brigade, according to military sources we have questioned since, had lost nearly 150 of the 230 tanks it had in Sinai when the war began. But with first light, its citizen army began to arrive – in the first wave, no more than 100 tanks, but supported by more than 20,000 infantry in five divisions.

By noon on Sunday, Arik Sharon's painfully-assembled reserve division was at last getting ready for battle. As commander of the central sector he deployed his by now considerable forces in positions in front of the Mitla and Giddi passes. Once he had done so, the immediate crisis in Sinai was over. But this is not quite how it seemed to the isolated pockets of resistance which were still holding out by the side of the canal – among them Avi Yaffe and his fellow warriors still in their beleaguered fort in the Bar-Lev line. The Egyptians, attempting to consolidate their position rather than press forward, were about to start an artillery barrage on the fort, and again Avi had his tape recorder switched on.

MEYERKE (as the shelling begins): Shuki! Go take a jump to outpost 3, and report when you're there. Signalman Shlomo [Avi's assistant] will run with you. Wait a moment. I want somebody in the northern outpost. They'll attack us from the north, possibly. Give me position 4.
AVI: You're connected to it.
MEYERKE: Hello! Hello! . . . Avi, they don't answer there.
AVI (on loud hailer): Position 4. Pick up your phone.
MEYERKE (on phone): Who's that? Dubbele? [nickname of look-out called Mordecai Eichebaum]. Bless ye the Lord every day (facetious greeting) . . . how are you? (powerful explosion). Where did it hit? In the bunker? . . . OK, but every now and again you· have to poke your head out afterwards because they might come from the north. You understand? . . . I should know what's going to happen! We'll soon see. I don't know where they're hitting us from.
Now a heavy mortar bombardment ranges on to the fort.
AVI: They say the shells are falling by the gate of the fort.
MEYERKE (to gate position): Pay attention the whole time. Lie down low and the moment there's any sort of let-up put your head outside right after the shell and watch the gate. OK?
Two direct explosions on the fort.
AVI: Shuki doesn't reply . . .
MEYERKE (snatching phone): Shuki . . . Shuki . . . Perhaps he went to position 3?
The shelling is increasing, and now almost every shot is on target. There are earth falls in the trenches and bunkers. Some of the telephone lines between positions are cut and the radio antennae are destroyed. Avi and Shlomo, the two signalmen, go out, exposed to the fire, to replace them.
MEYERKE: Give me HQ . . . Hello, Yigal, listen: they're hitting us hard. Artillery, perhaps also tanks. It's falling directly on me, I don't know where from. The tanks I think are shooting from the other side. A shell lands every minute. That's it.
DUBBELE (on phone): Moment. Shuki is in the bunker, position 4.

MEYERKE: Certain? Good. Are you looking out on that side? OK?
More shells and mortar bombs. Direct hits.

DUBBELE: Exchange. Exchange. The trench to positions 3 and
3A is blocked.

SHUKI (on loudhailer): The trenches to 3 and 3A are blocked.

MEYERKE (to Shuki): You'll stay in 4. OK?

Sergeant Baruch appears in Meyerke's command bunker,
bleeding from the head. Shrapnel has torn his helmet, and is
still lodged in the side of his head. His ear is also cut.

BARUCH: Give me some help, boys, give me some help.

The medic and the doctor take over. The shrapnel is extricated
and a sedative injection given. Baruch falls asleep on the doctor's
bed. The shelling continues . . .

AVI: We should explain to HQ things are getting serious.

SOLDIER: Tell them we have casualties. That's it.

MEYERKE: So what if there are?

SOLDIER: So they should hurry.

MEYERKE (to HQ): They're shelling us. I don't know where from.

AVI: Don't make things too easy for them.

MEYERKE: What should I do? I'll say they're shelling. So what?

AVI: Exaggerate a little bit. Put some spirit in it.

MEYERKE: I have exaggerated, so? (To HQ): Where to? I should
know where they're firing from. They're firing at us and that's
that. (To Avi): Give me Shuki in bunker 4.

AVI: I think the line's been cut.

SHLOMO (on the loud hailer): Shuki. Lift the phone.

MEYERKE: Give me HQ again . . . (Breaking off for the phone):
Shuki, where are you?

SHUKI: Bunker 4. It's impossible to be outside. Everything's
exploding.

MEYERKE: But someone should always be jumping up to see what's
happening to the north . . . (Breaks off again to try and get
headquarters).

AVI: HQ doesn't answer. I'm trying the whole time. They have
all the time in the world, those chaps at HQ.

SHUKI (on the loud hailer after another explosion): Bunker number 4 is blocked off. I'm stuck here. Can't get back. Somebody
should go out near the gate . . .

MEYERKE (finally getting through to HQ): Now listen a moment.
Yigal, Yigal . . .

HQ: Hello, you'll get it right away.

MEYERKE: Get what?

HQ: Artillery.

MEYERKE: On what? I want to tell you on what . . . I want it like
this. They should give artillery on the tank park . . .

SHUKI (on the phone): What's happening? They're still shelling.

I left the bunker. It's blocked between all the trenches to 3 and 3A. I'm in 4 at the moment, completely buried, trying to get out. Maybe something will work.

By now it is dark. Another powerful explosion is heard.

MEYERKE: What's that?

SHUKI: It's still falling on me . . . I can't see. I think the shell fell in the middle of the fort. What shells, honey! The trench in position 4 has also had it. Everything on top's collapsed on me.

Shuki asks for someone to be sent to clear the entrance to bunker 4, but he digs out an opening before this is done.

SHLOMO: Position A say they can hear armour. They don't know from where. And there are halftracks on the canal road opposite us.

MEYERKE: Give me HQ . . . HQ, listen, the fort again. We can see lights on the canal road . . .

HQ: Instead of talking give me targets.

MEYERKE (amid more explosions): I gave you the targets. First of all the canal road. All of it. Halftracks are moving on it. The question is whether ours or theirs. I don't know, can't see in the dark. Second thing, I understand you have lots of artillery, so if you can hit right away, do you hear, because they are wiping us out here. Our main positions we can't get to them because they are blocked. So I want as follows: shells on concentration point G. After that I want fire by the church in Ismailia. There's a tank position there. You'll see it on the map between the church and the mosque. Then in the tank park. Also to the north, 200 northeast . . . (another gigantic explosion) . . . Oh-oh. All the bunkers are collapsing . . . I want rapid fire now.

SOLDIER: Can't they send some sort of vehicle to take us away?

MEYERKE: Here? During the shelling? We'd get killed outside. Tanks would just get knocked up in a shelling.

SHUKI (phoning from ruins of bunker 4): We've just caught a whopper. We're completely covered in sand.

MEYERKE (Voice choking with dust): We can't see a thing. We're choking here. The ventilator has bust . . . .

It is, however, the last Egyptian salvo. The barrage subsides almost as abruptly as it began. The tape picks up the squeak of the ventilator as a soldier cranks it by hand, but otherwise quiet returns. Avi starts to speak a private message to his wife into the microphone: 'Dassy, do you hear me? I feel like talking to you . . .'. But he breaks off dispiritedly and switches off his tape recorder until the following morning.

On Golan, too, Sunday was the hardest day for the Israelis. In the Israeli newspaper *Ha'aretz*, the military correspondent Zeev Schiff wrote: 'The Israelis at home never knew or felt how great

The appalling toll of the Golan fighting: seven Israeli Centurions knocked out

was the danger nor how bloody the battle. Eight hundred tanks had broken on to the heights. . . . The pride of the Syrian armour was only a few miles from the Benot Yacov bridge.' Late on Sunday afternoon, in fact, the Israelis thought for two hours they had lost the battle.

The first shock had come at dawn. Contrary to their practice in previous wars, the Syrian tank crews had not wasted the hours of darkness. Using the infra-red night vision equipment with which many of their Russian tanks are equipped, they had redeployed through the night and at sunrise were waiting to attack in a long line abreast – 'Not regarded as a classic tactic these days, but perhaps that's what the Russians teach them,' observed one Israeli commander. At first light, the long line advanced. But now, in one sector of the battle, they faced the first Israeli reserves. Overnight, Brigadier Etan had been forced to make the decision to leave Janos' 7th Brigade to struggle on as best it could, and instead to throw the first limited formations of reserves into the battle to hold the southern sector.

The first group of reservists who had climbed the southern road to Golan were operating Israel's weakest tanks. They were driving World War Two Shermans, which though they had mostly been modernized with 105 mm guns were by modern standards hopelessly weak in armour plate (some, indeed, had only 75 mm guns). Ranged against them were large numbers of Russian T-54 and T-55 tanks – dating from the fifties and sixties – and even some of the latest T-62s. Several of the Syrian T-62s had only fifty kilometres on the clock. They had been driven off the tank transporters straight into battle. 'They're all modern, freshly painted and with the smell of fresh rubber,' was one Israeli report – with the bitter comment: 'Everything Russian except the food; that's Arabic.' Yet amazingly, in this unequal

on a single road, and (below) the common graveyard of three Syrian T-62s

confrontation, the Israeli reservists won.

Lieutenant Dov, a twenty-eight-year old civil servant working on the West Bank, was commander of one of those first Shermans. His signalman-loader was twenty-nine-year-old David Elimelech. When Elimelech heard from their tank squadron commander, Captain Gadi, that they could expect to face seventy to eighty Russian tanks, a shiver literally ran down his spine. It was about mid-morning as they approached the Syrian formations, carefully deployed around El Al. Lieutenant Dov said later that he was almost in a state of shock: 'We went into El Al in such a hellish noise of exploding shells.' He weaved his tank between the shell bursts, heading for the nearest cover. He could not believe his eyes when he saw the size of the Syrian column. 'Only when I saw our guys beginning to shoot at them did I grasp what was happening.' The squadron commander Gadi gave them a target, Elimelech loaded, and Dov's tank too opened up on the Syrians.

Some of the ensuing battle was fought at such close range that on one occasion a T-55 blundered into the midst of the halftracks carrying the reservists' headquarters company. 'Most uncomfortable,' the operations officer, Major Itzik, recalled. Nobody knew quite what to do. It was clearly unwise to provoke the tank, which could have obliterated them all, so none of the Israelis fired. Fortunately, the Syrian tank crew were as puzzled: the T-55 wheeled round and left without firing a shot.

It was no easy Israeli victory. As an Israeli gunner from Inverness, Scotland, observed of his Syrian opponents: 'They hit things; the days when they couldn't shoot straight are over.' While the reservists halted the southernmost Syrian thrust, the destruction of Colonel Shoam's brigade of regulars continued. At noon on Sunday, Shoam himself was killed. He had climbed one of the old volcano cones to reconnoitre and the Syrian artillery got him. His second in command took over what was left of the brigade. That was not much: the Israelis have not released precise totals, but so far as we can work out, by 5.00 pm on Sunday, nearly 150 of Shoam's brigade had been killed. On the Israeli rule of thumb that the dead roughly equal the crew of every other tank hit, Shoam's brigade was virtually wiped out.

It was at 5.00 pm that the Syrians made their last attempt to destroy the 7th Armoured Brigade as well. Over the ceasefire line rolled the main Syrian reserve force, 300 tanks of the crack armoured division, commanded by Rifad Asad, brother of the Syrian president. 'The next two hours, from five to seven, were the most crucial in the whole battle,' an Israeli officer told a *Sunday Times* reporter afterwards. Few details have emerged on how Colonel Janos tackled this daunting new task. An American account says that he concentrated upon channelling the Syrian advance, preventing it from spilling at will across the plateau. This fits plausibly with known Israeli tactics – and with the subsequent Israeli comment that 'the danger stemming from a long line of penetration was a disturbing factor'.

But the weight of the Syrian advance was unstoppable. By dusk on Sunday, their lead tanks had chopped down the Kuneitra road, past Naffak, to the Old Customs House at the top of the ridge above the Jordan. Less than five miles down the road ahead lay the Benot Yacov bridge. All that lay between were scattered squadrons of reserves coming up the road towards them – 'We could not wait to group our reserves,' an Israeli officer in northern command headquarters said later. 'As fast as we got them, we sent them up the road to stop the Syrians.' It seems inconceivable that a determined Syrian push could not have demolished these uncoordinated units in the hours ahead. Yet the Syrian advance got no further.

There is some evidence that the Syrian advance just ran out of steam. The few UN observers, still trapped in their bunkers on the ceasefire line, for instance, saw little fuel or repair gear coming up behind the armour. And, since the Syrians were fighting on the Russian pattern of consolidating one objective at a time, perhaps the top of the ridge was the Syrian objective for the night.

But perhaps the desperation of the Israeli counterattack really did stop them. The Phantoms and Skyhawks used the last minutes of light to make hair-raisingly low-level runs across the Jordan Valley and up over the Golan ridge, to strafe the advancing tank formations. One observer later saw an entire file of Syrian tanks obliterated outside Naffak by those air strikes. And the long swathes of burned earth testified that napalm was used. 'It was the supreme effort of our air force,' one Israeli commentator said later.

It was the turning point of the Golan battle. By dawn on Monday Israeli reserves were choking the roads up to the plateau. Around noon, reserves finally reached Colonel Janos's brigade. By that time, the 7th Armoured had lost 100 dead: half its tanks had been destroyed. In all, by mid-Monday – forty-eight hours after war began – Israel had lost 250 dead in Golan, and the same number in Sinai. On both fronts, the immediate crisis was now past. But at this price in dead – with at least 1,000 wounded – Israel could not afford to keep fighting with that intensity. The urgent necessity to limit casualties was to be one of the major factors governing Israel's strategy through the rest of the first week.

By Monday the casualties which most concerned the Israeli high command were their pilots. For it had become clear during the first two days of war that, in combating two deadly types of anti-aircraft missile deployed by the Arab armies, Israel's air force faced potential losses as harrowing as those already inflicted on Israel's armour.

The Israelis knew that these missiles were: the SAM-6 (NATO codename 'Gainful') and the SAM-7 (generally known by its Russian name of 'Strela'). But the Israeli pilots were encountering both for the first time. They had some forewarning about the SAM-7 which had been used in Vietnam: a highly mobile short-range missile, used against low flying aircraft. The SAM-6 was in action for the first time and still largely an unknown quantity: it proved to be devastatingly effective at both short and long range.

The first confirmed victim of this new weaponry was a Phantom coming in low over the desert to bomb the Egyptian bridgehead only a couple of hours after the crossing of the canal. It was almost certainly shot down by the portable sam-7s carried by the first wave of missile infantry. After the first wave of abortive strikes against the Egyptian bridges, however, the Israeli high command had decided that the priority task for its air force was to crush the Golan advance. And here the aircraft had been caught by the Syrians' cunningly deployed sam-6 batteries, interlaced with zsu-23 AA guns (each capable of spewing 4,000 shells a minute) which caught the planes as they dived to the deck in their attempts to avoid the missiles.

Over the following week, Israel was to lose eighty planes on the two fronts: the vast majority downed by sam-6s and zsu-23s as they flew close-support missions for Israeli armoured assaults. About two-thirds of these losses were over Golan. (The Israelis, indeed, claim that only four of the 115 planes they lost throughout the war were downed in dog-fights.)

As the Israelis caught their breath on Monday with the Golan crisis resolved for the time being, the grim task ahead of the air force was the destruction of these missile defences. The first problem was the missiles' mobility. The cumbersome sam-2 and sam-3 missiles which Russia had supplied to Egypt after the 1967 war were essentially designed for fixed or semi-permanent sites. (It takes at least eight hours to dismantle one.) Both the new sams, by contrast, could be shuttled around the war zones with bewildering speed.

The sam-6s were mounted in threes on a tracked launching vehicle which could travel over sand: the launcher and its accompanying radar vehicle could drive to new positions immediately after firing a missile. Camouflage and concealment was relatively easy – and the Syrians, in particular, exploited this cleverly. (They had moved their sam-6s, for instance, after the Israeli reconnaissance flights on the eve of battle but before the actual assault.) For most Israeli pilots, the first sign of danger was the thin white smoke trail of a sam-6 as it climbed towards them in a shallow curve at twice the speed of sound. By the time the Israelis – the pilot if he survived, or the watching ground forces if he did not – could call down artillery fire or bring in support aircraft for a diving counter strike (see appendix), the launcher and radar vehicle had disappeared elsewhere.

The sam-7 was even more mobile. Apart from the infantry-carried version – so light that it could be fired from the shoulder – the Israeli pilots realised by the second week of war that they were also confronted by sam-7s in a different mode. The Egyptians and Syrians put into action new vehicle-mounted launchers, capable of firing a salvo of up to eight Strelas simultaneously – reducing the possibilities of evasive manœuvres. There were many hits by sam-7, though these were not always lethal because its explosive charge is smaller than in other SAMs.

These missile defences had to be destroyed if the Egyptian bridgeheads were to be tackled, because the forward protection of these thrusts now comprised three methodically organized lines of defence: infantry dug in with Sagger anti-tank missiles; then tanks; and behind them batteries of SAM-6 missiles brought over the canal even before the Egyptians had moved up their armour. Somehow, the SAM missiles had to be outwitted by Israeli counter-measures before they – and the armour they protected – could be smashed.

In Vietnam, a good deal had been learned about the guidance system of the older SAM-2 and SAM-3, and the Israeli Phantoms and Skyhawks had been equipped by the Americans with elaborate systems of electronic counter-measures (ECM). An early-warning alarm – called by pilots the 'Sam Song' – sounded in the cockpit as soon as the missiles' ground radar began tracking an aircraft; another ECM device then jammed the missiles' guidance system by sending out rival transmissions on the same frequency.

The SAM-7 – and the SAM-6 in its homing phase – operate on a different principle which made these ECMs irrelevant. Instead of being guided by radar, they 'home' on to the aircraft by heat-seeking infra-red sensors which guide the missile to the hot exhaust from the plane's jet engines. The early part of the SAM-6's flight is controlled by radar, but even here the Israeli pilots found their existing ECMs ineffective. The electronics of the new missile proved to be far more sophisticated than those of the earlier SAMs. The SAM-6 guidance radar could switch between several frequencies to throw off jamming transmissions.

The Americans, as much with their own interests in mind as the Israelis', launched an intensive programme early in the war to find out more about the SAM-6 electronics. Their electronic detection satellites orbiting over the Middle East were no doubt used in this: the method being to fly over a high-altitude reconnaissance plane to trigger a SAM-6 launch at a time synchronized with the passing of the satellite. This way, the technicians in the United States could get an almost immediate read-out from the satellite of the transmissions from the missile's tracking and guidance systems. It was, however, a hazardous business for the pilot. It was not until the last days of the war that any modified ECMs on the Israeli planes showed signs of being effective. In the meantime, Israel's pilots could rely only on much cruder devices.

One of them, extensively used, was to pour out of the aircraft showers of 'chaff' – thin metallized strips which blur the plane's radar image. In order to be fully effective, the length of the strips must be 'tuned' to a multiple of the radar's wavelength so

The morale battle: General Elazar (above left) makes his 'break their bones' speech and (right) the opposing Chief of Staff, General Shazli. Below, Moshe Dayan, Israel's Defence Minister, tours the Golan front.

until the SAM-6's wavelengths were known this method was of questionable value. The device, developed in Vietnam, of dropping high-heat-intensity flares from the aircraft as decoys to confuse the missiles' heat-seeking sensors was also used against both SAM-6 and SAM-7. Here, too, the Israeli air force was in for a shock. The Russians, it seems, had developed the 'counter-counter measure' of equipping the sensors with filters which could distinguish between the infra-red frequency from jet exhausts, and the lower frequency of the flares.

There was one other – last resort – counter to the SAM-6s: violent evasive action. After the first few days, Israeli pilots were using pre-arranged evasive manœuvres – turning violently into and across the missile's path – in hope of breaking its homing lock. In some cases, helicopters were used to spot the puff of white smoke which followed a missile launch: even then, pilots had only a few seconds to react.

Over Golan on the first Wednesday of the war, October 10, *Sunday Times* reporter Philip Jacobson saw five Israeli planes – three Skyhawks and two Mirages – hit by missiles in the space of an hour near Kuneitra. A Skyhawk pilot who had bailed out safely landed nearby. 'Once that thing gets behind you, it's all over,' he observed while waiting for a rescue helicopter. 'We have orders to eject as soon as it locks on to our exhaust.' Israel faced enough problems ensuring replacements simply of its aircraft: its pilots were even more precious. Against the massive Egyptian missile presence in Sinai, however, it looked by the third day of the war as if Israeli counterattacks were going to be costly in both aircraft and armour.

On Monday evening, the Israeli Chief of Staff, David Elazar, put a bold face on things. 'This morning we embarked on a counterattack simultaneously on both fronts . . . I am happy to tell you it is succeeding. . . . We have begun to destroy the Egyptian army. In some place we have returned to the canal and in others our counterattack is still under way . . . We are advancing on all fronts . . . This war is serious, the fighting is serious. But I am happy to tell you that we are already at the turning point, that we are already moving forward.' He even dropped heavy hints of further Israeli expansion: 'I have to remind you that the ceasefire lines are not marked on the terrain . . . We are moving wherever it is possible, and we shall destroy him wherever it is possible. We shall strike them, we shall beat them, we shall break their bones.' Elazar's supporters later said that he was trying to bolster the confidence of the reservists going into battle.

But Israel's senior officers themselves needed bolstering. The Sinai commander, Major-General Shmuel Gonen, had moved from Beersheba to his forward HQ at Khiseiba, twenty-three miles from the canal on a hill guarding the Gidi Pass. Here the atmosphere was little short of despairing. Dayan and Elazar had spent most of Sunday in Sinai trying to restore morale.

Israel, according to a NATO paper filed in Washington, had reckoned it had the resources to fight a thirty-day war. Israeli military sources have explained the timing of this: one week for the reduction of the Syrian army: three weeks to beat Egypt. But this convenient belief in Israel's ability to fight on one front at a time hinged upon the role of the Bar-Lev defences in fatally impeding an Egyptian build up in Sinai. By Monday evening, that strategy was in ruins: Egypt had 600 tanks across the canal, with perhaps five divisions of infantry.

In Sinai, as Sharon said later: 'For the first week the concept was to hold against their attacks and try to destroy as many of their tanks as possible while we are in defence.' Sharon did not mention the other factor: Israel's need to cut the casualty rate. (In this, the Israeli commanders were successful. After the first two days, the toll of Israeli dead mounted at less than a third of the initial rate of 250 a day.)

Moreover, there seemed no way of halting the steady Egyptian pressure. Elazar claimed, truthfully, that an Israeli armoured unit had reached the canal. What he did not say was that this happened near Kantara, during a battle which Egypt won. The northern Egyptian bridgehead at Kantara had – because of the soft and marshy terrain – relied upon infantry more than the others. But on Monday night, after Egyptian missile-infantry had beaten off the Israeli armour Elazar mentioned, an Egyptian armoured brigade secured Kantara East. (The veracity of Egyptian communiques sagged a bit next day, however, when they talked of its Arab inhabitants thronging to greet the liberators. Kantara East has been a ghost town since 1968, when Israel evacuated its inhabitants a hundred miles eastward to El Arish.)

Further south, around the Ismailia and Suez bridgeheads, the Egyptians were steadily, methodically, expanding sideways – 'stretching their elbows in areas where they have been successful', was one Israeli military euphemism. The blunter truth was that the Egyptian bridgeheads were consolidating into an unbroken front the length of the canal.

Nor did there seem to be any way of really damaging the Egyptian build-up. Apart from close ground-support in Golan, the priority for the Israeli air force from Sunday onwards was the destruction of the pontoons over the canal. It was a costly failure: the attacks took a steady toll of gallant pilots, and the Egyptian Chief of Staff, Shazli, later explained why they were unsuccessful. 'The enemy air attacks were severe and sustained. They did hit some points. But military bridges [Shazli meant the new PMP pontoons] are built from linked sections which are replaceable. Repairing a bridge usually took from half an hour to an hour. We also moved our bridges from one location to another, to confuse pilots who were working from reconnaissance information. We put up heavy smoke-screens to make aiming more difficult for them, while dense anti-aircraft fire added to these difficulties.'

The most effective damage to the bridgeheads was achieved by the Israeli 155mm and 175mm guns, ranging in from the relative safety of the road fifteen miles back from the canal. But this revealed another Israeli muddle. The artillery were totally dependent on forward spotters – tank crews, and the last remaining forward strongholds such as Meyerke's on the canal. There is much evidence of confusion in the use of coded map references – 'concentration point G' and so on – which suggests that the artillery may have been using different maps or codes from the spotters'. There were even incidents when the Israeli artillery hit their own side, including one reported shelling of an Israeli tank unit that resulted in the deaths of the crew of the command tank, and possibly of two other tanks. Meyerke's bunker may also have been hit by Israeli shells. The Egyptians, of course, were not to know of this muddle and now intensified their attempts to destroy the forward spotting points. Late on Monday morning Avi and his colleagues faced their greatest crisis, as the Egyptians tried at last to capture their battered outpost. . . .

The doctor is being kept busy. Sergeant Baruch, wounded the day before, walks round carrying his infusion bag. Soldiers come in with backaches. They haven't urinated for two days. They are ordered to drink lots of water.

MEYERKE (suddenly): Armoured troop carriers are moving up.

DOCTOR (over loudspeaker): Back to your positions. Get back to your positions.

MEYERKE: They're advancing on us, do you understand?

SHUKI: What about the mortar and bazooka?

MEYERKE: Mortar, mortar. What bazooka? Honest! Let them hit with the artillery. (To Avi): Tell the artillery they're advancing on us and entering positions A and B. They should send some planes here.

HQ: One moment.

AVI: That one moment of theirs!

MEYERKE (impatiently): Eight armoured personnel carriers are firing on us.

Sound of shots. A plane is heard.

DOCTOR (excitedly): Excellent!

HQ: Are they attacking yet?

MEYERKE (with emphasis): Yes! But the plane is bombing . . . .

A bomb falls between the fort and the Egyptians. The Israeli troops' rejoicing ends abruptly as they realize the plane isn't theirs. Automatic fire is heard. The Egyptians fan out from their APCs but don't attack. Hand-to-hand combat is expected. Everyone grabs their personal weapons.

MEDIC: Avi, is that your Uzi [submachinegun]?

AVI: I don't know.

DOCTOR: It's mine.

MEDIC: So I don't have one.

AVI: Who took my Uzi? Don't take my Uzi.

The telephone rings . . .

HQ: What's your problems?

MEYERKE: What's our problems! Ten APCs facing us. Soldiers moving towards us. Aside from that their planes dropping on us. And you ask what are our problems?

HQ: Great, guys. Just keep beating into them as hard as you can.

MEYERKE: We're shooting at them. But where's your artillery?

HQ: OK. I'm already sending it.

MEYERKE: Yes, yes immediately.

Small arms firing is heard from the soldiers in the fort, but no artillery. The Egyptians eventually retire to the junction on the canal road, leaving casualties.

HQ: There'll be some artillery soon. We're a little short. Be patient, everything will be fixed.

MEYERKE (ironically): Sure, sure we'll be patient.

HQ (a few minutes later): What's the situation now? In order?

MEYERKE: In'alrabak! [Good God Almighty!] What should be in order? The APCs that were on the road turned around and dropped off men and left markers. Markers where to attack from. They're probably planning another attack, in the afternoon or tonight. Now they've gone to the north . . .

The Egyptian assault switches to the fort to the north. On the radio, Avi and Meyerke – the tape machine still recording – listen to increasingly desperate interchanges between the commander of the northern front and HQ as the assault develops. Eventually, repeated calls from HQ fail to get a reply: the northern fort has been wiped out. Meanwhile the situation in isolated forts to the south is deteriorating. The commander of the next main fort, by the Bitter Lakes, radios that hundreds of Egyptians are attacking with tank support and he can hold out no longer. Forty-two men in Fort 'Mezakh', at the extreme south of the Bar-Lev line by Port Tewfik, are still bravely holding on (and would continue to do so for four more days, before a highly publicized, televised surrender).

Terrifyingly, over the loudspeaker-telephone that linked together all the forts of the Bar-Lev line, Meyerke and his men now
begin to hear the screams of men being roasted alive in their
underground bunkers by tanks mounted with flamethrowers.
They know their luck cannot last. That night they decide on an
escape plan.

4: 'Not our sort of war'

The lack of Israeli resources to help the beleaguered Bar-Lev
forts stemmed from the fact that on the other front, Golan, they
were having a much tougher time than they had bargained for.
By Monday, Israel might be winning in Golan – but far too
slowly for comfort. 'Good starters, bad finishers,' a British diplomat in Amman said, prophesying that the Syrian advance, its
momentum slowed, would now quickly crumble. The Israeli
reinforcements going up to Golan thought the same. 'In the last
analysis, they're chicken,' the *Jerusalem Post* reported an Israeli
officer on Golan as saying. Yet the Syrians did not crumble:
instead, they fought back with tenacity and skill.

Why the Israelis so despised the Syrians is hard to fathom.
Elazar, of all people, had cause to know that the taking of Golan
in 1967 had been no walkover: as a brigadier he had commanded
the northern front in that war, marshalling the forces for the
Golan battle. (The commander of the actual assault was Yitzhak
Hoffi, now the northern commander.) The Syrians had fought
well before collapsing under pressure. 'We just pounded them
continuously,' said the then air force commander, Major General
Mordechai Hod. 'After twenty-seven hours they broke and ran.'
(Hod's memory speeded the sequence: most of the Syrian line
had held for about thirty-six hours.) Israeli intelligence must
surely have learned in the next few years that one reason for the
Syrian collapse was the corrosion of its command structure by
'political' officers. Most officers in 1967 had been members of the
Alawite Muslim sect; and under heavy fire they simply deserted
their men, mainly of the Shi'ite sect. Where officers and men
stuck together, they had done rather well.

But presumably the Israelis had discounted that. And, to a
people seeking bravura in their military leaders, the Syrian army
commander, General Moustafa Tlas, must have cut a dispiriting
figure in Israeli eyes. A former law student, Tlas – when he first

emerged in the Syrian army in 1964 – had been another of the 'political' officers: he then presided over the Damascus military tribunal. He saw no action in 1967 – he was commanding the 5th Division at Homs – yet was elevated to Chief of Staff in 1968. Now, clearly, he and his Chief of Staff, Yusif Shakkour, were considerably tougher than the Israelis had thought. It looked, for instance, as if rumours around the beginning of 1972 that President Asad had been persuaded to purge incompetent 'political' officers from the forces had been true. Certainly, there was now nothing incompetent about the Syrian defence of their gains in Golan. (Another possible reason for the Syrian improvement was advanced by an Israeli lieutenant – one-armed, it should be noted – midway through the Golan battle: 'You play good chess players,' he said, 'you get better at chess.')

To Syrians who recalled the humiliations of 1967, merely to have an army now capable of standing up to the Israelis was a victory. But the Syrian armour did much better than that. By Tuesday, the pattern of the Israeli assault was established. Israeli pilots would launch ferocious air strikes against the Syrian formations. Israeli artillery would then open fire. Finally, Israeli tanks would attack head-on. It was war reduced to a slogging match – 'Not our sort of war,' a tank commander on Golan said with a shrug, 'but what else can we do? We are used to taking the initiative, but this time the Syrians beat us to it.'

It was brave, but it was all taking Israel too long – and costing too much. For twenty-four hours now, Israeli pilots had been trying to knock out the Syrian SAM-6s, to open up their tanks and artillery to the full weight of Israeli air power. In the chilling euphemism of the Israeli military spokesman: 'Our air force suffered losses to establish its supremacy.' Yet despite optimistic Israeli statements about the 'destruction of the central sector' of the Syrian advance, the Israeli tanks had in fact only managed to consolidate their hold upon their first objective, which was their own brigade headquarters at Naffak. The Syrian headquarters set up at Khusniye in southeast Golan remained the hub of a solidly entrenched Syrian tank force of close on a division. The strikes against the SAM-6s were, however, meeting with some success, and Syria was forced to withdraw most of its missiles back nearer to Damascus.

During the early hours of Tuesday morning, the Syrians had launched a series of determined and coordinated counter-attacks. Simultaneously a division had broken into the Israeli lines in front of Kuneitra while another formation drove in by Khusniye on the southern sector. Only at 4.00 am Tuesday did the Kuneitra action ebb away as the Syrians retreated again. Three hours later, further north, another formation – this time

Machine gun guard over Kuneitra, centre of the Syrian assault

mainly of the Syrians' most modern tanks, the T-62 – thrust several miles into the Israeli front consolidating north of Kuneitra, on the 7th Armoured Brigade's old territory. By Tuesday mid-morning, that assault too had been broken, with eighty Syrian tanks burning in the 'graveyard' of the Kuneitra triangle. But the battle to contain the southernmost Syrian counterattack, near Khusniye, took the Israelis all Tuesday. A large part of that Syrian column had been cut off during the early hours: at dawn the Israelis called in air strikes to destroy the clustered Syrian formations of tanks, mobile guns and armoured personnel carriers.

So ended the last major Syrian counteroffensive. As the last bitter fighting continued into Tuesday night, however, Israel could not know that. And even at its end, the Israeli northern command estimated that Syria still had in reserve another 400 tanks – 'More than enough to make a good fight of it in the days to come,' one of the headquarters staff commented gloomily.

Somehow, Syria had to be crushed swiftly. On this fourth day of fighting – Tuesday, October 9 – Israel embarked upon a calculated escalation of the war. Its air force bombed the Syrian capital, Damascus – and then proceeded to destroy in the days ahead as much of Syria's heavy industry as it could.

There was an immediate reason for this. Shortly before sunrise, a Russian 'Frog' rocket launched from Syria had landed amid the buildings of Kibbutz Gevat, near Nazareth in central northern Israel. The resulting explosion wrecked twelve buildings and caused £100,000 worth of damage. Some of the buildings were the dormitories for 270 children of the kibbutz. The children were, in fact, sleeping in the kibbutz' underground shelters, as were most of the adults, so nobody was hurt. But it was a horrifying indication of how vulnerable Israel's civilian population was to rocket warfare.

The 'Frog-7' is the latest of a series of Russian battlefield missiles, launched from a wheeled vehicle. Even with a range of less than forty miles, it could be lobbed from the Syrian lines into the centre of northern Israel. This the Syrians had been doing on a small scale each night of the war.

At 8.00 am on Tuesday, Israeli radio announced: 'In the past two days, the Syrians launched some twenty Frog missiles on civilian settlements in northern Israel . . . ' (This was something of an exaggeration: the total was nearer ten.) At 9.06 am the Syrians – no doubt appreciating what was in store – broadcast back: 'Our forces shelled Ramat airport and other military targets in the area and . . . did not attack any civilian target.'

At 12.10 pm, six Israeli Phantoms approached Damascus, flying low and fast over the desert south of the town. In three waves little more than a minute apart, the Phantoms opened up with rocket and cannon on the buildings of the Syrian air force headquarters and the Ministry of Defence, wreaking havoc inside both. Inevitably, though, the strikes overshot. The air force headquarters backs on to the ancient fairgrounds of Damascus. But the Ministry of Defence, though not far away, stands amid the smart residential streets of the diplomatic quarter. As the rockets and cannon shells overshot, they destroyed one of the rows of houses. A reliable diplomatic source in Damascus later gave *Sunday Times* reporter Brian Moynahan his estimate that 200 people died in that strike. Among them were women of the Indian community, holding a coffee party for a visiting Indian singer; a rocket penetrated the house, killing four and injuring sixteen. A Norwegian United Nations official and his wife also died: he had presumably spotted the aircraft lining up on their approach run for he had hustled his wife into the basement of their home. But the Israelis were using delayed-fuse rockets to penetrate the military buildings: a rocket made a neat hole in his roof – and exploded in the basement.

Israel later claimed to have hit only 'strategic targets'. And through the days ahead, its strikes on Syria became even bolder. Not only did the bombing of obvious tactical targets such as airfields continue – that had begun on the second day of the war. A sizeable part of Syria's heavy industry was also shattered. Two oil refineries at Homs were hit; so were fuel tanks at Adra and Latakia worth £2.2 million. More oil tanks at the port of Tartous were destroyed, together with their loading terminal. Power stations at Damascus and Homs were bombed. The costliest blow of all was to Banias, the Mediterranean terminal for Iraqi crude oil: it was devastated. The Banias installation had been earning royalties for Syria of £25 million a year, and the Banias and Homs refineries together had employed 3,400 – a lot for a small, poor country. In 1972 Syria's growth rate had been 12%: the Israeli bombing was a massive setback to future hopes.

That was the point: Elazar's seeming bombast about 'breaking the bones' of the Arab armies *was* Israel's strategy. For, as Israel began to count the cost of war, it was clear by Tuesday – according to Israeli sources in Europe – that Israel was going to need at least six years to recover from this war: to repair the damage both to its military machine and to its economy. Therefore, the Arabs had to be so injured that they too would need at least six years to recover. Any more rapid Arab recovery would find Israel locked into a spiral of irreversible vulnerability. Hence the decision to destroy Syria's economic infrastructure. Also, as a warning to other neighbours, Israel on Tuesday bombed one of Lebanon's radar stations on Jebel el Baroukh, which was claimed to be tracking aircraft movements in northern Israel.

If the Israeli plan in Golan 'to pound the Syrians into cracking' – as the *Jerusalem Post* put it – was having slow success, Israel's initiative in Sinai on Tuesday, October 9, was a disastrous failure. In the early hours of that day, the Israeli southern commander, Major-General Shmuel Gonen, launched the first concerted counterattack by his newly-deployed reserves in an effort to push back the Egyptian bridgeheads. The attack failed, and an entire Israeli armoured brigade was destroyed. The verdict of Gonen's critics, given later to the *New York Times*, was that the attack had been made 'without sufficient preparation and with insufficient strength'. But the particular ruin of the 190th Armoured Brigade, by the Egyptian Second Army between Tasa and the canal, seems to have been a product of the lingering Israeli disregard for the lethal potential of massed anti-tank missiles. Israel released nothing about the defeat. But the commander of the 190th, Colonel Assaf Yagouri, survived to answer questions on Cairo television.

Yagouri clearly found the precise sequence of his defeat difficult to unravel – all he seemed to know was that he and many other tanks had suddenly been hit, that his tank had caught

Egyptian troops storm through the Bar-Lev fortificatións

fire and that he had no choice but to surrender. Brigadier
Abu Saada, commander of the Second Army's central sector
forces which destroyed the 190th, said later: 'Yagouri made
several tactical mistakes. He sent out ten tanks and we destroyed
seven. Then he sent out thirteen and we destroyed four. By this
time, we had been able to set up an ambush, and when Yagouri's
main force charged us at full speed they ran into a trap. They
were wiped out in three minutes, having scarcely fired a shot.
Yagouri's tank was hit trying to escape and fell into a ditch.'

The difficulty which the Israeli tank-crews had in grasping
the potential of Egypt's new infantry missiles was subsequently
conveyed vividly by the commander of a formation of Israeli
tanks, caught like Yagouri's in a Sinai battle. 'We were advancing and in the distance I saw specks dotted on the sand dunes. I
couldn't make out what they were. As we got closer, I thought
they looked like tree stumps. They were motionless and scattered
across the terrain ahead of us. I got on the intercom and asked
the tanks ahead what they made of it. One of my tank commanders radioed back: 'My God, they're not tree stumps.
They're men!' For a moment I couldn't understand. What were
men doing standing out there – quite still – when we were advanc-

The Israeli infantry begin a counter-attack

ing in our tanks towards them? Suddenly all hell broke loose.
A barrage of missiles was being fired at us. Many of our tanks
were hit. We had never come up against anything like this
before. . . .'

In the central sector, in the wake of the Israeli failure, Egypt's
Second Army even gained territory – notably a useful sand
ridge between Tasa and the canal, which dominated the surrounding dunes. When on Tuesday, Haim Herzog, the retired
general used through the war as official Israeli military commentator, disavowed Elazar's previous optimism, only the Israeli
military then knew how accurate his warning was. 'I have no
doubt that the struggle facing us will not be an easy one,' Herzog
told Israeli television viewers. 'I would not say we have moved
over to a major offensive yet.'

Naturally, Herzog did not talk of the counterattack running
into trouble. But it was still a far cry from Elazar's 'offensive on
all fronts'. 'So far,' Herzog said, 'we have been consolidating,
deploying and seizing the initiative.' And he was frank enough to
make the central point: 'I would not be lulled into believing
this can be an easy and very rapid operation.' This time, he
warned, there would be 'no easy and elegant victories'.

It was through these Tuesday Sinai tank battles that Meyerke and his men, unescorted and on foot, were to march to safety. The decision had been taken during the night, after another armoured personnel carrier had penetrated the gate of the fort and left a flashing marker, presumably to guide flame-throwing tanks in a night assault. (As it was doing so, the men had debated whether to try the desperate tactic of capturing the APC intact and riding to freedom on that.)

The preparations for departure are again recorded on Avi's tape, and the men subsequently recalled details of their escape in other tape recordings.

MEYERKE (after the debate about the APC): Boys, we're leaving this place on foot, tonight. (There is a brief argument, which Meyerke firmly settles): We're leaving tonight . . . But we have to ask for formal permission. This isn't a *bardak* after all. (*Bardak*: Russian for brothel.)

HQ (after Meyerke puts his request): It'll work out OK if you stay.

MEYERKE: I don't want any more promises . . . I want a reply within ten minutes.

The CO, Arik Sharon, comes personally on the line. Meyerke explains the plan.

SHARON: You haven't got much of a chance. We can't come out to help you.

MEYERKE: We're leaving anyway.

SHARON: Well, if you think it will work, do it.

MEYERKE: We'll report again next time when we're back there.

SHARON: Take care of yourselves.

The men, who have now gone sixty hours without sleep, get ready. Meyerke makes them all eat. They fill water flasks, put on heavy flak jackets and assemble their weapons – Uzis, two grenades each, a bazooka and six machineguns with ammunition and flares. They destroy other equipment and documents, except for the main radio set which is left in use until the last minute so as not to arouse Egyptian suspicions.

MEYERKE (giving his final briefing): Our aim is to get back safely, with a minimum of casualties. The main thing is to keep moving forward and not to get delayed. If we get fired on, try to fight, charge the enemy and move forward quickly.

Avi bundles up the tapes he has made and puts a new battery into his portable radio equipment. They wait into the early hours for the setting of the moon, and start out in pitch darkness. Outside they split into two groups, Meyerke and Avi heading one, Shuki and Shlomo the other. They go separately but in the same general direction: three kilometres southwards along a strip of sand parallel to the canal, then the risky crossing eastwards over the canal road followed by a long, thirteen kilometre march to the northeast over sand dunes. Barbed wire is in their way, and the dunes are pockmarked with craters. They are worried mainly about the two wounded, Marciano and Baruch, but both make their way without help. Flares flicker in the sky. The men freeze until the light goes out.

At 5.30 dawn breaks, and Meyerke changes direction into the rising sun. They take off their heavy, cumbersome flak jackets and bury them in the sand. At 6.00 a large tank battle starts up and the men find themselves trapped between the opposing armoured forces. They take cover in a dip in the dunes. Avi can't hear base on his radio because of his low position. He climbs to the top of the dune and makes contact again. Two MIGs are shot down and their pilots parachute to the desert nearby. The men debate whether to try to take them prisoner, but decide not to complicate matters. As the sun gets up, and the heat of day begins, they spot another group of men a kilometre away. It is Shuki's group. They join up in the same dip in the sand, and excitedly compare experiences.

It emerges that a mortarman called Meir Orenstein has a small battery-powered cassette recorder in his pack. Avi is annoyed with him for breaking orders and carrying excess weight. But with his unfaltering sense of occasion he borrows the machine and, as they shelter from the tank battle, records one of his by now quite practised commentaries. He also passes the recorder round for the other men to describe their experiences of the night.

MARCIANO : When we passed through them in the night, we actually heard them shouting. Enough to make you feel faint. All the way we kept seeing tanks, but when the Phantoms came . . .

DOCTOR : That made us feel good.

MEYERKE : When I set out I wasn't scared. And when we passed by them I wasn't scared. You know when I began to worry? You didn't even notice it. There was this embankment of sand and all sorts of guys lying in foxholes. I thought we were coming on the Egyptians so I got hold of that one who speaks Arabic – where is he – that's you Roni. I told him mutter something aloud in Arabic about wanting to get there quickly to smash those Jews . . .

BARUCH : You know he came to Israel after the Six-Day War . . .

MEYERKE (astonished) : Is that so?

Others join in and the recording ends incongruously – against the continuing background of the tank battle – with a discussion between Avi and Baruch about the cost of hi-fi equipment.

Burning tanks are now scattered in all directions, but Meyerke encourages the men to press on. They come under machinegun fire. Avi calls base on the radio. 'We're sending a tank to rescue

you', he is told. Meyerke says he will fire a green flare for
identification. A classic rescue operation follows. Armoured
infantry in halftracks suddenly appear over the dunes fighting a
quick, angry battle against the Egyptian infantry positions. Two
tanks, one giving cover, are approaching. Marciano fires the
green flare. Almost simultaneously, a green flare is fired from an
Egyptian position too. (Has the radio conversation been over-
heard?) Avi hastily radios a caution for the tank commanders,
and Marciano sends up another flare.

As the tank arrives the thirty-three men clamber all over it
holding on to anything available, even the gun barrel. Exposed
to fire, the tank zig-zags at full speed to where a halftrack is
waiting. The military road which they reach, just a little way
further, is still under full Israeli control.

After an Israeli naval strike on the Syrian port of Latakia – the listing Japanese
cargo ship was one of the victims.

The nearest the Israelis got to the old-style 'quick and elegant
victories', of which General Herzog had wistfully reminded the
televiewers, came on Wednesday. They were won by the service
Israel had always regarded as something of a poor relation, its
navy. And, as an additional irony, they came because the navy,
at least, had recognized that missiles revolutionized warfare.

The navy's attention to missiles is readily understandable:
on October 21, 1967, the Israeli destroyer *Eilat* was sunk off
Port Said by a Styx missile launched from a Russian-built
Komar class missile boat of the Egyptian navy. Israel's immediate
retaliation had been to destroy Egypt's Port Suez oil refineries.
But, as a longer-term response, Israel built up its own fleet of a
dozen fast missile boats – five of them smuggled out of their French
constructors' dockyard at Cherbourg on Christmas Day, 1969, in
defiance of de Gaulle's embargo on arms sales to Israel. These
'Saar' boats, plus two home-made models named *Reshef*, are
armed with a missile designed and manufactured by Israel

itself, the Gabriel. This has a range of only twelve miles – half that of the Styx missiles used by the combined Egyptian and Syrian missile fleets of twenty-eight boats. But the Gabriel's guidance system is known to be highly sophisticated.

Certainly from the first day of the war – when Israel wiped out four Syrian craft, mostly with the Gabriel – the Israeli navy had the battle all their own way. On the first Wednesday of the war, October 10, three Egyptian missile boats were sunk near Port Said and, in a more controversial action, Israel tackled Syrian missile boats actually in Tartous harbour – sinking four but contriving to damage Greek, Russian and Japanese cargo vessels in the port at the same time.

From then on, Israel had the run of the coastlines. Its boats were out twenty-four hours a day, rocketing and shooting up anything that moved. And their 76mm guns played a part in the destruction of the Syrian coastal oil installations, as well as damaging several radar stations, military complexes and supply depots on both the Syrian and the Egyptian coasts. One source even says that the navy tackled some of Egypt's most northerly SAM sites.

In return, Israel admits to one small shrapnel hole in a Saar – American estimates are that Israel, in fact, lost two and perhaps three Saars. Still, the engagements cheered the Israelis. Depending as they did upon superb manœuvrability and handling to dash well inside the Styx range before they could launch their own Gabriels, the Israeli boats were morale-boosting reminders of the heady days of 1967.

5: Ismail versus Shazli

By Wednesday, October 10, Syrian tanks in Golan still held a substantial pocket around Khusniye. And Egypt was steadily adding to the 700 tanks massed on the east bank of the Suez Canal, with an intact missile defence system to back them. The crucial question was: what did Egypt intend to do now?

'To me,' General Ismail said, 'rigidity was better than looseness, especially if it was a matter related to war.' Specifically, he was rejecting criticism of tight-mouthed Egyptian war communiques. But as War Minister and Commander in Chief, Ahmed Ismail was not merely overlord of the Egyptian planning of the assault; he directed the campaign itself. And 'rigidity' was its hallmark throughout. As Henry Tanner, the *New York Times* Cairo correspondent, wrote at the time: 'The Egyptian army has doggedly adhered to a comprehensive, preconceived strategic and tactical plan. Military spokesmen insist that there have been no departures from the plan, no improvisations and no unauthorized initiatives by local commanders.' That was Ismail's doing. 'Wars,' he said lyrically, 'are a dialogue between one plan and another . . .'.

Partly, this mystical faith in planning was a product of Ismail's temperament. At fifty-five, he was, as one British officer put it, 'a brilliant classroom soldier'. In 1950, already a highly experienced officer, he had graduated top of his year from the Cairo Military Staff Academy; in 1965, he was first again on graduation from the Nasser Military Academy for senior officers. In 1957 – in the wake of Nasser's rupture with the West after the Aswan Dam–Suez War debacle – Ismail had been one of the first officers chosen for training in Russia. Not that Ismail was short of practical experience. He had been through four wars: an intelligence officer in the western desert in World War Two; and an infantry commander through the 1948, 1956 and 1967 Arab–Israeli wars. It was Ismail's memories of 1967 which, along with his belief in planning, exerted the most potent influence upon his conduct of the October war.

In July 1967 – barely a month after Egypt's shattering defeat – President Nasser had appointed Ismail to command the Suez front. Years later, Ismail recalled the moment in moving terms: 'My memory still carries the picture of the situation then. There was no front. . . . There was no Army either. . . . Everything had been smashed into fragments and lay broken in ruins. We had to prepare for the stage of steadfastness, as Gamel Abdel Nasser called it.'

That time haunted Ismail – just as, through World War Two, British commanders were haunted by the losses of the Somme. With genuine passion, Ismail said to Heikal: 'The safety of my forces was my first preoccupation throughout the new war . . .'. He knew he would be criticized: 'There are those perhaps who think we should have taken greater risks. I was ready for any risks and for any sacrifices. But I had resolutely set my mind on one target which I kept all the time before my eyes, which I felt to the depths of my conscience: to preserve the safety of my forces.'

Ismail, who was close to President Sadat, knew the strain which 'no war, no peace' imposed upon the Egyptian economy. He knew that Sadat saw this war as the decisive catalyst, making possible a political settlement in the Middle East – as the final effort to rid Egypt of its monstrous military burden. 'I was aware,' Ismail said, 'of the effort which Egypt had exerted to rebuild its army. I had to reconcile my knowledge of the magnitude of this effort – which can never be repeated so easily – with the fulfilment of my military objective. I knew what losing our army once more would mean. It would have meant Egypt's surrender. And for Egypt to surrender would have meant its complete defeat for this generation and for generations to come.'

It was the thinking of a humane and sensible man. And those qualities served Ismail brilliantly during the preparations for war. After his 1967 appointment, Ismail had supervised the construction of the Egyptian lines along the Suez Canal – 'Egypt's Bar-Lev', he was called. He was appointed Chief of Staff in March 1969 (his predecessor had been killed in an artillery duel at the beginning of the 1969–70 War of Attrition). But he did not get on with Nasser – Ismail has since hinted that Nasser's grandiloquence grated on him – and he was swiftly sacked, to re-emerge only with the succession of Sadat in October 1970. Ismail became War Minister in October 1972.

He has explained in precise detail the task as he saw it then: 'The problem was our own forces. Circumstances had forced them to remain for six or seven years on the defensive – most of this static defence. Under those conditions, forces – any forces in the world – would be exposed to what we in the military profession call "trench disease". We had to dispel the effects of this.

'I concentrated at the time on a number of essentials, without which I believed we could do nothing, nothing at all. The first of these was that our forces should be convinced that fighting was inevitable – and that there could be no solution without fighting. . . . I visited the armed forces, in their positions, and I explained the circumstances to them, saying that the existing situation had to be changed – and that, if we did not change it, the enemy might force a change upon us . . . because for neither of us could the conditions of "no war, no peace" continue indefinitely.

'The second essential was that our men should have faith in their arms. I wanted to change the concept that arms make the man. It is man who makes the arms. Unless our men were confident of themselves, their arms would never protect them. If, on the other hand, they did have confidence in themselves, then any arms in their hands would protect them.'

Clearly, Ismail was exaggerating. The infantry he sent across the canal on October 6 were armed with some of the most formidable personal weapons yet devised. Yet there was still validity in Ismail's insistence upon the importance of the individual soldier. Ground missiles demanded courage of their operators. The RPG-7 (rocket propelled grenade) is best fired

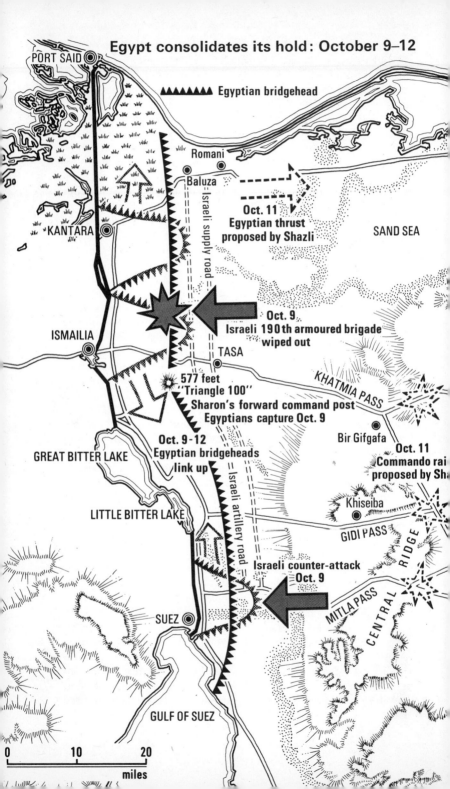

Egypt consolidates its hold: October 9–12

▲▲▲▲▲▲▲ Egyptian bridgehead

PORT SAID

Romani

Baluza

Oct. 11
Egyptian thrust
proposed by Shazli

SAND SEA

KANTARA

Israeli supply road

Oct. 9
Israeli 190th armoured brigade
wiped out

ISMAILIA

TASA

577 feet
"Triangle 100"
Sharon's forward command post
Egyptians capture Oct. 9

KHATMIA PASS

Bir Gifgafa

Oct. 11
Commando rai
proposed by Sh

Oct. 9-12
Egyptian bridgeheads
link up

GREAT BITTER LAKE

Israeli artillery road

LITTLE BITTER LAKE

Khiseiba

GIDI PASS

CENTRAL RIDGE

Israeli counter-attack
Oct. 9

SUEZ

MITLA PASS

GULF OF SUEZ

0   10   20
miles

at little more than 100 yards – and it takes considerable nerve to let an enemy tank get that close. (And even if the tank is then disabled, its crew usually survive to machinegun the infantryman.) The Sagger wire-guided missile has a range of only a mile. At that distance the missile is in readily visible flight – like a high-speed model aircraft – for about ten seconds, a long time in battle when you are exposed and at risk of being machine-gunned. Yet, throughout, the operator must coolly pilot the missile on to the target with a tiny joystick. The Israelis were certainly not expecting the new confidence of the average Egyptian soldier.

In part, that was a tribute to Ismail's 'third essential' – intensive training – and to his fourth and last stipulation, that this should be under realistic conditions – 'to get our forces to see plainly what we would have to face in the future and to remove any fear from it. I therefore began to select training grounds which bore as much resemblance as possible to the conditions and nature of the task which our forces would have to discharge later.' The training was meticulous. The commander of the engineers, Major-General Aly Mohamed, later revealed that his men had practised assaults on an accurate mock-up of the Bar-Lev line no fewer than 300 times. Ismail adds: 'There were water currents in our training ground, which had the same speed as the currents in the Suez Canal.'

They even practised the crossing on the canal itself – at El-Ballah, north of Ismailia, where the canal forks for a few miles into two channels. Egypt still held both banks of the western channel, so that stretch became a training ground. But even in training the emphasis was heavily on Russian-style set-piece battles. In a land ninety per cent of which is conveniently shifting sand, the mock battlefield at the Egyptian military training college was constructed of concrete.

By the fifth day of war – Wednesday, October 10 – Ismail's planning had worked out superbly. Operation Badr had overwhelmed the Israeli defences and thrown the whole Israeli strategy out of gear; and the Egyptian bridgehead extended virtually the length of the canal from Port Said to Port Suez – with Egyptian armour pressing to fill the few remaining gaps. In creating this long front, Ismail's thinking about the next phase of battle after the crossing was as follows: 'The enemy would have to disperse his aerial counterstrikes against our forces. In view of the extensive area of confrontation, this dispersal of effort would ensure that his strikes were weak everywhere.' Israel's land forces too would be thrown off balance by the length of front: 'The enemy would not be able to discover at an early stage the direction of the main thrust of our attacking forces and, consequently, would be unable to concentrate on it.'

But what did Ismail plan after that? Amazingly, he planned to halt, consolidate – and hand Egypt's brilliantly won initiative to the Israelis. 'Our original plan envisaged a "mobilizational pause" after we had completed the crossing operation and en-ensured the security of our bridgeheads,' he said. 'During the pause I could make a re-evaluation of the situation in the light of the enemy reaction, and prepare for the next move – taking adequate precautions before advancing.' Ismail's ideas on what to do next were essentially responsive. He did not want to keep the initiative. 'What comes after that?' he said. 'Several possibilities. We had calculated them all minutely. But every-thing ultimately depended upon what the enemy did. Accordingly, the crossing operation was a plan complete in itself, with an ending. What came after that was also covered by our planning although the choice of possibilities depended upon the enemy's reaction.'

It was when this phase had been reached, on the fifth day of the war, that major differences of opinion opened up between Ismail and his Chief of Staff, Shazli. The day before, the first concerted Israeli counterattack had been beaten off with heavy Israeli losses. Now, Shazli argued, Egypt ought to seize the initia-tive once more and press forward into Sinai. It was an argument between two opposing military philosophies.

'If Shazli weren't so deliberately low key – and if the Egyptian army had any flair for publicity – he would be Egypt's Dayan,' a western diplomat in Cairo observed in the middle of the war. If Shazli never sought that mythopœic status, he was nevertheless a hero to the Egyptian public even before the October war – a model of the 'new Egyptian officer'. It was scarcely overnight fame: since World War Two, Shazli had stood out as perhaps Egypt's most capable and aggressive field commander.

Saad Shazli was born in 1922, the eleventh of thirteen children in a landowning family in the Nile delta. He graduated from the Egyptian military academy in 1940, and first came to notice as a twenty-year-old second lieutenant in the Western Desert, when his post near Mersa Matruh was overrun by the Germans. Ordered to evacuate, Shazli apparently stayed behind until all the equipment had been removed. It was the start of a continuing reputation for personal bravery. In 1948, he commanded an infantry platoon; in 1950, by now regarded as one of Egypt's brightest young officers, he went to the Staff Academy; three years later, he trans-ferred to the arm which has since proved his greatest military interest: the paratroop special forces.

A friend, asked whether a theme ran through Shazli's life,

paused and then said: 'Unlike many of his colleagues, Shazli always thought Egypt could win.' The friend recalled Shazli saying during the 1956 war: 'Why are we despairing? We can beat them.' And the hectic pace of Shazli's career in the wake of the 1956 humiliation, suggests the deliberate grooming of a man on whose skills Egypt already knew it would one day depend.

In 1960, he commanded the Egyptian paratroop units sent to the Congo as part of the United Nations force. In 1961 he went to London as military attaché. Returning to Egypt, he was one of the few officers whose reputation survived Nasser's ill-fated Yemen campaign of the early 1960s – in the Yemen, Shazli put into practice his ideas on long-range helicopter-borne penetration by commando units.

He was then one of even fewer officers to gain credit from the 1967 disaster. Shazli's division in eastern Sinai was surrounded, but he got his men back over the canal in good order. The incident has become encrusted with legend: one story holds that he slipped into disguise; another that he was surrounded by the Israelis, but had in turn already captured Israeli prisoners, so bargained his way out. The simpler truth seems to be that Arik Sharon was given the job of cutting off Shazli's retreat but missed him in the dark. Whatever the circumstances, mere survival with dignity set the seal on Shazli's reputation – though critical Israeli tacticians have since noted that a bolder commander in Shazli's position in 1967 might have pressed *eastward*, taken Israel's southern port of Eilat, and thrown part of the Israeli offensive seriously off-balance. Given his reputation, however, Shazli's appointment as Chief of Staff in 1971 caused little surprise – even though Sadat plucked him from his relatively junior place at thirtieth in the ranking of major-generals.

It was a shrewd appointment. For Shazli brought to the post not only military talent – and a flinty determination to beat the Israelis – but a care for his men unusual in that army. The Egyptian army has always been cursed by a gulf between officers and men – the officers regarding themselves as a privileged elite, and their men as peasants. Shazli, by contrast, is close to his troops. Instead of the medals and gold braid he could affect, he wears the standard beret, jump boots and camouflage smock of a paratrooper. (Although balding and on the short side, Shazli – a keep-fit enthusiast – looks younger than his fifty-three years.) In May, 1972, he inaugurated an armed forces blood bank with a pint of his own blood – a simple enough gesture, but in that army a brilliant common touch. And although himself a stern disciplinarian, he stands up fiercely for those in his command: his almost legendary popularity inside the forces was finally cemented in 1972 when, in a public slanging match in front of his troops, he bawled out a Russian adviser unwise enough to claim that Egyptians were 'untrainable'.

By Wednesday, October 10, nobody would still have said that about the Egyptian soldier. But the irony was that although the Egyptian army's brilliant success was popularly ascribed in Cairo to 'the Shazli plan', the strategy so far had more nearly been Ismail's. By Wednesday, in fact, Shazli was vigorously trying to persuade Ismail to switch from his methodical set-piece approach to a more mobile exploitation of the Egyptian successes. He was unsuccessful (see map page 114).

Ismail and Shazli had first met in the 1960 Congo operation, when Ismail had some oversight of Shazli's role. The two men had not got on then, and according to Cairo sources, have never got on since. Given their different backgrounds, it is not hard to see why. Nor is it hard to understand why the two should by Wednesday have differed so strongly. Shazli, the more experienced field commander, wanted to follow up the Israeli defeat with a decisive switch to a more mobile and adventurous strategy. He is thought to have advocated another round of helicopter-borne commando raids to strike at the eastern ends of the passes, and to destroy Israeli supply dumps and communications centres throughout the area. One source reports that Shazli also wanted an armoured thrust along the northern coastal road.

Ismail vetoed Shazli's plan. Defensively, he later sought to explain his reasons: 'Were we unable to see the chance available to us? For me, the question was not one of chance but a matter of calculation. Whatever chances presented themselves to us it was my duty not to run risks . . .'. He could produce technical justification for this decision: 'We had begun the operation under the protection of our famous missile screen. If I had to advance after that, I was determined to wait – whether there was a chance which someone else could see or whether I saw it myself – until I had made sure that my forces had adequate backing. I had to give time for my armour and my anti-aircraft missiles to cross.'

From which it seems fairly clear that Ismail questioned even the existence of the 'chance' Shazli and the others saw. But Ismail's plea that even by Wednesday, he had still not got as much equipment as he wanted on to the east bank tends to confirm persistent reports in Cairo that in its later phases the Egyptian build-up was hitting severe logistical problems. Shortage of ammunition seems to have been one. Egyptian fire control in the early days of the war was apparently poor: they blazed away with everything and then ran short. An oblique reference by Ismail also supports the allegation that there were shortages of more basic stores such as petrol, water and even food. 'There was

Kissing Egypt's recaptured soil: the apex of the Arab triumph

a time,' he said, 'when we had soldiers who lived on half their food rations and yet their fighting ability was not in the least affected.' Some Cairo sources also think that by the middle of the first week supplies of SAM-6s may have been running short.

But the strongest reason for Ismail's alleged shortage of equipment on the east bank was that he had deliberately kept half his tanks on the west bank. By the end of Wednesday, Egypt had pushed more than 700 tanks over into Sinai (though many of these had already been destroyed, of course). But another 500 still remained west of the canal. Ismail was keeping them to defend the homeland against the possibility of an Israeli airborne assault from the rear.

Ismail could, and did, claim that he alone understood what Sadat wanted. And that was a more complex and subtle outcome than simple military victory. Sadat's strategy had not altered since the Cairo summit of September 10: to use the war simply as a means of sparking an international crisis sufficiently serious to persuade the superpowers that the Middle East situation was too dangerous to remain unresolved any longer. Ismail therefore saw no need to pursue Israel across Sinai.

Yet, finally, Ismail's temperamental differences with Shazli were the critical factor in his rejection of Shazli's plan. 'Those who had heard me speak to the forces,' Ismail said later, 'knew that I feared nothing more than that we should be conventional. I did not want to be conventional. But at the same time I did not want us to be adventurers.' Pointedly, he added: 'Wars are a much more momentous issue than adventures . . .' .

Shazli's daring strikes would have faced high odds. But Ismail's caution was fatal. Because the first phase of his assault had already failed in one crucial respect: Egyptian armour had not penetrated Sinai as far as planned.

Operation Badr had called for a bridgehead slightly deeper into Sinai than the Israeli military road – which means about twenty miles deep. (See map on page 66.) At that depth, natural features – mostly sand ridges – would provide an intermittent but serviceable defence line. But the first swirling Israeli rearguard actions on Sunday had deprived the Egyptians of that objective. And in repulsing Israel's concerted assault on Tuesday, the Egyptian armour had given still more ground. By Wednesday night, therefore, the Egyptian bridgehead stretched impressively almost the length of the canal. But it was at most ten miles deep – little more than half what it should have been.

The bridgehead thus suffered from one potentially fatal weakness. It was not deep enough to allow a resilient defence against a determined Israeli thrust. That was precisely the flaw which next day, Thursday, October 11, was to spark an argument among Israel's generals paralleling the Ismail-Shazli debate.

6: Sharon versus Gonen

The thirty-six hours from the morning of Wednesday, October 10, to the evening of Thursday, October 11, were as critical for Israel as the start of the war had been. For when Mrs Meir's ministers met on Wednesday morning – for the eighth time since war began – Israel's ability to fight on was in grave doubt. The failure of Tuesday's counter-attack had demonstrated Israel's weakness in Sinai – which Egypt would surely exploit – while Golan drained its resources. Syria had to be crushed.

But Israel now needed to do more. Syria had to be subdued not merely rapidly, but also in a sufficiently exemplary fashion to deter other contenders from entering the fray – most particularly, Iraq and Jordan. For Israel was uncomfortably aware that the longer the war of attrition continued on two fronts, the more likely it was that Arab political pressure would force King Hussein – whatever his military weakness – to open up a third front. Israel knew America was vehemently counselling Hussein to stay out of the conflict. But Hussein was, after all, an Arab – and a proud one. The taunts of President Gadaffi – who, himself keeping Libya safely on the sidelines, had taken to calling Hussein a coward – might be ludicrously inapposite, but they presumably stung just the same. More ominous was the possibility of Iraq's entry into the war: unlike Jordan, Iraq had considerable military resources. (Later on Wednesday, Iraq did proclaim its entry into the war – but that still gave Israel a couple of days in hand before Iraqi forces could actually deploy in support of the Syrians. Hussein ordered mobilization but did not yet commit himself.)

But the critical development was the growing likelihood that Russia was preparing to re-stock the Arab arsenals. Further supplies of SAM-6s to Syria would end the Israel Air Force's new and hard-won ability to strike the Syrian armour at will. That increased the urgency of a Golan victory. But although Israel, by Wednesday, still had the resources to mount twin assaults in Golan and Sinai, any set-backs – such as a repeat of the 190th disaster – would effectively leave Israel bare of reserves. Resupply by America would then be the only way in which Israel could continue the war. Mrs Meir's ministers knew, however, what Kissinger would want in return for a promise of arms: Israel's agreement to a ceasefire. And the only realistic terms for this would leave the Arabs in possession of their new gains.

Israel could bear the loss of a strip of Sinai. In the United Nations, its foreign minister Abba Eban, was already talking semi-publicly of 'concessions' amounting to withdrawal from most of Sinai. But Israeli pride and military security forbade any Syrian gains on Golan. Before Israel lost so much material as to have no choice but to accept the likely American terms, therefore, the Syrians must be driven from their last remaining pockets of armour around Khusniye and Kuneitra. That was the decision of Mrs Meir's ministers on Wednesday morning. By Wednesday evening, the job was done.

The battle for Khusniye was the harder. It began on Wednesday morning and was not over until evening. Here as elsewhere in their fighting retreat across Golan, the Syrians used anti-tank missiles in almost the profusion of the Sinai campaign; the Syrians seem also to have used Russian tank-to-tank missiles called Schmell far more than the Egyptians did. Dug into the fortified rubble of Khusniye behind weapons like those, they seemed impregnable. And, indeed, the Israeli forces in the end not so much captured Khusniye as overwhelmed it. They charged

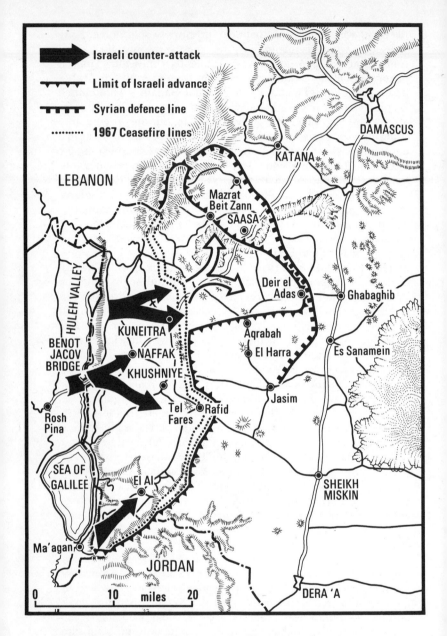

Israel's hard slog towards Damascus

Having broken the Syrian armour on Golan, Israel thrust down the road
to Damascus. But Syria's second line of defence held; Israel was pushed
back from Saasa; and the Moroccan troops along Mount Hermon's lower
ridge threatened Israel's flank. Jordanian and Iraqi armour attacked the
Israeli advance from the south. The Iraqis, mauled, were chased back to
Deir el Adas. Jordan's brigade headed up towards Kuneitra but, their attack
unsupported by the Syrians, they had to retreat to Jasim.

the Syrian defences in a frontal attack. Again it was a battle that cost a lot of tanks and men.

By contrast, the assault on Kuneitra began late on Wednesday afternoon, and it was over in an hour. This pile of rubble was taken in the same fashion as Khusniye. After a perfunctory barrage, Israeli tanks simply charged up the main road from Naffak and into what had once been the centre of the town – to relieve the Israeli garrison surrounded since the first night of the war. The Syrians had fallen back in the face of the Israeli charge, but one terrified prisoner was hustled away. The garrison was un-ruffled: 'We never worried when the Syrians came through,' a nineteen-year-old Israeli infantry captain, late of Brooklyn USA, said. 'We shot them up as they went through the first time and we shot them up when they came running back.'

It was a bloody affair though. Israeli air strikes caught the retreating Syrian column on the road back home about two miles north-east of Kuneitra. The road was cluttered with the ruins of their tanks. Two men from one T-54 had tried to run for it when the planes swooped down: their corpses lay as they had been hit, both staring back over their shoulders. Beside another tank, the driver lay beneath a blanket as if asleep, his head on a pillow. Perhaps he had been exhausted and trying to snatch a fifteen minute doze? His face was quite relaxed: he must have died in his sleep as the Israeli fighters' cannon blew off both his legs.

By nightfall, Israel had recaptured Golan. Its infantry were cautiously probing the outposts of the first Syrian defence works the other side of the erstwhile ceasefire line. It was clear that by the morning of the next day, Thursday, Israel would be in a position to attack into Syria. The only question Israeli military commentators thought it worth raising was whether Israel would strike due east, heading across the plain to cut Damascus' links with Jordan; or whether the tanks would spear north-east up the main road to Damascus itself? Just in case the Jordanians had not got the point, Thursday's *Jerusalem Post* reported that Israel 'will not be cowed into blind respect for the armistice lines.'

Syria fought back still. The dawn of Thursday, October 11, brought death to four helicopter loads of Syrian commandos, ambushed as they tried to land behind Israeli lines. The Israelis had been monitoring the Syrian wireless nets and an Arabic speaking officer had listened to the raid. Other infiltrators were more successful: Syrian infantry armed with RPGs killed more than one Israeli tank commander in this counter-attack phase.

Syria threw in more armour, too – in a counter attack on Thurs-day morning in the northern sector, straddling the Kuneitra-Damascus road. But it was the last effort; the fact of the attack at all came as an unpleasant surprise to the battered Israelis, but most observers felt that it did not compare in intensity to the earlier Syrian struggles. It seems, indeed, that it was this Syrian attack which precipitated the actual Israeli crossing into Syria: in a looping southward curve, the Israelis swung through the line of Syrian tanks to take them from the rear – and found themselves behind the first of the Syrian defence lines. By Thursday evening, the heart of that defence line had been smashed – and Israeli armour was six miles into Syria.

The wrong side of the ceasefire lines on Golan, Syria had left more than 800 tanks – blown up, burnt out and simply abandoned. A subsequent American estimate by the Defense Department was that Syria might also have lost 8,000 of its soldiers there – a relative handful captured, but the overwhelming proportion killed. Touring the scene in a helicopter, Dayan now announced that the Syrians were to be taught that 'the road which leads from Damascus to Tel Aviv leads also from Tel Aviv to Damascus.'

But if Dayan found it hard even now, after the debacle of the first six days, to distinguish between confidence and hubris, other military men were willing to murmur the truth: which was that Israel had barely reached the end of the first phase of the war; that on the Syrian front it still faced an exhausting slog towards Damascus; that the worst Sinai battles were yet to come; and that Israel's equipment was by now in terrible shape. By Friday morning, as the Syrians fought back in a relatively orderly retreat, cheerful Israeli promises about 'downhill to Damascus' were silenced. As he had pone to Elazar's blithe boast of 'breaking the bones' of the Arab armies, General Herzog now publicly punctured Dayan's facile optimism. 'Smashing such defence lines [as Syria's] cannot be done quickly,' he said. 'The defence is not a single line which we broke through yesterday, but a defence network which continues deep into the country and over very difficult terrain which is not ideal ground for a tank battle.'

But at least, by Thursday evening, the transfer could begin of some Israeli armour from Golan to Sinai. With more immediate impact, Israel's overworked and battered air force could not concentrate its efforts against the Egyptians. But just as the question of what Egypt should do next had split its high command on Wednesday, so these growing capabilities in Sinai fomented sharp differences among Israeli generals – divisions which were never really resolved, which later affected the outcome of the war in a critical manner, and which called into question the personal authority of the Israeli Chief of Staff, Elazar.

The Israeli regular army is small, only 11,500 men (omitting conscripts), and most of its senior commanders have fought together in four campaigns: as adolescents in guerrilla actions in

Palestine before the British withdrew; and then rising in rank together through the wars of 1948-9, 1956 and 1967. The strengths and weaknesses, failures and achievements, of each man are thus intimately known to his contemporaries. This has not left over-much reverence within the high command. Equally inevitably, there is a tendency to magnify the exploits of previous commanders to the disadvantage of the present generation. These stresses are reinforced by the straightforward bureaucratic point that the small scale of the army means that its officers' careers interweave – first in one job, then in another – to a remarkable degree. Inevitably, factions coalesce – with one officer advancing as the protege of this commander, another owing allegiance to that. The close connection of the army with politics – for officers are supposed to retire around forty, and several have in recent years chosen to go into politics – is an additional source of potential friction. The Israeli army is thus not easy to run – as Elazar had already found by October 6.

David Elazar's career encapsulates the story of Israel's army. He was born in 1925 in the Yugoslav town of Sarajevo – where his father, a former major in Tito's army, still lives. But in 1940, aged fifteen, Elazar emigrated to Palestine – joining his boyhood friend, Haim Bar-Lev, who had arrived from Yugoslavia the year before. Elazar first went into a kibbutz, where he met his future wife. But the cast of his life was set in 1946, when he joined the Palmach, the striking force of the illegal Jewish militia, the Haganah, which was then in open revolt against British rule – as well as fighting a savage war of terror and counter-terror with the Palestinian Arabs. In the full-scale war which followed the British withdrawal, the Palmach was regularized as the commando arm of the Jewish forces. And it was the attempt in May, 1948, by two platoons of the Palmach to relieve the heavily outnumbered defenders of the Jewish quarter of Jerusalem that first brought Elazar to his seniors' notice. Elazar, newly commissioned, commanded one of the platoons. Palmach had to withdraw, it was a gallant attempt, and Elazar afterwards rose swiftly.

The War of Independence, as the Israelis came to call it, was an infantry affair – the Israelis did have a few run-down tanks, but by far the most important vehicle was the jeep. And until the 1956 campaign Israel concentrated on its infantry, with paratroops as the elite strike force. Elazar rose to direct the School of Infantry in 1956 and, in the brief Sinai campaign that year, commanded an infantry brigade in the Gaza Strip.

But the relative failure of Israel's armour in 1956 – and the realization by the Israeli General Staff that, had they not attacked the Egyptian armour from the rear while it was facing the British and French, they might have suffered heavy casualties – forced a rethink. Israel decided that it too needed armour. The task of building it up was given to Haim Bar-Lev – from 1957, commander of the armoured corps. Elazar went into tanks too. He had comparatively little hand in the moulding of what was to become Israel's distinctive armoured tactic: mobility and deep penetration as the riposte to massive but static Arab tank formations. That was more the contribution of Yitzhak Rabin, later Chief of Staff during the Six-Day War – although further work on the techniques of large-scale tank manœuvres was then done by two other soldiers, Israel Tal and Bren Adan. But it was the soft-spoken, level-headed, unflamboyant Elazar who succeeded Bar-Lev in 1961 as commander of Israel's armour. (He still wears the tankman's black beret.) And it was Elazar who fostered among tank men – as before he had fostered among paratroopers – a conscious elitism. He devised the Wagnerian commissioning ceremony for young tank lieutenants: the midnight swearing of an oath of loyalty in a ring of flaming torches on top of the Masada plateau by the Dead Sea – scene of the Jews' last bloody stand against the Romans 1,900 years ago.

In 1967, Brigadier Elazar held the Northern Command – the Syrian front – and directed the successful assault on the Golan Heights. It was not, perhaps, an over-imaginative battle: with two possible plans of attack, Elazar chose the more straightforward and, some observers think, lost more men than he need have. Still, Elazar won – and in sufficiently dramatic fashion to gain public acclaim.

The 1967 war also saw Moshe Dayan back in the Ministry of Defence, after some years of comparative political eclipse. And the career of one of Dayan's favoured officers, Haim Bar-Lev – who since 1961 had also been in eclipse – prospered too. He was Deputy Chief of Staff during the 1967 war and became Chief of Staff in January 1968. Elazar took over as Bar-Lev's deputy.

Bar-Lev saw Israel through the 1969–70 'war of attrition'. Most of his attention went on the construction of the canalside fortifications which bear his name, while Elazar looked after Israel's famous tanks – whose success in 1967 had, of course, ensured their place as the keystone of Israel's tactical thinking. When Bar-Lev retired to enter politics, it was almost inevitable that Elazar would take over as Chief of Staff, which he did on January 1, 1972. As deputy, Elazar chose Israel Tal – joint creator of Israel's armoured strategy.

Elazar was a safe choice, even if his tactical limitations were known. 'Elazar has the bulldog technique of taking a big bite and then hanging on,' one Israeli journalist said. And he was popular: now 48, he is a stocky, darkly handsome figure; in a poll just before the war, readers of the Israeli women's magazine *At* chose him as their ideal husband.

In the months that followed, every single top Israeli commander was due for replacement. It was the most sweeping re-allocation of jobs the armed forces had seen. Most of Elazar's new commanders – including the head of military intelligence, Major-General Eliyahu Zeira – had been installed only in the spring of 1973. The GOC of Central Command – the Jordan front – had held his post for just six days when war began. Elazar – himself with barely eighteen months in which to adjust to his job – thus faced the war with an untried, unsettled team.

On Wednesday, October 10, the Israeli government called up six retired generals, mostly as 'special assistants' to the new commanders. The six carried famous names – among them Bar-Lev, the ex-Chief of Staff; Yariv, for nine years head of military intelligence and now a likely cabinet minister should Mrs Meir's government return to power; and Mordechai Hod, commander of the air force in its finest hour in 1967. (Hod's name had not been wholly free of controversy since. His appointment by Dayan to the lucrative managing directorship of Israel Aircraft Industries was one of the political scandals of Israel in the months before war.) But while the resurrection of the 'old war horses,' as Elazar called them, served to reassure the reservists – and the generals did take a burden off the shoulders of their successors – it did not ease the political problems.

The fullest discussion of these, albeit guarded in tone, was aired in the Hebrew magazine *Haolam Hazeh* – run by Uri Avneri, millionaire member of the Knesset who is the most outspoken critic of what he sees as Israel's drift towards militarism: 'Political figures who played key roles in the election campaign were suddenly compelled to cooperate in the battlefields. It was impossible to erase all at once the personal and ideological rivalry between them or the differences in their political perceptions and outlook. The belief which prevailed at the outbreak that this would be a swift war, at the end of which it would be necessary to return immediately to the election struggle, contributed its share to the creation of this intolerable situation. The fact that the war also led at once to an ideological debate about the validity of the various political views on peace and security – secure borders, strategic buffers and the deterrent power of Israel's forces – aided in fostering the political differences.'

The focus of these 'differences' was Arik Sharon – convinced he had been passed over as Chief of Staff for his right-wing political views, and now recalled to work in his old command, Sinai, under a man who, only three months before, had been *his* subordinate, Major-General Shmuel Gonen. Gonen was a brave and competent officer. But he lacked Sharon's bravura, and he had been unnerved by his setbacks. From the start, Sharon seems to have treated Gonen with contempt: 'If I were still in command, you wouldn't have much to do in this war,' he reportedly said. Against this strained personal relationship, the argument began.

By Monday, on the third day of fighting, Israeli units could have reached points on the canal once more. The Egyptian bridgehead was incomplete in places, and still thinly held elsewhere. But what purpose would have been served? Israel was concentrating on the Golan battle, and the Egyptians seemed intent on consolidating what they now held rather than pressing home their advantage. Sharon, in charge of the key central sector defending the passes, was an enthusiastic advocate of some such swift Israeli response. After the war, Sharon put this fairly outspokenly: 'Our aim was to check them in Sinai while we attended to the Syrians. I personally thought that this was a mistake and expressed my views several times. I saw that we did not have unlimited time. I saw that the Egyptians were not pressing forward, but were digging in; and that a ceasefire would see them strongly entrenched.'

Sharon has always implied two points: that he was overruled from the start; and that the position in Sinai through the rest of the week was stalemate. Neither point appears to be correct. Gonen had allowed the Tuesday counter-attack in Sharon's central sector. The result had been failure and the loss of the 190th Bridgade to Egyptian missiles. And from Egyptian sources, it seems that the middle of the week saw a major battle in Sinai, in which Sharon lost the site of his advanced headquarters. On November 10, the Cairo newspaper *Al Gomhouria* gave a detailed account of a four-day battle for 'Triangle 100'. (Their description fits the 577 feet hill of Katib-el-Kheil, west of Tasa.) This commanding point, the account claims, was the site of Israel's 'central sector headquarters' – presumably, Sharon's group of armoured personnel carriers laden with radio gear. Egypt took Triangle 100 on Tuesday night, in the wake of the Israeli defeat. And a series of Israeli counter-attacks through Wednesday were apparently beaten off with considerable Israeli losses. (See map page 114.)

If Sharon's position by Wednesday night was thus less assured than he has since maintained, it is true that Thursday morning brought a decisive change in Egyptian deployment. Ismail now began to bring over into Sinai the 500 tanks he had held on the west bank of the canal to protect the rear of his armies. In Egypt, Ismail has since been savagely criticized for thus committing Egypt's main reserves. But Sadat knew of the decision and could have vetoed it. And Ismail did it reluctantly. But Egypt was under intense pressure from Syria to take some of the Israeli weight off

A briefing in Golan. The Israeli officer is using a carefully hand-drawn
— though not very accurate — map of the Damascus plain.

Golan. Politically, Ismail had little choice but to prepare for a fresh assault in Sinai. The arguments which followed between the Israeli generals on Thursday, October 11, at the Ministry of Defence in Tel Aviv and in Gonen's Sinai headquarters were about how Israel could best take advantage of Ismail's unexpected move.

By this point, Sharon was claiming not merely that he could reach the canal but that he could cross it. In his four years as GOC Southern Command, Sharon had found ample time to study – even to prepare – potential crossing points. And his argument for doing so was straightforward: Israel should strike first, and the west bank offered better chances for traditional Israeli tactics. 'By carrying the war to the west bank, we would be in our element,' he said, 'fast moving armour in open, classic tank country.' Sharon, of course, was not a tank man. He did, however, get powerful support inside the Ministry of Defence from Brigadier Avraham Tamir – at 49, regarded as one of the two or three cleverest men in the Israeli army, though one of the least known. Tamir, backed by several other officers – on one account, even by some major-generals – urged a swift canal crossing on the grounds that an attack now, while the bulk of the Third Army was redeploying from the west bank to the east, would catch its armour unprepared – and with its rear unprotected by the missile screen in the Sinai.

Tamir commanded respect. (He was subsequently promoted Major-General and put in charge of a new army planning branch, answering to the Deputy Chief of Staff.) But he was reckoned short of combat experience. The Tamir-Sharon plan was overruled at the highest level: by the triumvirate, Dayan, Elazar and Bar-Lev – now attached to Elazar for 'special duties'. They decided to wait. Each succeeding day now would see more Israeli armour and air power concentrating in Sinai – improving the chances of a later assault. If the Egyptian eastward build-up continued, the succeeding days would also see ever fewer tanks remaining on the west bank of the canal – enhancing the chances of any Israeli force that might finally cross. As for the expected Egyptian assault, it seems to have been the Sinai commander, Gonen, who saw that this could provide the decisive opportunity for Israeli tanks to destroy the Egyptian armour – because the Egyptians, in advancing, would have to leave the protection of their infantry-borne missile screen. Bar-Lev's support of this appreciation was decisive in the rejection of a swift crossing – as Sharon realized: 'Bar-Lev said that we should wait and repel their armoured attacks. I believed that we should have crossed the canal and that we wasted several days. . . . But in an army you obey orders.'

But the underlying strategic reason for the rejection of Sharon's plan was one over which Israel itself had no control. By Thursday, a Russian airlift to resupply Syria – and to a lesser extent, Egypt – was in full swing. But America was making no similar effort to re-equip Israel. Dayan, Elazar and Bar-Lev were thus acutely conscious that the Israeli army was not in a position to risk the losses that an unsuccessful assault would bring. Israel's ability to do other than accept the new situation in Sinai, in other words, now depended on what terms Kissinger required of them.

7: The rejected victory

On the surface, the first week of war seethed with momentous diplomatic and political effort: at the United Nations, attempts to secure a Security Council resolution calling for a ceasefire; in Washington, agonized discussions whether to resupply Israel; most dramatic of all, a massive Russian airlift to the Arabs. The reality was less frenetic – but considerably more chilling.

At midday on Sunday, October 7, with the war just twenty-two hours old, the British ambassador to Egypt, Sir Philip Adams, was driven in his Rolls-Royce to the Cairo suburb of Heliopolis, to see President Sadat at his wartime residence, the Tahra palace. He found Sadat sitting, casually dressed, looking out of the big window over the palace grounds, puffing his pipe. Sadat made some casual remark about the view. There was a long pause, which Sadat finally broke. 'Well,' he said cheerfully, 'what's going on?' Adams had rarely seen him so relaxed.

Back in the British embassy lay a confetti of cables briefing Adams of the urgent international efforts to get a ceasefire. At the United Nations, the British representative Sir Donald Maitland was urging anyone who would listen – and many who would not – to support a meeting of the Security Council. Nixon and Kissinger had also called for one. But Maitland, by virtue of Britain's status as author of Resolution 242, was thought to have more chance of cajoling the Arab states into accepting the necessity for a ceasefire. The British Foreign Secretary, Sir Alec Douglas Home, was ready to fly to New York. All was set. Now, sitting comfortably opposite the man at whom all this activity was directed, Adams cautiously raised the critical question: would Sadat be interested in a Security Council resolution calling for a ceasefire? Sadat was brusque, almost angry. It was out of the question. In a few pithy sentences the President spelled out that this time, the only ceasefire Egypt would consider was one inseparably linked to a longterm settlement. The only acceptable basis for that would be Israel's implementation of Resolution 242 – the Arab interpretation of 242. Then Sadat dismissed the topic.

The lobbies of the United Nations hummed for the rest of the week with the sound of diplomats rehearsing the well worn peripheries of the problem. What about 242's 'constructive ambiguities', as the British delegation at the UN somewhat smugly called the crucial vagueness of wording on 'territories'? Would India and Yugoslavia make an acceptable peacekeeping force? What sort of international assurances of security would Israel accept: a joint superpower guarantee; a treaty with America? But unspoken at the heart of the debate was the crucial question: how could Israel be pressured into accepting, immediately, the substance of 242? And that in turn depended on a single issue: would America resupply Israel?

Kissinger's subsequent accounts of his diplomatic involvement in the war have all begun with the dramatic telephone call waking him at 6.00 am in New York – noon in Israel – on the Saturday war broke out. As we have seen, Kissinger's involvement actually went back some days earlier. And in persuading Mrs Meir to reject a pre-emptive strike, the American ambassador to Israel, Kenneth Keating, had been forced at least to open the door to an American resupply effort.

But Kissinger was unmoved. Phrasing it tactfully, he explained on October 26: 'Throughout the crisis, the President was convinced that we had two major problems – first, to end hostilities as quickly as possible; but, secondly, to end hostilities in a manner that would enable us to make a major contribution to removing the conditions that have produced four wars between Arabs and Israelis in the last twenty-five years.' In blunter terms, Kissinger wanted a limited Israeli defeat. The nicety lay in calculating the optimum scale of this defeat: big enough to satisfy the Arabs; modest enough to preclude a propaganda triumph for the Russians; sobering enough to bring Israel to the conference table; bearable enough to avoid the collapse of Mrs Meir's government and its replacement by rightwing intransigents.

In pursuit of this strategy, Kissinger refused arms supplies. At 2.20 pm on Sunday, October 7, the Israeli defence mission in New York received a coded cable from the Israeli embassy in Washington: the American response to the first Israeli request for arms was 'negative'. In this, ironically, the American government was nearly unanimous – for very different reasons. Kissinger wanted an Israeli defeat. But the American intelligence community that first weekend predicted a swift Israeli victory. Either way, resupply was a poor policy. As Kissinger later told Mohammed Heikal, editor of *Al Ahram*: 'All our experts believed that if you started a war, Israel's forces would deal you a knock-out blow. When the war did break out, it became clear that our calculations were wrong. Yet we continued to believe that our estimate of the likely result was still correct.'

By Monday, October 8, Kissinger was still advocating a ceasefire on the basis of a return to pre-October 6 positions. The proposition – amounting to unilateral Arab withdrawal – was so ludicrous that it could only have been founded on a total mis-understanding of the progress of the war. And Kissinger after-wards confirmed to Heikal: 'I imagined then that this was in your own interest before it was in Israel's interest.' Yet later that day, Kissinger seemed less certain of a swift Israeli victory. Israel's ambassador in Washington, Simcha Dimitz, cabled to the Israeli defence mission after meeting Kissinger that, although his request for arms had got a 'negative', Kissinger had added: 'There is a chance.'

By that afternoon, it had begun to look as if Russia had decided to wade in on behalf of its Arab client states. The timely evacuation of the Russian advisers had suggested prior know-ledge of the assault. So had the launching – on October 6 – of a second COSMOS reconnaissance satellite. By Monday, too, the Soviet party leader Leonid Brezhnev was urging other Arab states such as Iraq to join the battle. Most worrying of all, analysis of the Russian merchant traffic passing through the Dardanelles from the Black Sea suggested that a Russian re-supply effort might be under way.

Kissinger still had faith in the 'structure of peace' he had laboriously been putting together – by which he meant principally the detente with Russia and China. He got on well with the Russian ambassador in Washington, Anatoly Dobrynin. Kissinger pressed on him the likely damage to their relations should the superpowers become entangled in the war. As he put it later: 'We have also urged . . . all the parties in the conduct of their diplomacy now to keep in mind that whatever momentary advantages might be achieved in this or that forum, our principal objective should be to maintain lasting relationships . . .'. In a final public plea, Kissinger took advantage of a speech he had long been scheduled to give to a peace organization that Monday to warn: 'Detente cannot survive irresponsibility in any area, including the Middle East . . .'. But Sadat's strategy was precisely to involve the superpowers – though how well Russia appreciated this is uncertain.

Published accounts have so far agreed that, in response to the massive Russian airlift which began late on Tuesday, October 9, Nixon reluctantly agreed to a comparable American airlift on Saturday, October 13. The truth is much less clear-cut. By Tuesday, October 9, the pressure of the American Jewish lobby on Nixon was enormous – especially the lobbying of a group of Senators led by Jacob Javits of New York. It was effective. At 7.10 pm on Tuesday evening, the Israeli defence mission had yet another coded cable from their Washington embassy. It reported that the Israeli ambassador, Simcha Dimitz, had now seen President Nixon – and got a 'green light' on arms shipments.

The most likely explanation is that Nixon and Kissinger were divided – Nixon bowing to domestic pressures, Kissinger still trying to use supplies as a lever to prise concessions out of Israel. For the American administration now embarked upon two mutually contradictory courses: trying to force a ceasefire on Israel, yet simultaneously releasing hair-raising stories about the Russian airlift which, inevitably, strengthened the Jewish lobby.

The Russian airlift to Syria gathered momentum through Wednesday. Giant Antonov-12 freighters landed at the military airfield near the Roman ruins of Palmyra, north-east of Damascus. Longer-range Antonov-22s flew in to Cairo. Their cargoes – according to Israeli sources – were mainly SAM-6s. In Washington, the American government promptly and grotesquely exaggerated the scale of this airlift – alleging seventy flights a day and, by Friday, 100 flights. In fact, although the Russian aircraft bound for Egypt had to overfly Cyprus air traffic control zone, the controllers there logged no abnormal Russian movements until 3.00 pm on Friday, October 12, when a stream of Russian pilots began asking for permission to overfly at 26,000 feet. The pilots claimed they were from Aeroflot, the Russian civil airline – but were using military throat microphones. By Friday midnight, traffic reached its peak: eighteen an hour – a total of sixty flights in the first twenty-one hours. When the *Sunday Times* approached the Pentagon about the discrepancy between this evidence and the American accounts, Department of Defense spokesmen – blaming faulty intelligence – acknowledged that the Russian airlift 'was not quite as substantial as we first thought'. Their revised estimate was twenty-five to thirty flights a day. In paving the way for an American airlift, the exaggerations were certainly helpful. On Wednesday, October 10, an El Al Boeing, its markings taped over, took off from Oceana Naval Air Station, Virginia, loaded with bombs and air-to-air missiles for Israel.

Yet as the superpowers edged into conflict, Kissinger almost succeeded. He could have got Israel to cease fire, on terms which amounted to a victory for Egypt. Sadat rejected the offer.

Kissinger later described the first part of this exercise to

Heikal: 'My proposal was to have a ceasefire in the positions held at that time – that, I think, was October 10. . . . It was not easy to present Israel with a proposal for a ceasefire on the October 10 or October 11 lines. Their opposition to us was furious, because they thought that with the completion of full mobilization they would now be able to change the course of the war. But they acquiesced in the end.' British sources say he exaggerated: their account is that Israel first wanted a ceasefire on pre-war lines – an Arab withdrawal, in fact. By Thursday, Israel wanted to swap its Syrian gains for Sinai losses: again, back to pre-war lines. But by Friday, Israel was so desperate for arms that, although Mrs Meir was kicking, Kissinger was sure he could now force a 'ceasefire *in situ*' – as his crucial phrase said. Meanwhile, the Russian ambassador Dobrynin – after consulting Moscow – told Kissinger that the Russians were sure Sadat would also agree to a ceasefire on those terms. The miscalculation led to a spectacular row between Britain and America.

Late that Friday afternoon, Kissinger contacted the British Embassy in Washington and outlined the bargain he had struck with Israel. He had agreed with Dobrynin that Britain would now propose a ceasefire in the United Nations Security Council, making appropriate references to Resolution 242, but calling for a ceasefire *in situ*. America and Russia would second this. According to the Russians, Sadat would then agree. Would Britain please get on with it.

It was around Friday midnight in London. And the Foreign Office, considering the plan, was puzzled. Britain had tried to cement its reconstructed relationship with Egypt by banning arms supplies to the war. Now, the Foreign Office was unwilling to alienate Sadat by advocating a ceasefire on terms which he would find unacceptable. But Adams had consistently reported from Cairo that Sadat, whom he saw frequently through the war, would never agree to a ceasefire except as part of a long-term settlement. Now Kissinger was saying the opposite. The first thing to do was to check with Sadat.

At 4.00 am on Saturday morning, Adams returned to the Tahra palace. Sadat was in his pyjamas, but wide awake. He had just said goodbye to the Russian ambassador, Vladimir Vinogradov. The Russian had previously been euphoric about the war: 'I have seen sweet times in Cairo, I have seen bitter times. But this is the greatest moment of all.' Now, considerably sobered, he had been pressing on Sadat the terms which Russia had just cobbled up with Kissinger. The Russian argument, echoing Kissinger's, was that Egypt had made its political point: the superpowers would now enforce a long-term settlement. Sadat angrily rejected the proposal as devoid of adequate guarantees. Adams arrived to find Sadat still muttering rude things about Vinogradov. His view of Sadat's position was confirmed in less than a minute.

A few hours later, the Washington embassy gave Kissinger Britain's answer: there was no point in pursuing the plan, because Sadat would not accept it. Kissinger blew up – 'acting like a typical German bully boy', was the disdainful British comment. How dare the British contradict what Kissinger had been told by the Russians?

So the Foreign Office sent Adams back to Sadat at 4.00 pm. Sadat was apparently amused by the process, but he did not budge. That evening, Prime Minister Edward Heath called his Foreign Secretary, Sir Alec Douglas-Home, and a couple of senior Foreign Office men to a worried meeting at his country residence, Chequers. The problem now was not merely how to halt the Middle East war but how to smooth what was later described as 'this enormous hiccup' in Anglo-American relations.

They decided, unhappily, that Britain had no choice but to persist in rejecting Kissinger's plan as unworkable. At 11.00 pm, Douglas-Home telephoned Kissinger to tell him.

So America had no choice but to begin an airlift to Israel. Kissinger was still so cross that Britain, to its relief, was not asked to provide bases.

Britain's circumspection was echoed throughout Europe. No European government could ignore the fact that on Tuesday, the third day of war, the Kuwait Council of Ministers had announced that they were organizing a meeting of Arab oil producers to discuss the role of oil in the conflict. By next day, Egyptian and Saudi Arabian oil experts were already discussing ways in which the 'oil weapon' might be used. And Europe obtained over seventy per cent of its oil from the Arabs. In the end, America had to channel its airlift to Israel through the base it leased from Portugal in the Azores. For its permission, Portugal too demanded a high price: American help in staving off United Nations pressure to force changes in Portugal's African policy. Washington had no choice but to agree. The irony was that, only days before the war, it had been discussing whether to allow its lease on this Azores airfield to lapse.

On Sunday, October 14, the American airlift cranked into gear – to the relief of personnel on US air bases who, according to a Congressional source, had been driven demented since Tuesday with orders like: 'Get ready to ship such and such, but we don't yet know how. Maybe not in our planes.' For America did explore the possibility of mounting a covert resupply operation. But re-equipment on the scale that Israel now needed simply could not be hidden, and the US Defense Secretary, James Schlesinger, finally convinced his colleagues that open resupply was the only sane policy.

Surveying the rubble of the week's efforts, Kissinger could at least derive one crumb of comfort. All week, King Hussein of Jordan had wavered unhappily until – as one observer put it with a dazzling confusion of metaphor – 'he took refuge in his emotional anchor: the Arab nationalism which always comes to the fore when he is under great stress.' He finally entered the war on Saturday; but Kissinger could claim credit for having pressured Hussein into delaying this move for at least three days. And even announcing his troops' departure for the Golan front, Hussein was still careful to distinguish between 'defence of our entire sacred holy soil' and an attack on Israel. But the troops Hussein sent were, as he said, his best: the 40th Armoured Brigade – despite its title, one of the two Jordan possesses, but equipped with Centurions and formidably well trained. The Israelis had a healthy respect for them. Hussein's risk was that, if they achieved anything too spectacular in battle, Israel would be tempted to bomb Jordan itself.

On Israeli television that Saturday evening, Mrs Meir did not reveal that Israel had agreed to a humiliating ceasefire, only to have Sadat reject it. But, in retrospect perhaps shaken by Kissinger's failure, she went out of her way to signal Israel's willingness to talk. Should the Arabs propose any sort of ceasefire, she said, 'within a few minutes we would be at the cabinet table and making our decision.' She even hinted at the crucial concession Israel had made, indicating obliquely that it would accept a ceasefire with Egypt securely astride the canal. In Cairo, the latest issue of the newspaper *Al Ahram* – whose editor, Heikal, almost certainly knew of the Kissinger proposal – must finally have disabused her. 'The immediate target which Egyptian troops have set for themselves,' its military correspondent now wrote, 'is to inflict the heaviest losses possible on the Israelis.'

So ended the first week of war – and with it Sadat threw away a striking military victory. As Kissinger recalled later: 'This first attempt at a ceasefire failed, on Saturday, October 13, for a variety of reasons – including, perhaps, a misassessment of the military situation by some of the participants.'

Section III

Below: A small column of Israeli tanks, part of Sharon's task force, drive towards the canal, where they would lead the most daring stroke of the war – the crossing into the Egyptian heartland.

Week two: Israel's big gamble just comes off

1: The big tank battle

Meeting on Sunday October 14 to hear military and financial reports, the Israeli cabinet broke off to send congratulations for the eighty-seventh birthday of David Ben-Gurion, the man who led Israel through the War of Independence in 1948–9 (and who was to die soon afterwards, on December 9). It occurred to more than one of the ministers that the situation they found themselves dealing with had more in common with the first great crisis of Israel than with the swift campaigns of 1956 and 1967.

The comparison cannot be pushed too far. Firstly, modern Israel is a far more powerful entity than the 650,000 Jews who, in 1948, faced six Arab armies without having anything much more to defend themselves with than a United Nations resolution. 'This will be a war of extermination,' promised Azzam Pasha of the Arab League in 1948. It would be spoken of, he said, 'like the Mongolian massacres and the crusades'. Not even the Palestinian guerrillas, let alone Presidents Sadat and Asad, produced anything along those lines at the start of the 1973 war.

But the resemblance was that Israel, instead of winning spectacular, inexpensive victories against disorganized opponents, was facing a reasonably cohesive Arab attack – and having to take heavy casualties in order to repel it. On this second Sunday of the war, the Ministry of Defence announced that 656 Israeli soldiers had been killed so far. (Later, it emerged that this was an underestimate, because at least a hundred of those listed as missing were in fact dead.) This was still small compared with the 8,000 killed in the War of Independence. But whereas that war went on for more than a year, the 656 admitted dead were the result of only eight days of largely defensive fighting.

It is fair to say that on David Ben-Gurion's birthday the state he brought into being faced one of the most profound challenges in its brief and stormy history. Yet this was the day on which the balance began to tilt decisively away from the Arab side, in military terms at least. On the Golan front, it became apparent that the Syrian strength had been irrevocably broken. In Sinai, the Egyptian army made its supreme effort, and was repulsed.

'In the name of Allah the merciful and compassionate' – said Cairo Radio on Sunday morning – 'at 0600 today our armed forces began developing an offensive eastwards according to plan. . . . Our armoured and mechanized forces are successfully advancing along the confrontation line.' It was this Egyptian dawn attack, preceded by a ninety-minute artillery bombardment, which brought about the decisive test of armoured strength in Sinai. As the Israelis had predicted, Egypt was coming out to fight. And as Gonen and Bar-Lev had foreseen this presented the Israeli tank crews with the targets they had been seeking.

This attack did not come out of a period of calm, for fighting had been more or less continuous since the first day. But it was a dramatic increase in the scale of the Egyptian effort. For three days beforehand, men and tanks had been crowding eastwards across the pontoon bridges to prepare for the showdown. The best estimate was that during Thursday, Friday and Saturday, another 500 tanks crossed into Sinai, bringing the Egyptian total to more than 1,000. At the same time, Israeli tanks were moving west through the Sinai passes, their numbers increasing with the decline of the Syrian threat.

On the afternoon of Saturday, October 13, the Israelis deployed in the area west of the Gidi and Mitla passes could see a huge cloud of dust moving north from Suez along the banks of the Canal. The axis of the Egyptian attack, it seemed, would be in the area of the lakes.

Neither side's claims about the number of tanks which joined battle – and which were destroyed – on Sunday can be treated as quite reliable. But Israel claimed, with much conviction, that more were engaged than the 1,600 British, German and Italian tanks which fought the Battle of Alamein, 200 miles on the other side of Cairo, during the same month in 1942.

A veteran of Alamein would have found many familiar features in the Sinai battlefield, quite apart from the similarity of the sandy, slightly undulating terrain. He might have been puzzled by items like the ballistic computers carried in some of the Israeli tanks, but in general he would have found the rules of the game little altered by the passage of thirty-three years. Indeed, he might have caught sight from time to time of an Israeli crew, bringing up a 'Super Sherman' – re-engined and re-gunned, but essentially the same as the Shermans that Montgomery used at Alamein. Equally, he might have seen among the Egyptian support formations some T-34s of World War II vintage, and would have been able to trace quite clearly the descent from T-34 through T-55 to T-62. The Israeli Defence Forces' devastating combat advantages arose not from any difference in principle between the weapons on either side – but rather from the detailed improvements made over the years in western armour, and the skill with which the Israelis put them into effect.

Because tanks are regarded as the successors to cavalry, armoured warfare is often thought to be something like the Charge of the Light Brigade, mixed with a dash of old-style naval battle – fleets of tanks sweeping across the desert, exchanging broadsides with one another. The reality is usually less exhilarating. Under battle conditions, tanks grind slowly over the ground, and they rarely if ever fire their guns on the move. Tank fighting is more like a kind of brutal chess match, in which the contestants manoeuvre to find temporarily static positions of advantage, from which they can deliver sudden and unanswerable blows.

Because they must push engineering possibilities to the limit, tanks are a bizarre mixture of brute power and mechanical waywardness. Simply to build a fast caterpillar tractor which can carry tons of armour and still be highly manoeuvrable is no small trick. Then it must carry a gun of such monstrous power that each recoil hits the tank with a fifty-ton hammer-blow, roughly equivalent to its own weight. Add in radios, intercoms, power-operated controls, ventilation systems and the like, and the possibilities of malfunction are easy to imagine. The M-48 Patton, one of the Israeli mainstays, was found to break down once every thirty-six miles in US army service. Tanks therefore require the skills of an automotive society, and this confers advantage on a country like Israel.

One basic proposition dominates tank tactics in battle: no tank can carry enough armour to be safe all of the time. Standard armour-piercing shot, fired at close range, will go through armour more than twice as thick as its own diameter. As the gun of a T-55 fires shot about four inches in diameter, it can punch through eight inches of armour if it gets close enough. The thickest armour on a Centurion, an unusually tough tank, is just over six inches. And it cannot be much more, because any tank significantly heavier than the fifty-two tons of a Centurion would be too slow.

This means that any tank which reaches the right position can destroy any other tank – even one theoretically better than itself. Naturally, penetration falls off with distance, and at 1,500 yards most of the shots from a T-55 will glance off the angles of a Centurion's armour. But the best protection is invisibility, rather than distance. An undulation in the ground of nine feet or so, scarcely visible to the casual eye, will hide a tank from track to turret-roof.

The chief skill of a tank commander leading a squadron is to use such minor wrinkles in the surface of the battlefield – the 'dead ground' – in order to reach an attacking position without being detected by the enemy. Ideally, he and his squadron can then loom suddenly above the skyline like Red Indians in a movie, fire a swiftly-destructive volley, and slide back out of sight. Because visibility from even the best of periscopes is strictly limited, commanders must ride as much as possible with their heads in the open. This exposes them to daunting personal risks which are not shared by drivers, gunners and loaders inside the armoured shell. Nevertheless, Israeli tank commanders only close their hatches under heavy artillery bombardment, when the risk of splinter-wounds becomes too pressing to ignore.

They are helped by the fact that Centurions and Pattons – as we illustrate in an appendix on this book – are better-adapted to this kind of stalking warfare than are Soviet-built tanks. Firstly, they can point their main guns down ten degrees below the horizontal, whereas a T-55 or T-62 can only go down four degrees. This may seem trivial, until one realizes that a tank hiding behind a ridge must point its gun *down* to fire, unless it is to move up and expose most of its hull to return fire. And, as the appendix shows, the western tanks are better adapted to the long, rolling desert terrain in other respects. The Arab T-54/55 commanders had to estimate range by their own visual judgement – sometimes called 'Eyeball Mark I'. The Patton and M-60 crews had accurate, if delicate, optical-prism range-finding systems which allowed them to zero-in on a distant target in a matter of seconds, while the Centurion gunners could use a range-finding machine-gun with tracer bullets to avoid the slow process of correcting successive shots from the main gun by trial and error. This Israeli advantage at long range was heightened by their tanks' armaments. While the Arab T-54s and T-55s had only ordinary armour-piercing shot, which gives limited penetration to long range, almost all the Israeli tanks were equipped with more sophisticated APDS and HEAT ammunition (see appendix) which remains lethal at greater distances. Only the latest Russian T-62 tanks could match the Israeli armaments, and these were in relatively short supply despite Russian deliveries before the war.

In short, Soviet tanks are still better suited to the massed charge and the close-packed *melée*. And it was just such an attack which the Egyptians launched on Sunday morning. It was one in which the military arithmetic was heavily against them, but which they had to make because of the tactical poverty of their situation, closely hemmed in against the canal.

The main thrust was made in the direction of the Gidi Pass. Before the first wave of tanks went forward, an artillery barrage and several air strikes were directed onto the Israeli positions. An Israeli reconnaissance pilot recalled: 'There were four MIGs below us flying very low and firing rockets. Then four Mirages arrived, and we were very happy until we realized that the Mirages were also Egyptian and were attacking our tanks too.' Finally, said the

Death of a tank commander hit by an infantry-launched Syrian missile

pilot, Israeli Phantoms arrived and chased off the Mirages. (But Egypt has no Mirages. These were on loan from Libya.)

Attacking at dawn, the Egyptians were coming out of the dark, while the rising light in the east could be expected to produce crisp outlines when Israeli tanks lifted above the skyline. It is not difficult to visualize the drama and horror of the scene: the canopy of dust rising slowly as hundreds of tanks lurched and swayed forward over the sand, dashing ahead sometimes at twenty miles an hour, then being slowed to a crawl by patches of soft going; the clattering of steel tracks and the massed roar of 600 hp engines, rising and falling as sweating drivers wrestled with gears and clutches; the occasional bark of a gun as a lead tank tried a snap-shot at a fleeting Israeli silhouette (but with only thirty or forty rounds of ammunition on board, wise crews would conserve their stock for worthwhile targets). And amid the din of engines and tracks, over and over again, the harsh clank of tungsten bolts striking through armour, or the wicked crack of HEAT shells going off. Sometimes, crewmen would be seen leaping from a stricken tank. But equally often, the impact of shot would be followed by the fierce orange flames of an ammunition fire, and a trail of oil smoke rising to mingle with the dust. 'Within ten minutes we had lit twenty bonfires,' said an

Israeli tank commander, recalling the battle later.

The first wave, he said, 'advanced through a wadi and climbed up onto a plateau to our south.' (Probably the Jebel Shaifa, roughly half-way between the Gidi Pass and the Little Bitter Lake.) 'Our forces met them on the plateau, and there was a fierce battle. Within an hour most of their tanks were wiped out.

'After this it was quiet for a while. Then the Egyptians began shelling us, then it was quiet again, and then the second wave of tanks attacked. There were 145 tanks, and when they came into range I brought up the whole of my forces and we hit them with everything we had.' The Egyptians tried to bring up mobile artillery pieces to support their armour. 'After we had finished off the tanks, we began hitting their artillery.'

The Israelis claim to have destroyed 250 Egyptian tanks that day, many of them in the first hour or two of battle. At 7.00 am local time the Israeli military spokesman was already claiming that the attack had been 'checked'.

Israeli communiques were not nearly so reliable as in the Six-Day War. ('They've learnt how to fight from us', went a joke in the *Jerusalem Post*, 'and we've learnt how to handle information from them.') But the main claim was clearly something more than mere battlefield rhetoric. Just after 6.00 pm local time, the Voice of the Arabs, broadcasting from Cairo, said with truly remark-able frankness that during the fighting 'one hundred of our tanks were hit'. (BBC Monitoring Service, 1705 GMT October 14.) The statement, attributed to Communique No 38 from the Egyptian High Command, was dropped when the broadcast was repeated an hour later. But the fact that it was made at all may be taken as confirmation of terrible Egyptian losses.

Yet the attack had to be launched because the Egyptian bridgeheads, eight or nine miles deep instead of the planned eighteen, were simply too shallow to be defensible. Tanks, even in defence, must have room to move if they are to be effective: armour-plate alone is never enough. 'To stand still', in the words of the British military historian Kenneth Macksey, 'is to invite destruction'.

Reduction of activity on the Syrian front would enable the Israelis to transfer more and more tanks to Sinai. Assuming the eventual immobilization of the Syrian army, and the legendary efficiency of Israeli tank-repair shops, the Egyptians could expect to find themselves faced with a tank force 1,200 strong within a few more days. Ismail did not want to attack. 'We were forced to launch a wide offensive before the suitable moment', he said later. 'Our object in doing so was to relieve the pressure on Syria.' He would have preferred 'going back to the bridgeheads to pro-ceed with their consolidation, to render them a stubborn rock over which the enemy's counter-attacks could be smashed.' But one plank of Shazli's counter-argument had been that Egypt's bridgehead was so constricted that at their chosen point of attack, the Israelis would be able to build up a decisive five-to-one advantage.

The outcome of the Egyptian initiative – an Israeli crossing of the canal – might well have been the same even if Israel had attacked first (as Sharon had wanted). But the Egyptian decision to move out into Sinai enabled it to be achieved with relatively lighter Israeli casualties, and at much less risk.

In the event, what Gonen did was to draw the Arab tanks out from the protection of the infantry missiles – and out from under the SAM umbrellas. According to Israeli tank officers, the Egyptians tried to bring infantry forward with the armour on Sunday. Personnel-carriers and trucks were following-up close behind the tanks. But the attempt seems to have failed almost completely.

It is one thing for well dug-in infantry to resist tanks from carefully-chosen positions. But to face up to well-handled tanks in a fluid battle is something altogether different. Many of the 'bonfires' studded across the desert were personnel-carriers and rocket-launching vehicles, as well as tanks. Israeli tank crews, accustomed to firing live ammunition in practice battles, are supreme experts at juggling their repertoire of weapons: armour-piercing shot to smash tanks, high-explosive shell to stop personnel-carriers, bursts of machinegun fire to cut down the infantry in the act of deployment. If the Egyptian infantry suffered comparably to the armour – which seems likely – the total number of Egyptian dead may have been more than 600.

A long series of spectacular victories, plus total faith in the superiority of Israeli expertise, produced in the years before the war a kind of contempt among many Israelis for the canny, counterpunching style of warfare. General Sharon was clearly among them, having claimed that Israel was a 'military super-power', capable of conquering in one week 'the area from Khartoum to Baghdad and Algeria'. It was an absurd statement from an officer in an army which could only be fully-mobilized by bringing the economy behind it to a virtual halt. None the less, it was typical of the bravura which led even experienced officers to disregard banalities like guarding flanks and securing communications. To care about such matters was almost akin to cowardice, as in the days when the Royal Navy was so certain of its individual superiority over the French that 'for a British Captain to attempt manœuvring for position, even in the most approved and scientific way, would have been at grave risque to his Character . . .'

That spirit got its come-uppance in the war of 1812 when the British encountered opponents who were not to be disregarded. And if Sharon had been given his head by the Israeli command, something very similar might have happened to the Israeli forces in the Yom Kippur War. As it was, by the afternoon of October 14, the Egyptian attack had been so badly broken that many of the attacking units faced difficulty even finding their way back to the bridgehead. In the evening, an Israeli tank force was sent to take advantage of this confusion by cutting off the retreat from the Gidi Pass area.

Now was the time for the Israeli skill in stalking and navigation – based on their carefully-surveyed 'going maps' of Sinai – to take effect. 'We had to follow a very difficult, roundabout route to get into position,' the force commander said afterwards. 'As soon as we arrived, we got into formation and began kindling the bonfires. The battle lasted until three in the morning. We lit about fifty-five bonfires – half of them tanks, the rest artillery pieces and personnel-carriers. We didn't suffer one loss. It was a fine battle. That is the way to sum it up – a fine battle.'

Moshe Dayan was in Sinai on Sunday afternoon, and was therefore among the first to know that the crisis of defence was passing. He spoke publicly twice during the day: first, aboard a helicopter at the front, second, on the *Mabat* current affairs programme. Because Dayan's own character is poised between extremes – between decisiveness and vacillation, between frankness and circumlocution – his words often shed more light than anyone else's on the dilemmas of Israel policy-making. The need, said Dayan above the clatter of the helicopter, was not to conquer land but to smash the Arab armies. 'Should they sign a ceasefire today, their forces will remain, and they will violate the ceasefire as they did in the past. . . . The aim is to hit and deal blows – the word "destroy" is not so nice – and to defeat them completely. Then it will be possible to carry out a plan. Before doing this the rest is simply dreams.'

But what plan could be carried out? Dayan did not think that even a crushing Israeli victory would lead to peace: '. . . there is no guarantee, and the proof is that we are now in the third war. [Note: fourth by some counts, but many Israelis do not include 1956 as 'their war'; others, including Golda Meir, count it number five – including the 1969–70 'War of Attrition']. This is a basic situation of the State of Israel, which the Arabs do not want to accept. And every now and then they attack it and the Arabs must be killed. There is no limit to this matter . . .'

Seemingly, Dayan recoiled from this bleak prospect, because he later urged: 'We must do something positive, not negative. . . .

We must build up a state and search for [indistinct] . . . and establish the state on a mighty military force and good borders, until one day there won't be a guarantee but there will be neighbourly relations and acceptance . . .

'There is no miracle solution . . . . If there is such a solution I don't know what it is . . . I have heard and read that perhaps we should take southern Syria and eastern Egypt and the north of I don't know what, etc. But when we have finished, would it be better and easier, and would it solve the problems?'

On the *Mabat* programme, he was pressed very hard about the beginning of the war. Had Israel been caught unaware? Should Israel have struck first?

Dayan said that an Arab attack had been possible at any time since 1971. In order to be totally safe 'one has to mobilize the entire reserve force, as at present; and as from the end of 1971 – we are now nearing the end of 1973 – to sit opposite them, so as not to find ourselves in a disadvantageous position. Or, to begin the war. These two options are very, very difficult for us. We desire to live a normal life. . . . They are very difficult, in view of our image in the world . . .

'The Jewish adage, "If someone comes to kill thee, hasten thou and kill him" could be simply adapted to our situation. The Arabs want to kill us. Therefore we have to hasten and kill them, especially when they mobilize their forces and make declarations about it.

'I do not think we have erred by not doing so in the years between 1971 and 1973. Also with regard to the future, I do not think it would be good if we take the inference of this fateful hour, that whenever we see the Arabs desire war and are getting into a position for it, we should begin a war against them. We would never achieve anything.'

Had Israel launched the war herself, Dayan conceded, then Israeli losses might have been lower. But: 'After all, we want to reach some sort of settlement [with the Arabs]. Had we launched a war a year, half a year, or two years ago, would this have brought us closer to a settlement? I do not think it would.'

Dayan's words, tentative and almost self-contradictory at times, give a vivid impression of the problems facing Israeli leadership even with victory in prospect. Could Israel go on imposing military solutions – each time, at higher and higher cost? But could that lead to anything but a state of permanent warfare, and economic ruin? Dayan's reputation outside Israel is that of a 'hawk', and an advocate of military solutions. And without doubt particular elements of his policy, such as the sowing of Jewish settlements in the occupied territories, can only be seen in hardline terms.

At that same time, though, few Israelis have a deeper understanding of the cost of unremitting military effort, both in money and in lives. Before the *Mabat* interview, Dayan made a brief, moving statement on the casualty figures for the first week of the war: '... we are in the heat of battle, and we cannot express publicly our deep sorrow for the fallen ones. . . . Today, we can only say to the families how much we share their mourning. . . . We should know that we are a nation which is shaped by the fallen ones and the fighters, and we pave our way with the force of the past and the future, with the strength of our sons who build, fight and fall . . .'

2: The economics of caution

Israeli communiques were at pains to depict Monday, October 15, as a period of inaction on both the Sinai and Golan fronts. Monday, in fact, saw the Israelis achieve their furthest advance into Syria. That evening, Rafael Etan's tanks rolled into Saasa (though the combination of a Syrian counter-attack and their own supply problems forced the Israelis out again next day). Meantime, the best publicized shooting of the day occurred inside the city of Damascus, which reverberated with small-arms fire for more than an hour that evening. Western diplomats in Damascus thought it signalled an assault by Israeli paratroopers. Eventually, the police chief revealed that it was only a section of the Damascus garrison demonstrating their approval of a speech by President Asad. (Relieved, the staff of the British embassy sent down a glass of beer to their doorman, who was happily potting away with his rifle.)

From the text alone, it is not immediately clear why Asad's words should have rated such an exuberantly Texan endorsement. There was a fair amount of rhetoric about the 'glorious days of ferocious battles' which the war had witnessed. 'With chaste blood,' Asad told the Syrian army, 'you have charted on the map of Arab struggle a road which will never change after today . . .' Much of the speech was devoted to celebrating a new degree of Arab unity, 'the pan-Arabism of battle'.

Yet amid all the rhetoric, the objectives nominated for this new pan-Arabism remained limited. Asad claimed the 'liberation' of Mount Hermon, Kuneitra, Rafid and several other Golan towns and villages – but only ones on Syrian territory lost in 1967.

(As a matter of fact, all but Hermon had been de-liberated by the time he spoke.) The Arab aim, he said, was one of 'forcing the occupation forces to withdraw before them,' and the nearest he came to speaking in terms of destroying Israel was a claim to have inflicted 'losses which deeply shook the Zionist entity'.

At one point, Asad spoke of a determination to 'liberate the whole land', and this was cited in Israel as evidence that the Arabs were still talking in terms of overrunning Israel proper. But in context, this interpretation was clearly invalid. Asad used the phrase when acknowledging, rather tortuously, that the Syrian army had suffered considerable reverses: 'With the quick supplies he received and which were added to the calculated reserve force, the enemy heavily concentrated on one sector of our front and began to exert pressures with the larger part of his forces . . . and was able to achieve a limited penetration of our lines.'

What Asad was trying to suggest was that the Syrian losses in the occupied territories had been confined to a few positions. 'Our forces,' he went on, 'continue to pursue the enemy and strike at him and will continue to strike at the enemy forces until we regain our positions in the occupied land and continue then until we liberate the whole land.' In this context, 'whole land' meant the whole of the occupied territory.

That a speech of such restricted ambitions and such ambiguous news of victory should have evoked wild joy must be ascribed to the psychological aftermath of the Six-Day War (the crowds seem also to have believed that Asad had been claiming that the army had again pushed the Israelis out of Kuneitra). The facts were that the Syrian army had committed the bulk of its resources to gaining objectives strikingly less dramatic than those most Syrians had grown up with. This enormous military venture had made only small gains, and then been thrown back with heavy losses. By any normal military standards, it was a shattering defeat.

But compared to the rout of 1967, it seemed to Damascus like a triumph. In Asad's words, the fighting had 'restored self-confidence to the Arab individual after dressing his wounded dignity' (BBC transcript). For that purpose, it seemed, it was not necessary to prophesy the destruction of Israel.

Asad's speech was to be followed next day by a notably more moderate, and immensely more significant one by his senior partner in the Arab alliance, Anwar El Sadat. The Egyptian President's statement of aims said explicitly that, for the Arabs, this was a war of limited objectives. He also implied that its declaration was an act of rational calculation. And men capable of rational calculation are also capable of appreciating the stupendous sacrifices that would be required to achieve the total destruction of the State of Israel.

Middle Eastern military budgets now stand at levels not equalled anywhere in the world except Vietnam. For the major contestants – not countries with money to spare – arms expenditure even before the Yom Kippur war was beginning to consume nearly a quarter of the national wealth. The need to re-equip with new and still more costly weapons will increase the burden still further.

This burden falls most heavily on Egypt, the military centre of gravity of the Arab world. Egypt's armed forces (298,000) are as large as those of Syria, Jordan and Iraq put together (306,650). And Iraq, for all its fervent anti-Zionism, can never make a total commitment to war against Israel, because of the danger it faces from its heavily armed and ambitious neighbour Iran. Broadly speaking, it is true that there are 100 million Arabs whose nationalist emotions are directed against Israel. But most of them are simply too far away to do anything about it.

Syria and Jordan, whose borders are the ones most intricately involved with Israel, are quite small countries. Syria's population is just over six million, Jordan's just over two. Therefore no serious Arab campaign, whatever the objective, can be mounted against Israel without the support of Egypt and its thirty-four million people.

Egypt is not a rich country, but it falls into the upper bracket of the underdeveloped countries. Together with very large numbers of rural and urban poor, it has a considerable educated class, capable of dealing reasonably well with the technical requirements of modern war. But the task of maintaining the strength required for confrontation with Israel has grown steadily more onerous.

In 1969, Egypt's military budget was equal to thirteen per cent of the country's Gross National Product (GNP), a rough-and-ready but serviceable measure of the wealth produced in any given year. By 1973, it had risen to twenty-five per cent. This was almost certainly the highest proportion in the world. South Vietnam reached seventeen per cent of GNP in 1972, and North Vietnam's unpublished figures may be comparable. But the closest rival is – as might be expected – Israel, which in the same year had a military budget equivalent to twenty per cent of GNP. (For comparison, the Soviet Union and the United States run military budgets around seven or eight per cent of GNP, declining slowly in recent years. Most other countries are in the two to five per cent range, with Britain on the high side at 14·6%.

By making enormous social and economic sacrifices, Egypt is

In the lull of war: a brief respite before battle in a disused pipeline; a briefing interrupts an improvised shower; a religious service in the desert; and — as

the situation eases in Golan — a girl entertainer gives a concert for an Israeli armoured unit behind the front line.

able to support a military force which can undertake limited operations against Israel with a reasonable prospect of success. But the cost of setting out to fight a war of total victory – one aimed at the annihilation of the Jewish State – would be almost beyond sensible computation. Certainly any major increase in military spending would preclude even the semblance of normal life, let alone social reconstruction, for many years to come. Indeed, such an increase could probably not be imposed without the destruction of the Sadat regime, and its replacement by a monolithic military government.

Possibly, some Israelis would favour the idea of breaking the Egyptians economically, just as some Americans used to hope that the burden of the arms race would destroy the fabric of Soviet society. The likely result, however, would be a more rather than less intransigent opponent. And in any case, the burden on Israel is also close to overwhelming.

It is chiefly because of the need to import weaponry that Israel has accumulated a foreign debt of about £1,600 million: in per capita terms, the biggest in the world. Interest payments on this debt now run at more than £100 million a year. The particular tragedy for Israel is that before the October war, the rise in its balance of payments deficit had at last been halted, and there was a sign of improvement. The cause was a levelling-off in arms imports – but of course, the need to re-equip will more than wipe out the improvement. Inevitably, re-equipment will mean steep taxation increases in what was already the most highly taxed country in the world.

Of the other countries seriously involved, only Jordan comes close to matching the Egyptian and Israeli spending, in per capita terms. But in any case Jordan, with a gross national product not much bigger than the turnover of, say, the Colgate-Palmolive Corporation – about £300 million – is simply too small to make much difference in a time when one new combat aircraft costs about £1·5 million.

Syria has much lower military expenditure than Egypt, and this is not only because of its smaller size. Its population, though distinctly wealthier in terms of per capita GNP, spends somewhat less per head on defence.

Until very recently Syria took a much more militant anti-Israel stance than Egypt. It is hard not to think that this may have had something to do with the fact that Egypt was footing the larger part of the bill, both in lives and money. Much of the disparity, particularly in lives, must have been made up in October 1973. But, as Asad's speech demonstrated, the war was accompanied by a new moderation in Syrian attitudes.

The same phenomenon, in more marked form, appears in the

case of Iraq. Iraq takes a tougher line again than Syria, and during the war some communiques from Baghdad had a flavour of 1967 about them. Iraq is better off in per capita GNP than either Syria or Egypt, but spends still less per head on defence.

But the evidence for an inverse relationship between rhetoric and actual military spending becomes most impressive in the case of the wealthiest Arab countries – classically Colonel Gadaffi's Libya. Libya's oil gives it a GNP of about £704 per head, not strikingly inferior to Israel's. But Libya's military budget is a pacific 2.6% of GNP. When the Yom Kippur War came to an end, Gadaffi gave an angry interview. 'The war should have gone on,' he said, 'for years if need be, until the Arab or the Israeli side finished each other off completely.' It is not difficult for Colonel Gadaffi to call for a long war. He is not paying for it.

On Tuesday, October 16, the fighting on Golan also demonstrated the simpler point that, however unified and limited the Arab political aims might be in this war, basic military co-ordination was harder to achieve. By now, the Iraqi and Jordanian contingents had arrived – the Iraqi armoured division taking position around Kafr Nasij on the Israelis' southern flank; the Jordanian brigade further south still at Jasim (see map, page 122). But Israel caught the Iraqis in a dawn ambush as they were still deploying, wiped out seventy tanks with air and artillery strikes, then pressed on southwest to Kafr Shambs, to destroy another thirty. The Jordanians might have fared better. Their Centurions thrust north, aiming to cut into the narrow Israeli advance and re-capture Kuneitra. But neither the mauled Iraqis nor the Syrians fulfilled the prearranged plan to move in and protect the flanks of the Jordanian attack. The Israelis outflanked Hussein's crack Centurions outside El Harra and destroyed twenty-two of the Jordanians' eighty tanks. 'Now,' one of Israel's commanders on the northern front said with grim humour, 'they are letting us pick them off one by one.'

Had the war been merely a matter of such tactical victories, Israel could have relaxed. But this was an altogether more serious struggle – as the leader of the Arabs proceeded to spell out. That Tuesday, an open car drove through the midday Cairo crowds, carrying the man who was bearing the responsibility for the Arab war – Anwar el-Sadat. For a man who rations his public appearances, the open car was an unusual touch of flamboyance. But Sadat must have known that by the eleventh day of war, a gesture was required to assuage the Cairo crowd.

Sadat was on his way to address the People's Assembly, and to make what might be the most critical speech of his life. Yet he remained, as usual, cool to the point of impassiveness, making little response, apart from an occasional slightly stiff-backed wave, to the boiling enthusiasm of the crowds.

Sadat, who is now fifty-four, was a lifelong friend of Gamel Abdel Nasser, whom he succeeded on Nasser's death in 1970. But it would be hard to imagine two more dissimilar personalities. Where Nasser was physically overwhelming and theatrical, Sadat is slightly-built and withdrawn. His forehead bears the *sabiba* mark, acquired by regular contact with a prayer-mat, and marking him out as a devout Muslim. But despite that – and the fact that he spent a reckless youth as an agitator against British rule in Egypt – Sadat's present-day style has marked Anglo-Saxon overtones. He wears the casual khaki shirt and breeches of the off-duty officer, with an old pipe gripped in his teeth, and diplomats, groping for an account of his personality in western terms, have sometimes compared him to Clement Attlee, leader of Britain's first post-war Labour government. Western ambassadors who saw him during the war found him unmoved even when news from the battlefield was dramatically bad. 'We can lose three tanks for every one Israel loses,' he told one such visitor. 'But they will reach bottom before we do.'

Nobody, quite certainly, was more aware than Sadat of the importance of the speech he had to make, or of the fact that the war aims contained in it might decide the future of the Middle East for generations to come. 'I do not think you expect me to stand before you,' he told the Assembly in his flat, slightly pedantic manner, 'in order that we may boast together about what we have realized in eleven days . . .' (English translation from Ministry of Foreign Affairs, Cairo.) None the less, he claimed that the Egyptian armed forces had performed 'a miracle by any military standard' in crossing the canal. That was putting it a little high, but he was certainly justified in claiming that the Egyptian army had been regenerated.

'I would like to say briefly that this nation can now feel safe and secure after the period of fear. It is now armed with a shield and sword. . . .' Then: 'We are fighting for the sake of peace – the only peace which is worthy of the name, that is, peace based on justice. . . . It was David Ben-Gurion who laid down for Israel the theory of imposing peace. . . . I really do not know what David Ben Gurion would have thought had he been in command in Israel today. Would he have been able to understand the nature of history, or would he have remained in a position contrary to history as we see Israel's leadership doing today?

'Peace cannot be imposed, and the *fait accompli* peace cannot stand or last. . . . Today, we would like to ask Israel's leaders where is the theory of Israeli security which they attempted to apply sometimes by violence and other times by brute power for twenty-five years?'

Sadat, reading from a prepared text, moved on to the vital business of the speech: the statement of war aims. It came after a long passage upbraiding the United States for 'setting up a naval and air bridge by means of which it is pouring into Israel new tanks, aeroplanes, guns, rockets and electronic equipment . . .'

Sadat had thought of sending a letter to President Nixon. However, he said drily, 'I hesitated for fear it might be mis-interpreted, and instead I have decided to address to him an open message from here. . . .

> First: We have fought and we shall go on fighting to liberate our land which was seized by Israeli occupation in 1967, and to find the means towards the restoration and respect of the legitimate rights of the Palestinian people. In this respect, we accept our commitment to the decisions of the United Nations, the General Assembly and the Security Council.
>
> Second: We are prepared to accept a ceasefire on condition that the Israeli forces withdraw forthwith from all the occupied territories to the pre-June 5, 1967 lines, under international supervision.
>
> Third: We are ready, once the withdrawal from all these territories has been carried out, to attend an international peace conference at the United Nations. I shall try to persuade my colleagues, the Arab leaders, who are directly responsible for leading the conflict with our enemy. I will also do my best to convince the representatives of the Palestinian people to participate with us and with the whole international community in laying down rules and measures for peace in the area based on the respect of the legitimate rights of all the people in the area.
>
> Fourth: We are willing, at this hour and at this very moment, to start clearing the Suez Canal and opening it to international navigation so as to contribute, once again, to world welfare and prosperity. I have in fact given the order to the head of the Suez Canal Authority to start this task immediately after the liberation of the eastern bank . . .
>
> Fifth: Throughout all this we are not prepared to accept ambiguous promises or flexible expressions which lend themselves to various interpretations, draining our time needlessly and returning our cause to the stalemate . . .

For a military leader, speaking in wartime, it was certainly not a violent speech. Nor were Sadat's remarks about the Israeli 'theory of security' very different from those Dayan had advanced. The whole speech indicated that he was prepared to come to terms with the existence of Israel. But Mrs Meir, speaking just a few hours later to the Knesset, took the view that Sadat's show of reasonableness was merely camouflage.

'There is no doubt in our minds,' she said, 'that war was launched once more against the very existence of the Jewish State: our survival . . . is in the balance. The armies of Egypt and Syria, with the help of other Arab states . . . went to war with the aim of reaching the lines of June 4, 1967 on their way to achieving their main purpose – the conquest and destruction of Israel.' (Text from Ministry for Foreign Affairs, Jerusalem.)

'The Arab leaders profess that their objective is confined to reaching the lines of 4 June 1967. *But we know that it is really the total subjugation of Israel.*' (Our italics.)

'It needs no fertility of imagination,' said Mrs Meir, 'to realize what would have been the nightmarish situation of Israel had we stood on the lines of 4 June 1967 . . .'

In saying this, Mrs Meir expressed one of the most important of all Israeli responses to the war – it proved we were right to hold on to the land gained in 1967. If we had bargained it away, the Arabs would have had us at their mercy. The argument carries such emotional appeal inside Israel that it is almost impossible to refute it. And even to criticize it from outside brings the natural allegation of callousness towards the proper fears of a beleaguered people, or equally the claim that one is being brave about other people's dangers. But the point of bargaining away territory would have been precisely to prevent war breaking out. Many Israelis, of course, will argue that the war would have happened anyway. Perhaps that is right, but if Israel's 'theory of security' is that war with the Arabs is always inevitable, then this leads straight back to the Dayan nightmare.

Mrs Meir devoted much of her speech to attacking the Soviet Union for supplying arms to the Arabs – in terms very similar to those Sadat had used against the United States. Even more bitterly, she denounced the embargoes on Middle Eastern arms exports announced by Britain and France – theoretically 'even-handed', but undoubtedly of more help to the Arabs than to Israel. 'What lover of peace,' she asked, 'but must view with trepidation the cynicism and partiality displayed in international politics, the selfish and unethical policy followed by enlightened states towards a small country beleaguered and under assault?' She was flintily precise about Israel's war aims: 'The time for a ceasefire will be when the enemy's strength is broken. I am certain that when we have brought our enemies to the verge of collapse, representatives of various states will not be slow in "volunteering" to try and save our assailants. . . . Anyhow, now as in previous wars, the ceasefire depends first and foremost on the strength of the IDF . . . a people's army in the truest sense.'

Even so, in terms of policy, it was contradictory. 'We have never held war to be a means of solving dilemmas in our region . . .' Yet: 'The repelling of the enemy and the crushing of his strength are the only conditions for safeguarding our future.'

And the most important line in her speech – the one which brought the most emotional response from the members of the Knesset – was a brief announcement that the Israel army was already on its way to a military resolution of the issue with Egypt. 'An IDF task force,' said Mrs Meir, 'is operating on the western bank of the Suez Canal.' It was the world's first news of Arik Sharon's bridgehead.

3: Battle of Chinese Farm

General Sharon had picked out a spot for a canal crossing well before the war, when he was running the Sinai command. Between Lake Timsah and the Great Bitter Lake, the north-south canal road runs a mile or two east of the bank. But just above the entrance to the Great Lake, two side roads branch off within a thousand yards of each other and link up at the side of the canal. At this point, roughly thirteen miles south of Ismailia, Sharon had the massive ramparts of the canal bank thinned down, and marked out the weakened section with red bricks. Nearby, he had a vehicle park laid out, 100 yards by 400 yards, protected by high earth walls.

When General Gonen was at last satisfied with the havoc wrought among the Egyptian tanks, and permission was given for a drive across the canal, Sharon found himself commanding the Central Sector, near Tasa (see map page 114) some eighteen miles north-east of the potential crossing point. He had with him three armoured brigades – originally of 90–100 tanks each, but somewhat decreased by a week's fighting – a brigade of infantry, including paratroops, and a special force of engineers with earth-moving equipment, self-propelled barges, and bridging equipment. Facing him was the Egyptian 21st Armoured Division, with about as many tanks as he had himself – the core of Egypt's Second Army, commanded from Ismailia by Major-General Saad Maamun.

The Egyptians, with large numbers of missile-equipped infantry formations, were well astride both of the roads leading from Tasa to the canal. 'The problem,' said Sharon, 'was how to reach the water and establish the bridgehead in the same night. We had to do it before daylight, because if we lost surprise no doubt we would have found quite a number of tanks waiting for us on the other side.' Sharon's solution was, by his own account, 'complicated'. But, he said, 'it worked'.

At dawn on Monday Sharon began to brief his officers for a canal crossing, anticipating that within a few hours he would get permission to attack. The engineer in charge said that with only ten bulldozers allotted to him, he would not be able to breach the ramparts of the canal in time to have the bridgehead established at first light. 'I told him to look for the red bricks', Sharon recalled. 'And when the time came he found them in the dark and he did it.' (*New York Times*, November 12, 1973.) Clearance for the attack came through on Monday afternoon, when it was clear beyond doubt that the Egyptians would not again attempt to break out of their constricted bridgeheads.

The essence of Sharon's plan was to use one of his armoured brigades to divert the Egyptians' attention, while another brigade won control of the road leading southwest from Tasa to the Great Lake. This road (see p. 132) links up with the main canal road only a few thousand yards short of the southernmost of the two junctions leading to the selected crossing-point. The area of the junctions was known as the Chinese Farm, because some time before the Six-Day War Chinese agricultural experts had conducted irrigation experiments there. Once Sharon was in control of the roads and junctions, he would be able to send his engineers, motorized barges and paratroops through to secure a crossing – together with a fresh tank brigade to go across and fight on the other side. After ferrying a few tanks over on the barges, the engineers were to push a sectional bridge across the canal.

The operation was timed to start at twilight on Monday, and it would be an understatement to call the schedule a bold one. The first paratroops were supposed to be crossing the canal in rubber boats by 11.00 pm. That meant the vital sections of the tank force had just about five hours in which to cover a complex twenty-mile route behind enemy lines, fight a night battle, link up with the engineers, and lead them and the paratroops through to the crossing-point. Large parts of the route were through trackless dunes – and tanks, travelling off the road at night, can rarely average more than five miles an hour.

At 5.00 pm, an armoured brigade, positioned north of the Tasa-Great Lake Road, launched an attack westwards towards Ismailia. This was the diversion: a hard-fought one, which gradually drew the main weight of the 21st Armoured Division north towards the axis of the Tasa-Ismailia road. 'Right through the night,' said an Israeli survivor of the battle, 'we advanced slowly, slowly, against fierce resistance.'

One hour later, in rapidly deepening twilight, the second armoured brigade swung off the road southward. Under cover of darkness, they turned west and, with no interference from the Egyptians, drove through sand ridges and dunes towards the Great Bitter Lake. Here they were heading for the 'gap' between Maamun's Second Army, and the badly battered Third Army to the south. Israeli field intelligence, maintaining its usual high efficiency, had identified the traditional weak spot that occurs in areas of overlapping command. That, together with the tactical skill of the Israeli tank commanders, largely explains the lack of opposition. Reaching the road by the lake shore, the column of tanks turned to race north, with the water securing its left flank.

Before they set out, the tanks had been divided into three 'task forces'. At the junction of the Tasa road, one task force swung northeast, to drive up the road and take the Egyptian blocking forces in the rear. At the first of the side roads leading to the canal (the 'y-junction' the Israelis called it) the second task force swung west to secure the crossing site. The largest part of the brigade drove straight ahead to the north, passing both canal junctions. Its job was to establish a secure perimeter as far north as possible. Only a few thousand yards past the second canal turn-off (the 'T-junction'), this task force ran into heavy Egyptian fire. Deploying hastily off the road, the force joined action in a bitter tank battle which – with occasional pauses – was to last through most of the next two days.

This heavy Egyptian resistance meant that the road-junction area could not be fully secured. And by this time the operation was running well behind schedule: the men who should have been paddling across the canal were still in Tasa.

But the eastbound task force, taking the Egyptians on the Tasa road from behind, broke through successfully. About midnight, they linked up with the paratroops, mounted on halftrack personnel-carriers. Reversing direction, the tanks led the halftracks back towards the canal, with the engineers and their equipment coming behind. Swinging north on the canal road, they went through the y-junction to the canal. Around 1.00 am Sharon himself, with a command group of about 200 men, had paddled across the hundred-yard width of the canal, and clambered up the western bank.

There, to begin with at least, they found themselves without opposition – looking out over a moonlit landscape, lightly wooded. The trouble was all behind them: two miles from the eastern bank, around the Chinese Farm road junctions, the night was

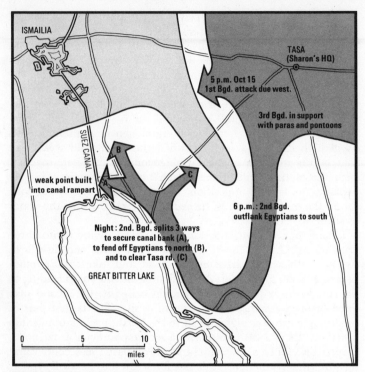

ISMAILIA

TASA
(Sharon's HQ)

5 p.m. Oct 15
1st Bgd. attack due west.

3rd Bgd. in support
with paras and pontoons

SUEZ CANAL

B

A

weak point built
into canal rampart

C

6 p.m. : 2nd Bgd.
outflank Egyptians to south

Night : 2nd. Bgd. splits 3 ways
to secure canal bank (A),
to fend off Egyptians to north (B),
and to clear Tasa rd. (C)

GREAT BITTER LAKE

0   5   10

miles

Sharon's crossing: the Chinese Farm battle

For 'Operation Gazelle', General Arik Sharon's plan for crossing the Suez
Canal, the essentials were speed and surprise. Sharon aimed within the
first night to reach the canal through the gap between the Egyptian Second
and Third Armies discovered by Israeli intelligence, and to bridge it by
dawn. Starting at dusk on October 15, one of his three armoured brigades
launched a diversionary attack to the west, while another swung southwest towards the Great Bitter Lake (top left). From the lake shore, it raced
north to the crossing-point. As it did so, the brigade split into three: one
group headed for the canal, another to the east to link up with the third
brigade, and a third went north to establish a secure perimeter (top right).
By midnight, the linkup had been achieved with the third brigade's paratroopers, and an hour later Sharon himself was over the canal, with about
200 men.

But the crucial objectives were not achieved: by dawn, the bridge was
not established, and even the roads leading to the crossing-point were not
secure. And the northbound group had run into heavy Egyptian fire after a
few kilometres: it was now deployed for a battle which was to last (lower
right) most of the next two days. On the night of October 16, a coordinated
Egyptian attack launched what became the battle of the Chinese Farm. A
few hours earlier, and with strong air support, this move would probably
have liquidated the Israeli crossing force. As it was, it came close to cutting
it off, but the Israelis just held on to the approach to their bridgehead. It was
only when fresh Israeli tanks under 'Bren' Adan crossed the canal that the
bridgehead was properly secured behind the Third Army.

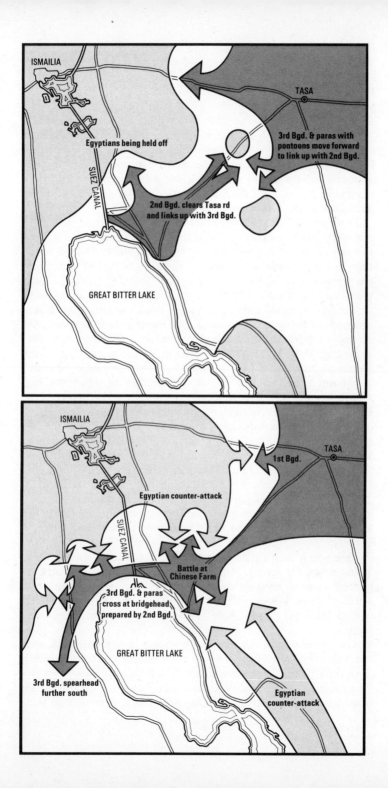

ISMAILIA

TASA

Egyptians being held off

3rd Bgd. & paras with pontoons move forward to link up with 2nd Bgd.

SUEZ CANAL

2nd Bgd. clears Tasa rd and links up with 3rd Bgd.

GREAT BITTER LAKE

ISMAILIA

TASA

1st Bgd.

Egyptian counter-attack

SUEZ CANAL

Battle at Chinese Farm

3rd Bgd. & paras cross at bridgehead prepared by 2nd Bgd.

GREAT BITTER LAKE

3rd Bgd. spearhead further south

Egyptian counter-attack

lit by gun-flashes, rocket trails and streams of tracer. Some of the paratroops had been dropped off to secure the y-junction in readiness for the heavy equipment to come through. But a force of Egyptian infantry had managed to infiltrate the t-junction area, to the north. They had rocket-launchers, and wire-guided missiles – so that the t-junction was impassable, and the spur road from the y-junction was under attack from time to time. Meanwhile, a considerable tank action was being fought another few thousand yards to the north, and another (the original diversion) was still going on some ten miles to the northeast. Minor tank skirmishes were exploding here and there half the way back to Tasa.

Through all this, bulldozers, excavators and barges had to be conveyed. As Sharon said, traffic control in the dark was the key to everything. 'If important equipment like the rafts (motorized barges) had missed the y-junction, and gone on to the t-junction, the operation would have been over right then,' he said. As it was, it was running desperately late. The paratroop force was supposed to have been established on the west bank by 11.00 pm. But it did not get there until 3.00 am, four hours behind schedule. At dawn, the barge units still had not reached the crossing-point: so far from there being a bridge thrown across the canal, even the ferrying operation had not begun. One of the officers in Sharon's command group looked out of the bunker in which he had established himself, and surveyed the empty water. 'Where is the bridge?' he asked. 'No bridge', said the man next to him.

Arik Sharon reacted with characteristic insouciance to the fact that he and a small party of infantry were isolated on the wrong side of the canal. 'Fellows', he said, 'don't worry about a thing. The secretary of the Likud Party is here with you.'

With first light, the Egyptian artillery zeroed in on the road-junctions, making it a nerve-testing journey for the men who had to bring through the barges – cumbrous, rectangular steel floats, carried on flatbed trucks. The navigator of the lead barge, a sergeant from Netania, described his unit's 'baptism by fire': 'There was a tank battle on both sides of the road, and we were going down the middle. It was a battle for the junction and the junction was in their sights and they hit every vehicle that went through there. We were a slow convoy, very easy to hit. . . . There were a few hits . . . a few holes. With dawn, we got to the crossing area.'

On either side of the new-cut breaches in the ramparts, anti-aircraft guns were being set up as the barges splashed weightily into the still water. With one barge, said the sergeant, there was 'a problem' – presumably, it had been holed by shellfire at the road junction. But at the crossing area itself, there was no shellfire, nor any other resistance. 'The barges began to ferry the first force which positioned itself on the other shore, a force of armoured infantry and an armoured force.' Working in life-jackets, half-submerged in water, the engineers lashed tanks, one at a time, onto barges, and sent them chugging slowly across.

Not far from the western end of the crossing was the wreckage of four Egyptian tanks. They had turned up at some point in the dark hours – possibly investigating, but equally possibly bound on some routine military excursion – and the paratroops had knocked them out with missiles. But as the sun gathered strength, there was no further interference from the Egyptian Army. By 9.00 am, thirty tanks and about 2,000 men had crossed the canal. On the western bank, the sergeant from Netania found that 'there was a very pleasant atmosphere. Blue skies, very quiet, like on training. We still hadn't been ranged in on from the ground. . . . It was a peaceful atmosphere, really pastoral.'

A few miles away on the eastern bank, there was nothing pastoral about the scene. The two Israeli armoured brigades which had started the whole operation on Monday night were still engaged in savage fighting all along the northern perimeter of the corridor leading back to Tasa. Aharon Bar, a tank driver who had been in action throughout the night, gave this account of how the war ended for him: 'In the morning, fog covered the area. As it dispersed, we found that we were facing huge masses of missile-carrying infantry. . . . We got into a hollow, behind a crest. From time to time we tried to get out, but the missile fire against us was too heavy. Then we got an order to attack.'

The whole crew agreed that it was 'suicidal', but they went forward over the crest. After a few minutes, Bar felt 'something I had never felt before in my life. I didn't understand what was happening to me, but I knew it was something very serious. . . . The tank was full of gas. . . .' A missile had hit the tank low down, and the explosive jet had taken one of his legs off below the knee. 'I opened the driver's hatch and got out: only then did I realize there was an empty space below my left knee. I stood on one foot, holding onto the tank.' Under small-arms and artillery fire, the crew abandoned the wrecked tank and dragged Bar painfully out of the battle zone. Remarkably, this fierce, discontinuous fighting scarcely affected the tenuous Israeli salient on the western bank.

On any orthodox military measurement, Arik Sharon's attempt to establish a bridgehead was a disaster. Starting with a division, he had managed after sixteen hours of frantic activity to get a force of rather less than battalion-strength across the canal, plus a little armoured support. There was no bridge, and because of shell damage done to the bridge-sections on the way through, there was no chance of establishing one within the next twelve hours. Considering the amount of shooting that had been going on in the whole Tasa–Bitter Lakes–Ismailia triangle since the previous evening, the Israelis had no right even to hope that they still had the advantage of surprise.

Sharon himself had said that if the Israelis lost surprise, they could expect to find 'quite a number of tanks' coming in to attack them. Had a force in any kind of strength turned up on Tuesday, there would have been nothing whatever the Israelis could have done about it. To get a division-strength force of their own across the water by barge ferry would have required about a thousand trips.

The Israeli high command had launched the crossing venture knowing that they faced a complex set of options, and had only limited resources available. They needed to win some major prize before the imposition of a ceasefire, which could not now be many days away. The risk they faced was that one incautious move could cost them several high-class armoured brigades – a loss which simply could not be permitted to occur.

An apparently glamorous option would have been to drive west and south until Cairo could be put under threat from artillery. To do so would have brought deep satisfaction to a great many ordinary Israelis, seeking emotional release after the first anxious days of Arab success. But in military terms, it would have been a wild gamble, requiring a fifty-mile advance, leaving to both north and south of the resulting corridor large Egyptian armies, which had been battered but certainly not destroyed.

There were physical difficulties about going north, because of the 'agricultural barrier' west of Ismailia: that is, the Ismailia Canal and the irrigation works built around it. To make a way through this, and cut off the Second Army from its base in Egypt, would be a long and costly job. It would require a north-ward advance of some forty miles, after which the whole right flank of that advance would have to be turned into a front capable of resisting a break-out attempt by the Second Army. True, missile sites could have been knocked out. But some of the sites in the northern sector had been knocked out by the navy.

The best option was to wheel south and cut off the Third Army. The route lay over firm, open sand where the Israeli columns could make maximum speed. And better still, for some twenty miles the Israelis would have one flank protected by the Bitter Lakes – a barrier which neither side could cross in strength. Once in position to the south, the Israelis would only need to control a front of some fifteen miles between Shallufa and Suez in order to have the Third Army trapped.

Given the slenderness of Israel's resources, the southern thrust was clearly the correct move. But even that general decision left a hundred questions of tactics, supply and organization unresolved: in short, exploitation on the western side of the canal was as subtle a problem as any commander of mobile forces could be faced with. Speed and concentration were required: but above all, the chief need was a well-protected bridge, so that 300 tanks could pass quickly over the canal with their supplies pouring along in a steady stream behind them. The high command's plan had been for Sharon and his division to establish the bridgehead, so that Major-General Avraham 'Bren' Adan, one of the foremost tank experts in the Israeli army, could cross over at once and begin the long sweep southwards.

On Tuesday morning, all that was in ruins. What happened next was the result of remarkable ineptitude on the part of the Egyptian army – and of behaviour on Sharon's part which his friends would regard as a manifestation of genius, and his enemies as a descent into military dementia. The development of the story also owes something to the wide discrepancies in personal outlook between, on the one hand, Ariel Sharon and on the other hand Shmuel Gonen and Haim Bar-Lev.

Nowadays, not many Israeli generals go in for touches like attaching a professor of ancient Hebrew to their staff. Sharon, who took his degree in oriental history, does just that. He is an almost implausible mixture of intellectual brilliance and physical *machismo*. What he is not is an expert in mechanized warfare. Sharon acquired his first military reputation as a brave and ruthless border raider: later, diligent training in Israel and at the British Staff College at Camberley turned him into a hard-fighting but not particularly subtle infantryman. He has some record of success in political manœuvre, which many professional soldiers find strange and confusing. But he has no comparable record in the equally confusing business of mobile warfare.

In spite of the Patton legend, success in this department of military life is not automatically correlated with flamboyance, incaution, or even personal ferocity. Some of its most effective practitioners have been studious technicians like von Thoma or cool administrators like Richard O'Connor. Success in a war of movement depends chiefly on an ability, while under emotional pressure, to juggle with considerations such as the speed of tanks over various terrains, the availability of fuel, or the likelihood of a rendezvous coming off.

Sharon's record is one of fairly straightforward lust for battle. He first became known as founder and commander of 'Unit 101', making raids across the Jordanian border in response to Arab terrorist attacks. In 1953 Unit 101 acquired some international notoriety when, in response to an Arab raid which killed an Israeli woman and her child, Sharon and his men blew up a Jordanian village, killing sixty-nine Jordanians in the process, half of them women and children. Sharon said Unit 101 had not known there were people hiding in the houses when they were blown up.

Dayan valued Sharon because in the fifties Dayan was trying to create an officer corps whose philosophy would be to take any objective 'by frontal attack . . . paying for it with lives'. (*Moshe Dayan*, by Shabtai Teveth, 1972). His aim was to exorcise 'Jewish cleverness' from the IDF. Apart from being an act of intellectual self-mutilation, it seems an impractical outlook to imprint on a people whose opponents have many more lives to spend. Possibly, in the context of Dayan's subtle, contradictory character, this was never more than a dialectical exercise designed to counter-act the defensive spirit engendered in the War of Independence. But in Sharon's case at least, it worked quite literally.

During the 1956 Suez Campaign, he was dropped with a parachute brigade to harass Egyptian movements near the Mitla Pass. He was ordered not to attack the heavily defended pass itself, because this was totally superfluous to the plan Dayan had devised. Obtaining permission for a 'patrol', Sharon sent a large detachment straight up the pass into an Egyptian ambush. He then had to commit the rest of his brigade to extricate the trapped force, and after losing 38 killed and 120 wounded – more than in all the other 'breakthrough battles' of the campaign – Sharon took the pass, killing some 200 Egyptians. It was magnificent, but it certainly was not clever; if it had not been for the friendship thirty-year-old Colonel Sharon had already established with David Ben-Gurion, he might have been severely disciplined.

In 1967 Sharon commanded an *ugda* (task force) which was to break through into Sinai along the Central Route. It was first necessary to capture the road junction at Abu Ageila, but this turned out to be much more strongly-defended than Sharon's field intelligence suggested. A swift 'regardless of cost' assault failed, and Sharon had to reduce the defences with a massive, set-piece attack. According to Edgar O'Ballance in *The Third Arab-Israeli War*, this was conducted with skill and determination, but it left the Sharon *ugda* battered and weary, with much of its potential mobility gone. Sharon was then given the task of catching an armoured formation under General Shazli, which had been stationed at Kuntilla and was virtually cut off. However, the last of the Shazli force managed to slip away behind the Sharon *ugda* after nightfall on the third day, leading Major O'Ballance to suggest that Sharon was 'more expert at positional battles than mobile desert warfare'.

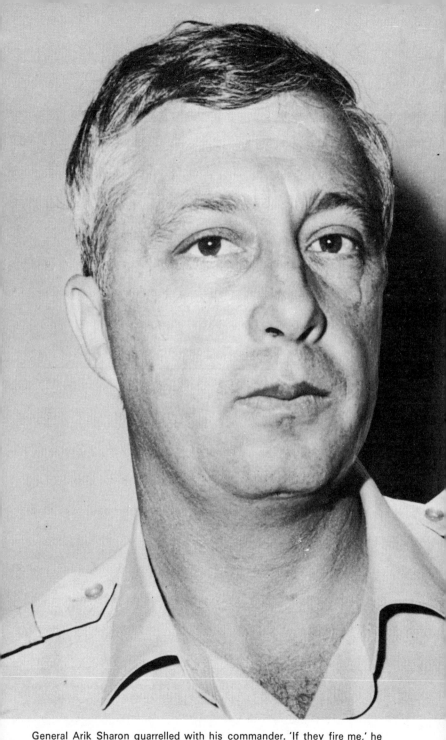

General Arik Sharon quarrelled with his commander. 'If they fire me,' he said, 'I'll join up under another name.

Sharon none the less sees himself as a custodian of the grand tradition in the Israeli army. Bored by planning and logistics, he professes a large contempt for those like Bar-Lev, Gonen and Adan, who excel in such matters. This contempt is expressed at personal level: Sharon, whose own life-style resembles that of a Texan rancher (or perhaps a Border chieftain) genuinely thinks it is improper that the Israeli army should be led by respectable suburbanites with degrees in economics.

Granted his aptitude for a hard-fought positional battle, Sharon was probably a good choice in theory for the task of seizing and securing a bridgehead across the canal. In the event, the complicated manœuvres got hopelessly behind schedule – and when that happened, Sharon ceased to be the carefully trained infantryman, and reverted to type.

'He was very sophisticated', said one officer who was with him. 'He said: "To hell with the bridgehead, the important thing is to get behind the Egyptian lines".' When General Gonen heard that Sharon's plan was simply to abandon the western crossing-site and make off into the Egyptian rear areas, he did not think it was a 'sophisticated' response. Gonen told Sharon to dig in around the bridgehead, and hold it until a new attempt at bridging could be made. It was the correct move, according to the book – indeed, anything else would leave the engineers virtually unprotected. Sharon replied that to dig in would merely make the little force conspicuous, so that even the Egyptians would realize what an easy target was being offered. These were not viewpoints that could be reconciled and the conversation ended on an abusive note, with Sharon entirely unrepentant.

'Gonen', Sharon shouted into the radio, 'if you had any balls, I'd tell you to cut them off and eat them.' With that, he started splitting up his tiny force into raiding parties, and sent them out to search for SAM sites, fuel dumps and anything else that seemed worth attacking. Slightly awed, one of Sharon's staff said that the army might well respond by kicking Arik out. 'So?' said Sharon. 'I'd join up under another name.'

Leaving only a token force at the crossing-point, the raiders fanned out through olive groves and patches of scruffy pine. The larger parties were led by a couple of tanks apiece, with half-tracks following – but in keeping with the piratical nature of the enterprise, anyone who could make a case for striking out on his own was more than welcome to do so. Two officers, for example, began by hijacking an Egyptian armoured car. Meeting a convoy, they waited for it to pass them, then shot it up from behind and made off. Finding a fuel dump by the road, they drove in and threw some grenades around to fire it. When the armoured car ran low on fuel, they hijacked a jeep for the return journey.

Inevitably, much of the damage inflicted was relatively trivial. But by midday, according to Sharon, four SAM missile sites had been knocked out, so that a wide area of sky was opened out in which the Israeli jets could operate without inhibition. And the raiders had enjoyed themselves and perhaps rattled several Egyptian units in Sinai by firing occasional shots into their rear from the west bank and then hoisting the Israeli flag conspicuously on the canal ramparts. As Sharon observed, nothing so demoralizes an army as finding its enemy behind it.

Meanwhile, why was there no coordinated effort to cut the Israelis off, or to destroy them on the west bank? What was going on inside the Egyptian command centre? What was being registered on the illuminated glass maps, which were supposed to show all the details of the ever-changing front?

General Ismail had gone down into the command centre to take charge of operations on October 2, four days before the war began. And Tuesday, October 16, was the first day on which he came out onto the street again – to go to the People's Assembly with President Sadat. According to his own account, in an interview with *Al Ahram*, he knew nothing about the Israeli crossing when he set out to drive to the Assembly. That was about midday, by which time the Israelis had been on the western bank for about eleven hours.

When Sadat failed to mention the invasion in his speech, the Israeli political and military command assumed that this was deliberate. According to Israeli spokesmen, it showed the existence of a 'political dilemma' inside Egypt. Complex speculations were mounted about the various degrees of face the Egyptians might lose according to which troops they used to try and destroy Sharon's force.

Understandably, it did not occur to the Israelis that perhaps Sadat and Ismail just did not know what was happening. Yet Ismail's version is that the first he knew of the invasion was 'information . . . which I found waiting for me after my return from the People's Assembly session.' This, he said, referred to 'the infiltration of a small number of amphibian tanks'. The message added that in the estimation of the local command 'it was possible to destroy them quickly', and a 'storm battalion' had been moved to face them.

Not only had Sharon's men been operating on the western bank since 1.00 am. Since Monday evening, there had been continuous Israeli activity in the Ismailia sector. On the eastern bank, the Israelis had suddenly pushed their front forward ten miles, and in the process gained control of the important Tasa-Great Lake road. Egyptian and Israeli tank and infantry units had been battling in and around the Chinese Farm road junc-

Israeli troops and Egyptian prisoners under fire near the canal

tions since ten or eleven o'clock on Monday night. On the west, immediately opposite the Chinese Farm, four Egyptian tanks had been put out of action some time between 1.00 am and dawn. And, most significant of all, four SAM sites in the area had ceased to function. It should have been obvious that, however small a party was actually across the canal, there was something a good deal larger brewing up. Yet nobody formed this into a coherent picture, either in General Maamun's HQ at Ismailia, nor in the war room run by Ismail and Shazli. And it seems that the Third Army, under Major-General Abdel-Moneim Wassel, did not know that anything unusual was happening at all.

Just as its own canal crossing had shown the virtues of the Egyptian army, so its response to the Israeli thrust on October 15–16 cruelly exposed the faults. According to western military attaches in Cairo, the Egyptian military machine does best in set-pieces: working out and carrying through large, elaborate plans. It has some competent administrators, and a sufficient number of men who can handle tanks, guns and rocket-launchers with courage and tactical skill. But these two qualities are not sufficient for success in mobile warfare, where the most vital of all commodities is information. 'Speed of reaction in command decides the battle,' Rommel had written in *The Rules of Desert*

Warfare. Therefore, he said, 'results of reconnaissance must reach the commander in the shortest possible time', and 'commanders of motorized forces should be as near as possible to their troops'. On both counts, the Egyptian army failed in 1973.

There was no equivalent to the incessant Israeli patrol and reconnaissance activity. Field intelligence – mapping out enemy dispositions by using radio intercepts, noting the unit affiliations of prisoners, and the like – remained an undeveloped art. At the most basic level, the Egyptians simply did not tell each other what they were doing. Radios and field telephones were rarely used. Junior commanders simply fought the Israelis as and when the Israelis presented themselves, and gave no priority at all to making combat reports. And even divisional commanders – men on the equivalent level to Arik Sharon – had little or no independence of action. This meant, in effect, that there were no real command centres closer to the fighting than Ismail's war room. An Egyptian officer, asked after the war who had been the overall *field* commander, replied that it was Ismail, sitting in front of his multi-coloured maps.

The paradox is that ordinary Egyptians are scarcely uncommunicative at the personal level. Lack of military communication is due to the fact that the army, like most other Egyptian institutions, remains a strictly hierarchical bureaucracy, in which promotion under Nasser's rule depended upon seniority and orthodoxy, not on individual claims to merit. Communication within the system in peacetime follows elaborate formal procedures – involving, usually, large amounts of paperwork. Rather than being modified by the strains of war, it simply goes into suspension. It is a question of the first importance for Israel whether this will remain so, now that the upper levels of the Egyptian army are beginning to be penetrated by younger officers promoted on merit. But it was still the case for the eighteen or so crucial hours of October 16, 1973 while the Israeli crossing was in its most vulnerable stage.

In order to mount an operation involving both the Second Army and the Third Army, it was necessary to circulate orders bearing signatures from four different staff officers. Not until after dark on Tuesday, October 16 did the Egyptians mount a coordinated attack on the eastern approaches to the crossing-point.

Late as it was, it nearly succeeded. The Second Army came down from the north in full weight, and the Third Army came up from the south. Their aim was to relieve and reinforce the Egyptian infantry holding out in the Chinese Farm area – and if that had been achieved, it would have been the end of the

Israeli plans, because a serious volume of fire from the farm would make the crossing-point untenable.

All night, a savage tank-to-tank conflict raged. Darkness cut down the value of the Egyptian infantrymen's anti-tank missiles. But because ranges close in at night, it also cut down the Israeli tank crews' advantage in long-range gunnery. It was a complicated battle, in which the outnumbered Israeli tanks were under fire from two and sometimes three directions at the same time. But the engineers at the canalside had no difficulty in appreciating its practical significance. 'They closed off the road behind us', said a sergeant-navigator simply.

The Israeli engineers had stopped ferrying during the night but they still had not had time to put a bridge together. At dawn, while the tank battle raged on, they began ferrying again – but almost at once the Egyptian artillery intervened. 'I was on the barge when we got to the bank on the other side,' recalled a veteran of the battle. 'We were taking two halftracks and a jeep. The moment they got off, exactly, the shelling started. The first shell fell some twenty metres away in the water. The next shell fell beside the barge on the shore . . .'.

Sergeant Zvi, from Netania, found that Tuesday's 'pastoral' atmosphere was replaced on Wednesday by 'a murderous pace'. The Egyptians, he said, 'had both shores ranged in. The moment a barge set out from one shore there'd be a terrifying barrage on it. When it got to the other bank they'd shell it again.' Now, men were being killed and wounded in considerable numbers. 'I haven't seen the wounded of other countries', said the sergeant, 'but I saw our injured. I saw wounded who refused to let people help them, walking with their infusion flasks in their hand to the collection station. . . . You see amputees, you see them writhing with pain, but they don't make a sound.' Soon the banks were littered with dead fish, killed by the shock of exploding shells, And shellfire began to sink barges. 'Two miracles occurred', recalled a lieutenant. 'Our company commander got his foot caught in a crack in the barge [when it sank]. I think he was the only person to go down to the bottom of the canal and come up with nothing worse than a fractured foot. He went wild down there in the water – and that freed his foot. The other case, one of our navigators didn't know how to swim. . . . He began sinking [with the barge]. At that moment, a lifebelt floated out of the crew cabin and got hooked around him from below and brought him to the surface . . .'.

Slowly and bloodily, the Egyptian resistance at the Chinese Farm was reduced, and the fire at the crossing-point slackened enough for the Israeli engineers to get the pontoons in position for their much delayed bridge. Even so, artillery fire and occasional air strikes made it a dangerous and nerve-testing

At last the tanks roll freely across the canal bridge at Deversoir,
belatedly established by Sharon's task force

job. 'We were under fire the whole time, very serious fire', recalled the officer who commanded the bridging teams. 'Our boys were . . . a target for all the guns and planes in the neighbourhood. . . . Everybody here lost a friend.'

'When a plane comes down on you', said a soldier, 'it's something frightening. Everybody who isn't shooting back at him dives for the ground with his head in the earth. But when our Mirages came in, they were shooting down MIGs one after the other. People . . . stood on the embankment, clapping like at a football match.'

Such air cover was possible because Sharon's raiders had torn a hole in the SAM umbrella – and that, perhaps, was the best argument in favour of his defiance of Gonen. None the less, the fact was that a plan which had originally failed dramatically was essentially being baled out by the fighting qualities of the Israeli rank and file. Around the middle of Wednesday, thirty hours behind schedule, the bridge was in place and the first of Bren Adan's three tank brigades began to roll across.

Surprise, of course, had been totally lost, and for the rest of the week the bridge and its whole environment remained a perilous place. But the Egyptian attacks were more distinguished for their stubbornness than their coordination : confusion in the Egyptian command continued to work powerfully for the Israelis. After Tuesday night's battle, Major-General Izz ad-Din Mukhtar announced confidently that the Israeli force on the west bank had been cut off. This, it appears, was based on a claim from General Maamun in Ismailia that the Chinese Farm attack had achieved all its aims. By this stage, according to Arik Sharon, the Egyptian communication system was 'perverted by lies' – but it could well have been yet another genuine failure to come to terms with Israeli resilience in attack.

On Wednesday night, the unhappy Maamun attempted an attack against the growing force established on the western bank, and was badly beaten. Now, Ismail bitterly regretted having committed virtually all of Egypt's front-line armour to Sinai. When a western diplomat asked one of Ismail's officers why Egypt did not move up its reserves against Sharon and Adan, the officer, near hysteria, replied : 'Reserves, what reserves?' Some of the 500 tanks Ismail had just sent to the east bank could have been withdrawn once more. But Sadat vacillated for thirty-six hours before agreeing to that humiliation. And then, on War Minister Ismail's admission, 'information was interrupted due to changes of responsibilities which we had made in some commands in the emergent circumstances.' A few days later, it became known that General Maamun had suffered a heart attack, and been replaced by Major-General Abdul Moniem

Khalil. Maamun was said to have been in poor health for some time and to have had a history of heart attacks.

Clumsily-aimed though they were, the Egyptian blows had somewhat slowed the Israelis. But the chief responsibility for delay lay within the Israeli army itself. Sharon, of course, blames it on a failure of nerve in the higher command: a swifter back-up on Tuesday would have made the vital difference. Arguably, Sharon's bold response to the situation on Tuesday morning was tactically correct. But all the same, it was his failure to get the bridge across on schedule which lost the vital twenty-four hours. By the time Bren Adan's tanks began to pick up velocity for the long run south to Shallufa and Suez, time was running against the Israeli army and its hopes of total victory.

4: Enter the oil weapon

In the second week of war, the 'oil weapon' began to bear against Israel – indirectly, but with considerable effect. It could only be indirect, because Israel itself has no need of Arab oil, or at any rate not while the wells on the west of Sinai remain in Israeli hands and the Shah of Iran is friendly. It was doubly indirect because the United States, Israel's one indispensable supporter, is of all major industrialized countries the least vulnerable to a Middle East oil embargo. Many of the countries which could be most seriously damaged by an embargo were already well-disposed towards the Arabs before the war began – at least, insofar as the Arab aim was recovery of occupied territories, rather than obliteration of the state of Israel. The theory, of course, was that pressure on western countries in general would bring pressure upon the United States, and the US would in turn bring pressure upon Israel to accept a ceasefire on terms favourable to the Arab cause.

It was the same method as the one used by the old woman in the nursery rhyme who made the water quench the fire, to make the fire burn the stick, to make the stick beat the dog, to make the dog bite the pig because the pig would not go and she wanted to get home to supper. The trouble was that applying the method to international politics turned out to be a tricky and unpredictable business. The Persian Gulf section of the Organization of Petroleum Exporting Countries (OPEC) was due to meet on Wednesday, October 17, in Kuwait, and in spite of the presence of the non-Arab Iranians, this was clearly a suitable time for the Arabs to produce their manifesto.

Two days beforehand on Monday, October 15, while Sharon and his officers were getting ready to cross the canal, an Egyptian delegation arrived in Riyadh, the Saudi Arabian capital, for talks with Ahmed Yamani, King Feisal's Oil Minister. The purpose of the talks was to ensure that Egypt, the major Arab political power, and Saudi Arabia, the biggest oil producer, would turn up in Kuwait preaching the same line.

Although the Egyptians, led by Oil Minister Hilal, wanted to go further than the Saudis, both sides were prepared to be fairly moderate – or at any rate, moderate by the standards of what actually began to happen a few days and weeks later. Saudi Arabia's Oil Minister Sheikh Yamani is not one of the world's radicals. He studied law at New York University and at Harvard, and at thirty he was serving on the board of Aramco, the chiefly American-owned company that handles Saudi oil. Although twenty years younger than King Feisal, he is just as much a Moslem conservative: his relationship with the King is said to be one of 'father and son'. Largely at Yamani's insistence, the Saudi–Egyptian talks ended with an agreement to go for five per cent monthly cutbacks in oil production, plus a pro-gramme of selective embargoes. It was a cautious policy and one which allowed considerable flexibility for negotiation between individual countries.

Nothing was to be said until after the meeting in Kuwait. Unfortunately, there was already a certain amount of confusion in the air when the Arab oil delegations went into session at the Kuwait Sheraton around 11.00 am on Wednesday. And by nightfall, it was almost total.

During the small hours of Wednesday, the Gulf members of OPEC (five Arab states plus Iran) had announced through their Iranian chairman that they were demanding a seventy per cent rise in the posted price for crude oil. Throughout the day, the distinction between the continuing attempt of *all* oil producing countries to get more money for their oil, and the immediate attempt of the Arab oil-producers to affect the outcome of the Yom Kippur War became steadily more blurred. So did the distinction between the Organization of Oil Exporting Countries (OPEC) and the Organization of Arab Petroleum Exporting Countries (OAPEC). Several reporters stated that the OAPEC production cuts had been announced through the Iranian chairman of the Gulf OPEC. The Iranians, of course, far from cutting off any western oil supplies, are major suppliers to Israel, and the entire Iranian delegation tactfully left town as soon as their business with price negotiations was over.

Nor did the crucial communique make things altogether clear when it was finally produced around 9.30 pm. There was only one copy of it, hastily handwritten in Arabic. Some essential phrases were lightly crossed out and others pencilled in. When the two flimsy sheets of lined writing paper were grabbed from the OAPEC spokesman, they were put through on the hotel copying machine for distribution to those journalists who could read Arabic. But the alterations did not show up well on the copying paper. Thus many reporters failed to notice that at the last moment the OAPEC members had changed the basis on which they would be prepared to resume full oil deliveries – substituting the vaguer term 'United Nations Resolutions' for a specific mention of Resolution 242.

Nor was that the only important provision which did not show up clearly. An arrow pointed to the inclusion of the phrase 'and the legitimate rights of the Palestinian people must be restored'. This was added only after members of the Kuwait Palestine Liberation Organization heard that the draft being discussed did not mention them, and descended on the Sheraton by taxi to complain to the oil ministers. Even so, the point was missed in many cases, and none of the oil ministers was prepared to stay behind and help with the interpretation of the communique. Indeed Sheikh Yamani, its chief architect, was en route back to Riyadh in his private jet even before it was issued.

But however it was reported, the document's moderation was a victory for the Saudis. The Arab radicals wanted to go much further. Iraqi Oil Minister Sadoon Hammadi wanted 'total nationalization of all American oil interests; withdrawal of all funds invested by Arab States in the US . . . breaking of diplomatic relations between all Arab oil producers and the US.' Libya's Izz al-Din al-Mabruk, once one of King Idris' civil servants, but now Colonel Gadaffi's nationalization expert, wanted expropriation extended to all foreign-owned oil companies, not just American ones. Belaid Adbessalam of Algeria considered that a five per cent cutback would not hit Europe hard enough.

But there was no stopping the combination of Saudi oil-power and Egyptian political clout. The communique, once the text was established, emerged as brief and cautiously worded. It asserted that the Arabs are under no obligation to accommodate the world by pumping out their finite reserves of oil at a pace dictated by others. Then came the immediate diplomatic point: 'the international community is under an obligation to implement UN resolutions and to prevent the aggressor from reaping the fruits of his aggression.'

More bluntly, the industrial nations were expected to force

Israel to withdraw. As one of the delegates at the Sheraton said: 'This time, neutrality is not enough. Countries must be positively for us. Those who are not for us are against us.' Those words were to be translated within a few days into concrete moves against Holland and Japan. The document went on to say explicitly that the members of the 'international community' (which really meant Western Europe and Japan) must not only bring their own pressure to bear on Israel over the question of the occupied territories. They must also persuade the Americans to do likewise. Only then would the oil flow freely again.

After this threat of the stick, a carrot was offered – one which was immediately to be munched by Britain, France and Spain. 'Any friendly state which has extended or shall extend effective material assistance to the Arabs' would get as much oil as before the cutback. And this exceptional treatment would be extended to 'any state which takes important measures against Israel.'

The statement ended with a conciliatory appeal for support, addressed to the American people. That was a Saudi addition to the communique, for most of the other producers had already indicated that they intended to boycott the United States completely within a few days. But the Saudis still hoped, despite the fact that America was airlifting arms to Israel, to win some kind of concession from their American friends. Sadoon Hammadi of Iraq regarded the communique as so feeble that he refused to sign it.

Alone among the Arab oil producers, King Feisal wanted to give the Americans time. Privately, he had assured James Akins, US ambassador in Riyadh, that he would anyway not embargo the United States until the end of November.

While the oil ministers were meeting in Kuwait, the Saudi foreign minister, Omar Saqqaf, was in Washington talking to President Nixon. The talks, which also included the foreign ministers of Kuwait, Algeria and Morocco, appeared to be remarkably cordial. When they were over, Saqqaf described Nixon as 'the man who had put an end to the Vietnam war' and as a figure who might well play an important role in a settlement for the Middle East. Nixon himself said that there would be a settlement, which would be 'peaceful, just and honourable'.

Saqqaf, as the American must or should have known, is so close to Feisal that Feisal would expect the minister to be treated as an extension of himself. On the basis of such assurances, the Saudis felt that the Americans, if not on the point of changing their policy, were at least not going to exacerbate the situation.

Then on Thursday, the day after he talked with Saqqaf, President Nixon asked Congress to make a loan of $2,000 million for emergency military aid to Israel. From the American viewpoint it was probably no more than a routine financial arrangement to cover military aid which was already being sent to Israel, the dispatch of which had been announced before Saqqaf met the President. Feisal, however, saw it as a personal betrayal, and on Friday the Saudi Royal Cabinet went into a lengthy emergency session. Next day, Saturday, October 20, it was announced that all oil exports to the United States were being suspended forthwith and 'at the instructions of King Feisal . . . a Jihad is called. As Jihad is the duty of all Moslems, every citizen in this country is called on to back the freedom fight.'

The Royal Court said that the abrupt change in policy was due to 'increasing American military aid to Israel'. The significance of the statement was not confined to the loss of 638,500 barrels of oil a day – although no other Middle Eastern contribution really matters to America. Far more important was the fact that, as a Beirut oil consultant put it: 'If Saudi Arabia moves to B, then every other oil producer must move at least that far if not to C.' The most conservative power in the Middle East had moved to a starkly anti-western position. The game was becoming dangerous for the backers and spectators, as well as the players. And the necessity for both superpowers to bring it to a halt was becoming too powerful to be denied.

The Soviet Union had become convinced of the need for a ceasefire after a very few days of fighting. Indeed, this conviction was so powerful that it caused the Soviet Union to imagine that President Sadat was ready to talk peace before that was in fact the case – causing, as described earlier, considerable loss of sleep to President Sadat, and to Sir Philip Adams, the British Ambassador in Cairo.

The urgent Soviet desire to see the Egyptians quit while they were still ahead no doubt sprang from a profound pessimism about the ability of the Egyptian army to deal with a powerful Israeli counterattack. They feared, correctly, that the longer the war went on the more likely it was that the Egyptians would suffer major military reverses, which would lead in turn to incalculable prospects of escalation. By Tuesday, October 16, the Soviet Union was ready to apply major pressure on its own 'client', Egypt. And to judge from the evidence available so far, what happened between the two superpowers over the next few days was not so much a detailed bargaining over diplomatic points as a simple process in which the American anxiety grew rapidly to match that of the Soviet Union – producing, by the weekend, a situation in which their joint approach to the Security Council was not merely possible, but inevitable.

On Tuesday, Mr Kosygin cancelled a meeting with the Prime

Minister of Denmark, and flew to Cairo, arriving just as the news of the Israeli bridgehead was beginning to filter through the Egyptian military intelligence network. Starting on Tuesday evening and going through to Thursday night, October 18, Kosygin had five sessions with Sadat, all shrouded in deep secrecy. But there is one source which suggests the settlement Kosygin was trying to achieve – and may even have got – before Bren Adan disrupted matters.

The Egyptian position was that there would be no ceasefire until the Israelis agreed to withdraw to the pre-1967 lines. It was a fine, bold negotiating position, but it was based on what Henry Kissinger later called, delicately, 'a mis-assessment of the military situation.'

Also in Cairo while Sadat and Kosygin met was Milos Minic, the Foreign Minister of Yugoslavia. Yugoslavia has traditionally close links with Egypt, which date back to the years in which Tito, Nasser and Jawaharlal Nehru developed the principle of nonalignment. And an immediately practical reason for his presence was that the idea had been canvassed – seemingly by Egypt – that the Yugoslavs should provide a large part of any peacekeeping force that might be required for the Middle East. Therefore it is likely that the Cairo correspondent of the official Yugoslav news agency *Tanjug* knew what he was talking about, when he reported the results of Kosygin's trip on Friday morning. According to *Tanjug*, Kosygin had obtained Egyptian agreement to a four-point plan which would stop the fighting – but at the price of bringing the superpowers very directly into the arena.

The first of the four points modified the precondition on which Egypt would be prepared to stop fighting. Instead of total Israeli withdrawal to the pre-1967 borders, it became withdrawal to those borders 'with minor corrections'. It was scarcely a large concession – and nor could anyone say that the ceasefire lines which Egypt had to accept three days later were really 'minor corrections'. But in the context of Sadat's confident speech on Tuesday, it represented movement of a kind.

The problem was the price that, according to *Tanjug*, Kosygin had been forced to pay. The remaining three points said that: the borders of the conflicting states would be guaranteed by the two superpowers and by the Security Council; that there would be international forces to police the ceasefire; and that the Soviet Union and the United States would safeguard the borders 'by virtue of their physical presence, separately or in concert with other parties'. The report was little noticed at the time – although just one week later the very question of the introduction of a superpower military presence in the Middle East was to provoke a quasi-nuclear dispute between America and the Soviet Union.

But western diplomats closely involved in the repercussions of this visit think that Kosygin's discussions with Sadat were far less orderly. On their account, the first couple of days may indeed have been spent thrashing out some deal on the neat *Tanjug* formula. Sadat, meanwhile, either himself did not know – or if he did, concealed from Kosygin – the true state of affairs on the west bank. Several days later, when it was clear that the Egyptian Third Army had been totally cut off, officials in the Kremlin told western reporters bitterly that the Egyptians had 'misled' Kosygin and his party about the true state of military affairs. 'There had been a Stalingrad in Sinai and they would not admit it,' was the way the Russians put it. But, according to western diplomats, Sadat did confess the truth to Kosygin on Thursday morning. (Kosygin may have had his own suspicions by then. He had telephoned the Kremlin several times during his visit.) Kosygin's reaction was apparently one of horror. More practically, he told Sadat to hang on militarily at all costs while Russia tried to get the best ceasefire deal now possible.

Once Kosygin got back to Moscow, after a detour via Baghdad and Damascus, the Russians wasted no time getting on the hot line to Washington. 'We began exploring a new formula for ending the war that evening, although it was still unacceptable to us', said Secretary of State Kissinger later. 'And while we were still considering that formula, Secretary-General Brezhnev sent an urgent request to President Nixon that I be sent to Moscow to conduct the negotiations in order to speed an end to hostilities that might be difficult to contain were they to continue.'

The Russians outlined to Washington the debacle facing Egypt, stressing that they simply could not allow this to happen even if, to prevent it, Russia had to take drastic steps. The Americans needed no persuading about the urgency of preventing this. At five on Saturday morning, Kissinger and a team of nine officials, including the veteran American Middle East negotiator Joseph Sisco, left Andrews Air Force Base just outside Washington, bound for Moscow. The question was whether a deal could be struck, and pushed through the Security Council, before Bren Adan's tanks could divide the Egyptian Army into three roughly equal parts.

Section IV

Below: Men of the Israeli Golani Brigade wave triumphantly after winning the epic battle to recapture Mount Hermon — the highest peak of Golan — just eight hours before the first ceasefire.

Week three: Superpowers decide to call it quits

1: Kissinger cobbles up a truce

On Sunday, October 21 – the sixteenth day of the war – the Egyptian high command in Cairo held its first press conference since the opening of hostilities. The chief military spokesman, Major-General Ezz Eddin Mukhtar, advanced the theory that Egypt had already beaten Israel in the field but now had to contend with the might of the United States; even so Egyptian troops covered the Sinai front from the Mediterranean to Suez. He put total Israeli losses on the Egyptian front at 600 tanks, 400 armoured vehicles, 23 naval vessels, 25 helicopters and 303 aircraft. When a correspondent pointed out that the combined Egyptian and Syrian totals indicated that Israel's air force of just under 500 planes had lost 600 in action, Mukhtar said smoothly that the apparent discrepancy was explained by the scale of America's resupply operation. (In fact, Mukhtar's air loss figures were inflated tenfold: more than eighty of Israel's 115 aircraft lost were destroyed over Golan.)

He was curtly dismissive of the Israeli bridgehead on the west bank of the canal. Mukhtar was willing to concede that there were two small pockets of Israelis about ten kilometres into Egypt in the Deversoir area – both were hopelessly beseiged by thousands of Egyptian troops. (This grudging admission was an advance on his assertion, made on the previous Wednesday, that the Israeli task force had been 'wiped out'.) Mukhtar now admitted the bridgehead as a pinprick in the Egyptian grand strategy, but no more. In response to a questioner, he said that the Egyptian supply arteries, the main Cairo–Ismailia road and the Cairo–Suez roads to the south, were not threatened.

While these assurances were being given, the northern extension of the Israeli forces west of the canal were taking up positions on a line two miles south of the Cairo–Ismailia road, bringing it well within range of Israeli artillery. But the bulk of the Israeli forces – and the reinforcements who came surging over the pontoons north of the Great Bitter Lake all day – were driving south towards Suez, stopping only briefly to dismantle a few missile sites, the last of those that had provided the Egyptians with their air umbrella for the original advance. The comparative freedom of the skies enjoyed by the Israeli Mirages and Phantoms on that day testified to the success of the ground action. Increasingly, the

Egyptians found themselves having to commit their own precious MIGs in an effort to halt the Israeli advance. The Israeli information service, which became more cautious and precise as Arab claims got wilder, claimed that seventeen Egyptian fighters were downed in the day's action.

By nightfall the Israeli bridgehead extended west of the canal to a distance of eighteen miles from the waterway along a front some twenty-five miles long, from just short of the Ismailia–Cairo road in the north to the Little Bitter Lake in the South. Within this area there were pockets of determined Egyptian resistance and the advance guard of the Israeli troops were still some miles short of the Cairo–Suez road, the main lifeline of the Egyptian Third Army, which still held to the wedge of territory on the west bank extending from the southern tip of the Little Bitter Lake to a point a few miles south of Suez. By any intelligent military assessment the Third Army, numbering some 20,000 men, and with an estimated three to four hundred tanks still intact, was highly vulnerable.

In Moscow the accelerating Israeli *blitzkrieg* concentrated minds wonderfully. The implications of the Israelis' success west of the canal were not lost on the American Secretary of State, Henry Kissinger, and the Soviet leader, Leonid Brezhnev. Brezhnev knew, and Kissinger appreciated, that the Soviet Union could not stand idly by while the Egyptian war machine was systematically smashed and the Israeli army fulfilled David Elazar's graphic promise to 'break the bones' of the opposition. Willy-nilly the two superpowers were being drawn into confrontation by their respective client states. By Sunday evening a situation existed – with the Egyptian and Israeli armies ranged in fighting order on the *wrong* sides of the canal – in which both sides could claim a victory for domestic consumption. It might obtain for another twenty-four hours, or forty-eight at best. Thereafter, given the pace of the Israeli advance, even Cairo's propaganda machine might find it impossible to conceal the military humilation; Arab pressure on the Soviet Union to even the scores would intensify.

For the architects of the detente policy in Moscow, the only remedy was to 'freeze' the battlefront situation before this happened – which meant within hours. Kissinger did not begin work in Moscow until early Sunday morning. By Sunday evening the main outlines of another ceasefire agreement had been hammered out between the armourers of the Middle Eastern combatants. In Cairo President Sadat was being kept abreast of developments by the Soviet Ambassador, Vladimir Vinogradov, forcing an uncomfortable intimacy on two men who normally find it difficult to remain on speaking terms. At 9.30 pm Vino-gradov informed the Egyptian leader of the superpowers' fresh agreement. For Sadat, the terms of the Kissinger-Brezhnev pro-posal must by then have come as a reprieve, though he knew he would have an uphill task selling it both to his own cabinet and the other Arab governments who did not yet appreciate the gravity of the Egyptian Third Army's position.

Israel's Prime Minister Golda Meir received word of the Moscow agreement at about the same time and promptly called a cabinet meeting which did not end until four o'clock the next morning. While the Israeli cabinet was considering a proposal that threatened to snatch an equivocal compromise from the jaws of imminent victory, the rusty machinery of the UN Security Council began to clank into motion.

Shortly after 10.00 pm on Sunday in New York (just after four o'clock on Monday morning in the battlezone), the Security Council was called to order by its President, Sir Laurence McIntyre of Australia; he presented to its members a draft of a resolution, number 338. Co-sponsored by the US and the Soviet Union, it was mercifully brief but left much unexplained. Its terms were summarized in three main points and read:

> The Security Council:
> 1. Calls upon the parties to the present fighting to cease all firing and terminate all military activity immediately, no later than twelve hours after the moment of the adoption of this decision in the positions they now occupy.
> 2. Calls upon the parties concerned to start immediately after the ceasefire the implementation of Security Council Resolution 242 in all of its parts.
> 3. Decides that immediately and concurrently with the ceasefire, negotiations will start between the parties con-cerned under appropriate auspices aimed at establishing a just and durable peace in the Middle East.

Of all the Security Council members only China could find much to say against it. Peking's representative, Huang Hua, said that his country could not go along with any resolution that did not 'condemn all the acts of aggression by the Israeli Zionists in the strongest terms . . .' and showed his disdain by abstaining from the voting. The other members reflected the unanimity of the two superpowers and, after only two and a half hours of debate, voted unanimously, 14–0, for the proposal. The resolution, shrewdly perhaps, did nothing to resolve the ambiguities of its predecessor 242; but it contained elements of incentive for both sides. For the Arabs it offered the prospect of recovering Israeli-occupied territories; for the Israelis it offered the opportunity, which they had long sought, for face-to-face bargaining with their Arab neighbours – though the vague 'auspices' might worry Israel, which has a well-founded fear that one likely auspice, the UN, is heavily against it. In the immediate context of the battlefield, however, the Israelis were unquestionably being asked to make the larger concession. Moreover, the only sanction against their pressing home their military advantage was self-restraint – never a very convincing deterrent in time of war. Still, as a British diplomat remarked: 'Henry and the Russians did a pretty good cobbling job' – but with one flaw.

Between the first clause of Resolution 338 – calling for a cease-fire within twelve hours time – and the subtle incentives held out in two and three, there was what the British Foreign Secretary Sir Alec Douglas-Home later called, with masterly understatement, 'a gap'. Despite urgent diplomatic representations to the United States by both Britain and France before the UN vote, the agreement contained no proposals for observation or enforcement of the ceasefire. It was an ominous omission.

At 10.53 on Monday morning – eight hours before the ceasefire resolution was due to come into effect – the Israelis successfully completed one of their most costly single actions of the war on the Syrian front. Since Sunday afternoon, helicopter-borne paratroopers and infantry of the elite Golani Brigade had sustained fifty dead and about 200 wounded during an assault on the Syrian-held positions on the 7,000-feet ridge near the summit of Mount Hermon.

The Syrians had captured a heavily fortified Israeli emplacement on the mountain during the first Sunday of the war and this was the Israelis' second attempt to retake it. By losing the position at the outset of the war the Israelis had lost, as we have seen, a considerable military advantage. But the loss of Mount Hermon was much more than a simple military defeat. Nine months before Yom Kippur the Israeli secret service, Shin Bet, had uncovered a spy and sabotage ring based in the Druze village of Majdal Shams – at the foot of the road which leads up to the mountain fortress. The ring was found to be linked with an operation run in Haifa by a local bookseller. It was one of the largest and most sophisticated networks ever uncovered in Israel.

The investigation into the ring revealed that native-born Jews, or *sabras*, were involved – for the first time since the establishment of the state. The affair, which ended with the conviction of two Jews and three Arabs as ringleaders, left its mark on the national psyche. During the trials it was said that top secret information of a military nature had been passed to the Syrians – it concerned a 'secret weapon'. At least part of the information

Attack on the 7,000-foot stronghold on Mount Hermon, the key observation
post overlooking the Golan plateau and Damascus

Aftermath of the bloody Mount Hermon battle. The body of a Syrian soldier lies in the wreckage of the Mount Hermon ski lift

passed, however, concerned the elaborate Israeli fortification on Hermon. Detailed drawings of the entries and exits to the labyrinth of bunkers and connecting corridors, specifications of the relative strengths of the armour-plated doors and layouts of minefields and boobytraps had found their way into Syrian hands.

In spite of this, when Syrian paratroopers landed by helicopter on the first Sunday to take the fortress, it contained only a token Israeli fighting force. The Syrians got into the fort through one of the easiest ways – a door that was normally reserved for escape in case of emergency, and could be opened more easily than the others. An Israeli military expert later observed: 'Someone should be court martialled for this.'

The Syrians were unable, however, to flush out the entire Israeli unit. Some literally locked themselves in; others managed to escape and took word back that, although in military terms the fort had fallen, some troops were still inside. An expedition was launched, by members of the Golani Brigade, to rescue them. It failed with the loss of thirty dead. Those Israelis still inside, weakening through lack of food and, particularly, water, gave themselves up. The Israelis complained to the International Red Cross that five were killed as they came out with their hands up.

The second attempt to recapture the position was more determined. It included the use, for the first time on the Israeli side, of helicopter-borne troops in the Golan. They were helped by infantry, artillery, armour and the air force. The assault was extended along the ridge into Syria to ensure full command of the strategic position on Hermon. At two o'clock on the afternoon of Sunday, October 21, paratroopers were landed behind the Syrian positions further along the ridge towards Damascus while a frontal attack was made up the side of the mountain. The Syrians responded immediately with MIGs, nine of which, the Israelis claim, were shot down.

The Golani Brigade began their gruelling climb up the side of the boulder-strewn mountain under cover of the early evening dusk. They had a rough time. The Syrian commandos on top had had a fortnight to select – and strengthen – their sniping positions covering the slopes and they inflicted heavy casualties.

A Golani infantryman recalls: 'We climbed in the dark, vertically, with almost no handholds. We climbed for eight hours feeling all the time someone was spying on us from above. We knew that once we reached the top we were on our own. The armour stayed below near the end of the cable railway. [The Israelis have had a ski-run on Hermon for the past two years]. Aircraft and artillery couldn't operate in case they hit us. On top they had a warm welcome for us. In every nook and cranny they had not one but seven snipers. In the first light we suddenly found ourselves at arms-length with them. We actually had fist fights. Everyone was shouting at everyone. Then there was a Syrian air attack.'

Another remembers: 'The snipers used the classic trick of raising helmets on a stick to draw our fire; they had made positions for themselves round the fort, not in it. Most of them were lying down; they used telescopic sights and the sun was behind them – right in our eyes. They threw grenades at anything that moved; many of our wounded were from grenade fragments.' The fiercest fighting was from 6.00 am onwards. By eleven o'clock the Israeli and Golani flags were fluttering from the radio antennae on top of the fort.

Henry Kissinger arrived in Tel Aviv that same Monday morning fresh from his diplomatic labours in Moscow. He waved cheerily to the pressmen assembled at Lod airport and walked deliberately past the microphones set up for an impromptu press conference. The most recent secrets of the Kremlin were for the ears of the Israeli leadership alone. By this stage, the Israeli cabinet had reluctantly agreed to the ceasefire, though no official word had come through from Egypt or Syria. The Israeli agreement was, of course, contingent on Egyptian and Syrian acceptance of

An Israeli Centurion under bombardment from a Sukhoi-7 near Saasa

UN Resolution 338. But within Israel itself, there were already the beginnings of a sour reaction to what many considered a premature cessation of hostilities just as Israel was getting on top. Before the day was over some of this opposition was focused through the right-wing Likud coalition. It rejected the ceasefire and announced that it would oppose it in the Knesset: 'Out of a sense of national responsibility we call on the people in this grave hour to strive for cancellation of this deplorable policy of the government . . .'. Even the normally mild-mannered General Haim Herzog complained of the 'unprecedented haste' with which the Security Council had endorsed the Russo–American deal.

With both popular and military sentiment running against a ceasefire, the Israeli leadership was anxious for reassurance from the American Secretary of State. Kissinger was in the country for five hours, and spent three and a half of them in a secret meeting place just north of Tel Aviv. With him were Mrs Meir, Deputy Premier Yigal Allon, Defence Minister Moshe Dayan, and the Foreign Minister, Abba Eban. Much of the time was spent reassuring the Israelis that there was no 'secret deal' between the superpowers. Kissinger told Mrs Meir that he had tried to telephone her from Moscow with the text of the ceasefire agreement, but that 'technical factors' had prevented it.

Kissinger was at much pains to stress that the Russians – if not yet the Arabs – had at last agreed to the idea of face-to-face Arab–Israeli talks, rather than negotiations through third parties. Still better, he said, the draft the Russians had produced did not refer to the 'rights of the Palestinians' – a concept which the Israelis claim implies the dismemberment of Israel. Instead, it followed UN Resolution 242, which refers to 'a just settlement of the refugee problem', thus remaining open to economic and social interpretations, rather than political ones.

Kissinger also spelled out, according to Israeli sources, the reason why a truce was urgently required – the big powers feared a total defeat of Egypt. No doubt the need to leave Egypt with some kind of negotiating base was obvious enough to the winner of the Nobel Peace Prize, but Mrs Meir and her colleagues are of another and starker cast of mind.

Subsequently, it was claimed that Kissinger did not adequately impose his authority on Mrs Meir; but this stemmed from a confusion over the relative weight of their personalities and the strength of their personal power bases. Kissinger is a man of nuances who can normally afford to speak softly because the big stick of American power is always implicit. But in the context of American–Israeli relations this implied authority did not exist, since it is unthinkable that American power could ever be used *against* Israel. (Certainly, a Jewish Secretary of State could not even hint at such a contingency.) Despite the fact that the Israeli war machine was dependent on American aid, Kissinger's role was that of a man come to ask a favour, not to impose a solution. He could expect a sympathetic hearing but no more, and Mrs Meir's track-record, both in and out of office, suggested a flinty attitude to any idea that might compromise Israel's security.

When she became Prime Minister in March, 1969, after the death of Levi Eshkol, there were many who doubted the wisdom of appointing a woman already over seventy whose health was suspect and who, although she had been Foreign Minister before retiring in 1965, was hardly regarded as a national figure at home. The doubters were rapidly silenced by her firm control of the cabinet and her flair for personal negotiation with world leaders. Her popularity reached a peak of 89·4% in a national opinion poll in 1972 and has fallen little since then. The standard joke about Mrs Meir being 'the strongest man in the cabinet' has a core of seriousness. She speaks in a low growl and this, with her large head and shoulders – all that most people see of her on the television screen – gives an impression of natural authority.

Mrs Meir evidently sees no contradiction in the fact that a woman should head a nation in a constant state of readiness for war. She is as much concerned with security as any man in the military establishment, believing that an independent Israel is the only guarantee of the Jewish people's survival. 'When people ask me,' she once said, 'if I am afraid, because of Israel's need for defence, that the country may become militaristic, I can only answer that I don't want a fine, liberal, anti-colonial, anti-militaristic, dead Jewish people.'

She was born Golda Mabovitch, daughter of a carpenter in Kiev in May 1898. The family emigrated to the United States and settled in Milwaukee when Golda was eight years old (she still speaks English with a strong American accent). In 1921, after marrying Morris Myerson, she left with her husband for Palestine. Both her children were born in a kibbutz and, as they grew up, she became more and more involved in Zionist politics. When the British arrested most of the male Jewish leaders in the 1940s she became acting head of the Jewish Agency's Political Department in Jerusalem and was among those who negotiated with the British up to the creation of the state of Israel. Before the state was established Golda went to Trans-Jordan, disguised as an Arab woman, to meet King Abdullah and try to persuade him not to join in the expected attacks by the Arab states on Israel. She became Israel's first envoy to Moscow and a year later joined the cabinet as Labour Minister. After her long spell as Foreign Minister (1956–65), she spent four years as secretary to the Labour Party before taking over as premier.

Mrs Meir and Kissinger had never met before; on her visits to Washington, he had kept out of the way. Now, she and her ministers found the American Secretary of State's presentation a shade cryptic. Asked after the meeting about her impressions of the famous Nobel Prize-winner, Mrs Meir replied curtly: 'Metternich'. Sometime after the war, when Mrs Meir visited the White House, President Nixon is said to have remarked on the coincidence of their both having Jewish ministers in charge of foreign affairs. 'Yes,' was Mrs Meir's alleged reply, 'but mine, I think, speaks better English.' Kissinger was wryly impressed by Mrs Meir, though. 'Golda's quite a woman,' he told his aides, 'but she's not the sort of dame I like to have around me at midnight.'

In the light of later events, it is clear that Kissinger did not impress the 'kitchen cabinet' strongly enough with the urgency of the ceasefire, but at the time he had every reason to be pleased with his mission. Before the American party left Israel, word came through that Sadat had accepted the truce. In Jordan, King Hussein seemed strongly disposed to acceptance, despite an Iraqi rejection and a deafening silence from Damascus.

The northern front still remained problematic as Syria wound up one last abortive attempt to retake Mount Hermon; but that was not where the danger to international peace lay. In the south, where the really explosive situation existed, Kissinger appeared to have secured his objective. In the space of twenty-four hours, he had contrived to bring all the elements together – superpowers, United Nations, and the two main combatants.

He left Israel with a reasonable assurance that a ceasefire would take place at 6.52 pm local time – precisely twelve hours after the passage of UN resolution 338.

2: The battle of the ceasefire

An hour before the scheduled ceasefire, Major-General Shlomo Gazit summarized Israeli achievements in the war at a press briefing in Tel Aviv. The army, he claimed, was in control of 1,200 square kilometres on the western bank of the canal. In Syria the line had been extended to include 600 square kilometres of territory beyond the 1967 truce line. Since the beginning of the war the Egyptians had lost 240 planes, the Syrians 212. One thousand 'enemy' tanks had been taken out on the Egyptian front and another thousand on the Syrian front. Gazit claimed that Israeli troops were now straddling the main roads and railway leading from Cairo to Suez in the south. Asked how he would describe the overall position, Gazit replied: 'It is a very big victory which could have been bigger.'

Over the next forty-eight hours, in what was theoretically a ceasefire situation, the victory became very much bigger.

The Israeli claim to 'control' so much Egyptian territory, including the vital supply route to the Egyptian Third Army, was somewhat exaggerated. While it was true that some Israeli units had reached the main Cairo–Suez road at a point about ten miles from Port Suez, these were well in advance of the main Israeli force. Moreover, in the areas of Israeli 'control' there were still Egyptian troops in fighting order. No hard and fast line existed between the two armies. The task of deciding where the line ran would in all probability utimately fall to tidy-minded men from the United Nations. In such a complex situation, the Israelis ran the risk of having their potential stranglehold on the Third Army tidied out of existence. This process might not be long delayed, although the Security Council had inexplicably failed in Resolution 338 even to alert the men of the UN Truce Supervisory Organisation who had kept watch on Israel's borders since 1967. At the time of the ceasefire there were some forty-two UNTSO men kicking their heels in Cairo, to which they had been evacuated from the Suez Canal area after the war started.

But before anyone could propel them towards the new front

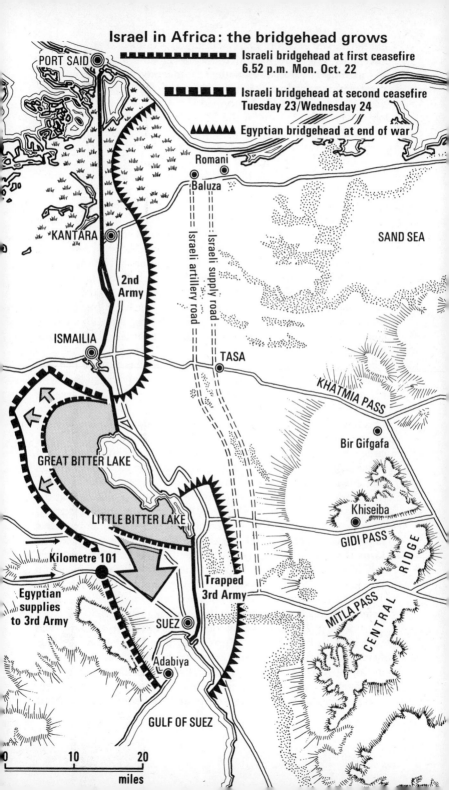

Israel in Africa: the bridgehead grows

▬▬▬▬▬ Israeli bridgehead at first ceasefire
6.52 p.m. Mon. Oct. 22

▬▬▬▬▬ Israeli bridgehead at second ceasefire
Tuesday 23/Wednesday 24

▲▲▲▲▲ Egyptian bridgehead at end of war

PORT SAID

Romani

Baluza

KANTARA

SAND SEA

2nd
Army

Israeli artillery road

Israeli supply road

ISMAILIA

TASA

KHATMIA PASS

Bir Gifgafa

GREAT BITTER LAKE

Khiseiba

GIDI PASS

LITTLE BITTER LAKE

RIDGE

Kilometre 101

Egyptian
supplies
to 3rd Army

Trapped
3rd Army

MITLA PASS

CENTRAL

SUEZ

Adabiya

GULF OF SUEZ

0   10   20

miles

lines, the war was on again. Both sides claimed that the other started it. The most extended version of how it happened was provided by Israel at a subsequent UN meeting. Its representative, Yosef Tekoah, claimed that there was 'virtually no time during which the Egyptian forces stopped shooting'. Tracing the official Israeli version of events in the hours immediately after the 6.52 pm ceasefire deadline Mr Tekoah said: 'The shooting became particularly violent at 2038 hours when Egyptian forces opened fire on the Israel bridgehead on the west bank of the Suez Canal from the east and from the north. At 2056 hours the Egyptian forces opened fire on the Israel bridgehead from north of Dever-soir. Later, Israeli forces were shelled from bazookas. At 2132 hours there was bazooka shelling. . . . While this was taking place the spokesman of the Israel defence forces repeatedly drew attention to these Egyptian attacks. . . . At 0555 hours [on Wednesday morning] the IDF communique stated that the Egyptians had opened artillery fire on Israeli forces toward the end of the night of 22–23 October; at 0800 hours that the Egyptians had opened fire on Israel forces on the west bank of the Suez Canal; and at 0900 hours, that the Egyptian forces were continuing to violate the ceasefire in the southern sector of the Suez Canal.

'Facing this situation, the Israeli defence forces were ordered to continue fighting in this sector of the front. It is clear who accepted the ceasefire and who rejected it, who has observed it and who has violated it.'

Allocation of responsibility for renewed fighting was less clear to war correspondents in the area. The truce resolution, after all, called not only for a halt to all firing but also for the termination of 'all military activity'. There was scant evidence of Israel terminating its build-up of men, supplies, ammunition and armour in the bulge west of the canal. (It seems probable that the Egyptian artillery attack was a response to this build-up.) Many of the Israeli tanks were emblazoned with the provocative label 'Cairo Express', while the supplies came in every conceivable form of wheeled transport, with huge Tnuva milk tankers (now full of water) and Egged Tours buses especially prominent. In the early hours of Tuesday morning, *Insight* reporter Philip Jacobson joined the convoy to observe the first day of the 'cease-fire'. After his tour, he cabled the following dispatch:

'A little matter of twenty-four hours after the ceasefire was supposed to have begun, I was lying face down on a pontoon bridge across the Suez Canal while Israeli troops blazed away at a pair of Egypt's 'Frog' missiles sailing majestically overhead in the dark. I had just begun crossing the bridge back towards Israel when the firing started, strings of bright red tracer, trailing up from both banks. For one heart-stopping moment, we appeared to be the targets: it seemed a good idea to get off the bridge. I was rolling vigorously to one side when the strong right arm of the *Daily Mirror*'s Anthony Delano stopped me from dropping into the canal.

'When we did raise our heads, it became clear that the "Frogs"– big, free-flight rockets packed with 1,000 pounds of high explosive – were the real targets. You could see their bright orange exhaust quite clearly, followed by streams of tracer fire; when last seen, they were still heading east, presumably aimed at Israeli positions beyond the canal.

'It was a suitably dramatic finale to what was, even by Middle East standards, a comprehensively flouted ceasefire. Earlier, a mile from the bridgehead on the Egyptian side, we had passed an uneasy hour in a fœtid Egyptian slit-trench while an artillery battle was fought out. The Egyptian gunners were going for the pontoons which the Israelis had thrown over the canal at the northern end of the Great Bitter Lake. Their shells were falling well short, uncomfortably near us.

'A few hours before that, I had enjoyed a grandstand view of what was quite clearly the beginning of a major Israeli armoured attack, scores of tanks roaring down a sand road while crewmen secured equipment and checked their guns. We could hear heavy guns firing in the distance and great plumes of white smoke were rising on the southern horizon. "What's going on?" someone asked our escort officer, a greying colonel with a splash of medal ribbons on his chest. "Just deploying to new positions, I imagine," he replied. Simultaneously, two Egyptian MIGs passed overhead with Israeli Mirages in hot pursuit. After a perfunctory dogfight, both MIGs spiralled down, bright flashes marking explosions of their bombs and fuel.

'What we were watching, it turned out, was the Israelis' attack round the town of Suez, ten miles to our south – the last major action of the war. Perhaps our colonel really didn't know. "You must remember, Philip," he had explained, "that we made it clear we would return blow for blow."

'This was the official line, and he served it up with a commendably straight face. But after jolting for hours around Israeli-held territory on the Egyptian side of the canal in an open army truck, I can only say that it did not look that way to me. From where I stood – occasionally lay – the Israelis appeared to be engaged in what I believe is known as "line straightening" among military men. On this occasion, it involved cutting the main roads from Cairo to Suez and tightening a huge ring around the Egyptian Third Army.

'I should have realized we were in for an eventful day when,

Suez town under fire during the battles of October 22 after the 'ceasefire'.
During this day, Egypt's Third Army was encircled

before we left Tel Aviv, the escort handed out steel helmets and
field dressings. The helmets were sand-coloured, bowler hat type,
vintage Dad's Army; they were painful to wear, and occasioned
much rude comment from the Israeli troops. The instructions
stamped on my field dressings were in Hebrew and German,
neither of which I speak, and which, I later discovered, could
hardly be hacked open with my newly acquired Japanese version
of the famed Swiss Army knife.

'An hour out of Tel Aviv, we began passing huge military convoys grinding towards the canal. It all looked, as someone said,
like business as usual. The bridgehead was a shambles. There
had been heavy fighting around it and the Israeli engineers were
still cannibalizing wrecked trucks and halftracks with blow-
torches. On the Egyptian side, we met Haim Topol, Israeli
actor, film star, and volunteer driver for the duration. He seems
to have been following me around for days, popping up in every
trench and dugout: he had acquired a brand-new Uzi sub-
machinegun since our last encounter. All round the bridgehead
the ground had been torn and furrowed by shells; smashed
bunkers and wrecked gun positions marked the path of the Israeli
tank force which had fought its way across the canal five days
earlier. We stopped for a moment under some pine trees; glanc-
ing up, I saw a helmet caught high in the branches. "Look out

for the steps of Moses" a tank driver shouted as we passed, "He came from the other direction, you know."

'The smell of death came very quickly. First, a faint whiff of corruption: the Israelis are scrupulous about burying enemy dead, and you could see neat lines of graves with individual markers. Those were the early casualties. Further on, Egyptian corpses had been collected in hastily dug pits, still awaiting proper burial, and the smell became much worse. In the back of the truck, you smelt the corpses before you saw them: the most recent dead, killed the night before, perhaps even that morning, lay sprawled along the road near the charred tanks and lorries.

'The flat, hard sand on both sides of the road was crowded with blackened and twisted vehicles. One convoy of halftracks had clearly been attacked from the air: the smashed armour lay in almost perfect line at right angles to the road where the panicking drivers had fled. The Egyptians had dug many of their ageing T-34 tanks hull-down into the sand, for use as fixed artillery: it is tactically sound, but only if you control the air. In half a mile, I counted eighteen tanks, all incinerated in their pits, neatly winkled out by Israel's pilots. The crews never stood a chance.

'As the day wore on, our escorts became noticeably more glum. As far as I could see, the whole idea of taking us so deep into Egyptian territory – more than twenty miles from the canal – had been to show us Egyptian violations of the ceasefire. These were in short supply, where we were at least. There was, it is true, a continuous rumble of heavy artillery from the south. "Incoming" announced our escort. "How can you tell from here?" I asked. "Experience."

'By late afternoon, we remained sadly unviolated. As we drove towards Suez for a prearranged briefing, there was a flurry of activity among the tank crews lounging by the road. Squadron after squadron started engines and moved south at speed, roaring up behind our truck. The radio jeep which had been guiding us stopped suddenly and the escort officers gathered round in the swirling dust. They hurried back looking worried. "Sorry, no briefing; arrangements got a bit confused."

'It must have been the last straw – a bunch of nosey journalists turning up as the attack on Suez got under way. As we drove back to the bridgehead, escorts muttering to each other in Hebrew, the big guns began firing more heavily behind us.

'Then it happened. A mile from the bridgehead, traffic was halted: there was shelling, indubitably Egyptian. The escorts hustled us happily into nearby trenches and we celebrated with soft drinks liberated from a canteen lorry. An American radio reporter started work: "Under fire near the Israeli bridgehead." '

By nightfall on Tuesday the Israeli army had closed the trap on the Egyptian Third Army. Driving forward on the ground, bombing and strafing from the air, the Israelis pushed well south of the main Suez road to envelop the city. Advance units pressed on to the port of Adabiya on the Gulf of Suez, near the oil refineries south of the city. All conceivable supply routes – for ammunition, food and, above all, drinking water – to the Egyptian forces over the canal were menaced by Israeli armour and artillery. Provided they could maintain these positions, the capitulation of the Third Army was only a matter of time.

In its summary of the day's fighting, the *Jerusalem Post* quoted 'a military source' with the demure observation: 'The line may have changed somewhat, and not to our disadvantage.' An Israeli infantry sergeant put it a little more bluntly to a correspondent near the front. 'If they let us,' he said, 'we can make them come out of the east bank with their hands up and their tongues out.'

3: Washington's nuclear alert

Egypt responded to the deterioration of its military situation by intensifying its diplomatic effort. Even before the Israeli encirclement was complete, President Sadat briefed three envoys to tour Arab capitals and explain why, only a few days after Egypt had declared it would never agree to a truce unless Israel withdrew to its 1967 frontiers, a ceasefire was a vital necessity. Dr Azid Sidki went to Syria, Mahmoud Salem to Libya and Algeria, while Sayed Marei was assigned Saudi Arabia, Kuwait and the Arab Gulf emirates.

At Sadat's request the Security Council convened for another emergency session on Tuesday, October 23, and, once more, it was the two superpowers who came up with a joint resolution. Although it made no attempt to allocate blame for the breakdown of the ceasefire, Resolution 339 had a stormier passage than its predecessor. The Chinese Deputy Foreign Minister, Chiao Kuan-hua, deplored 'the malicious practice of using the Security Council as a tool to be juggled by the two superpowers at will', and the session had to be suspended for twenty minutes after an angry shouting match developed between Chiao and the Israeli and Soviet delegates. When passions cooled the Council endorsed by fourteen votes to none (with China abstaining) the following:

The Security Council, referring to its resolution 338 (1973) of 22 October 1973,

1. Confirms its decision on an immediate cessation of all kinds of firing and all military action, and urges that the forces be returned to the positions they occupied at the moment the ceasefire became effective;

2. Requests the Secretary-General to take measures for immediate dispatch of United Nations observers to supervise the observance of the ceasefire between the forces of Israel and the Arab Republic of Egypt, using for this purpose the personnel of the United Nations now in the Middle East and first of all the personnel now in Cairo.

The resolution, with its specific mention of UN observers, at least provided a mechanism for monitoring the truce. But the provision for the immediate dispatch of observers did not guarantee their immediate arrival. Nor was there much chance of their finding agreement between the Israeli and Egyptian forces about their October 22 ceasefire positions when they did arrive. The new ceasefire was, hopefully, scheduled for 0500 GMT (7 am in the battle-zone) on Wednesday morning.

Before it came into effect, Syria announced acceptance of the October 22 ceasefire, although on terms that seemed likely to create a fresh *casus belli* in the future. The Syrian acceptance was made 'on the basis that it means the complete withdrawal of Israeli forces from all Arab territories occupied in June 1967 and after . . .". (In presenting her acceptance of the ceasefire to the Knesset some hours earlier, Mrs Meir had given the assurance that it did not imply a return to the pre-1967 borders which made Israel 'a temptation to aggression'.) Even so, the fact that Syria had endorsed a UN proposal that referred to Resolution 242 and direct negotiations with Israel – neither of which had previously been acceptable in Damascus – was a hopeful sign. (The Syrian decision, reached after extreme Russian pressure had been put on Asad, did not prevent it in December from boycotting the Geneva peace conference at the last minute.)

Shortly after 10.00 am on the morning of Wednesday, October 24, seven UN patrols left Cairo on their way to the forward Egyptian positions. By early evening, two had established themselves on the east bank of the canal – one just east of Port Fuad, the other east of Qantara. Another two took up positions on the west bank at Abu Suweir and south of the Abu Sultan roads. The three patrols which had headed southwest down the roads to Suez never reached their objective.

They made it as far as Jebel Oweida and Bastat El Hemira, only to learn that there was still a war going on. The UN Secretary-General, Kurt Waldheim, later explained to the Security Council that they 'had to withdraw westward due to the intense exchange of tank and artillery fire between Egyptian and Israeli forces'. Soon afterwards a convoy of Red Cross lorries, laden with medical supplies and blood plasma for the beleaguered Egyptian Third Army, was turned back by the Israelis outside Suez. In Tel Aviv, General Haim Herzog, interviewed for an Israel overseas broadcast, observed that the only option open to the Egyptian Third Army was 'surrender with honour'.

Confronted by Israel's evident determination to humiliate the Third Army, President Sadat requested yet another Security Council meeting. This time his Foreign Minister, Dr Zayyat, had instructions to urge the Council 'to call on the Soviet Union and the United States . . . each to send forces immediately from the forces stationed near the area to supervise the implementation of the ceasefire . . .'. The unenforced ceasefire was turning out to be worse than useless. Something a little more potent than a few jeep-loads of UN observers would have to be injected into the truce-keeping operation.

Wednesday evening's Security Council meeting was an edgy occasion. Although the Soviet Ambassador Yakov Malik did not comment directly on the readiness of the Soviet Union to commit troops, he indulged in some cudgelling rhetoric about 'the war criminals of Tel Aviv'. In his view Israel's 'brazen violations' amounted to a 'carefully prepared criminal and hypocritical imperialist provocation'. It was not the kind of talk calculated to foster a spirit of cooperation between the two superpowers.

Malik went on to say : 'The only possible way of correcting the situation and directing the course of events is that Israel must immediately be compelled to comply with the decisions of the Security Council, and the United States is obliged and bound to play a decisive role as a permanent member of the Security Council and as a co-sponsor of the two resolutions.' Egypt's call for the superpowers' troops as guarantors of the peace was, Malik felt, 'undoubtedly justified and . . . entirely in accordance with the Charter of the United Nations'. The implication seemed to be that, if the Security Council felt troops ought to be committed, Russia was ready to do its duty and the US should do likewise. The US ambassador to the UN, John Scali, did not much like the implication. 'This is not a time,' he said, 'in which involvement by the great powers, through the dispatch of their armed forces, could be helpful in creating conditions of peace.'

While the Security Council talked on until past midnight without reaching any decision, the first steps towards escalation were being taken in Washington.

The crisis erupted when Washington was in a nervous condition for reasons totally unconnected with the Middle East. The

Watergate scandal – an amalgam of electoral and national security abuses that had defaced Nixon's re-election in 1972 – had just gone critical as a result of the President's decision a few days earlier to fire his Special Prosecutor, Archibald Cox, who had been investigating the scandal. Cox's dismissal caused an uproar and the idea of impeaching Nixon, or forcing him to resign, was publicly canvassed by erstwhile supporters in his own party. In an attempt to restore his position, Nixon announced that he would, after a short retreat to Camp David, his rural residence, address the nation on network television.

While the President was in Camp David, the thankless task of mollifying a by now thoroughly roused Washington press corps fell to his White House chief of staff, Alexander Haig. At a briefing in which Haig tried to explain the President's position on the Watergate tapes – the secret White House tape-recordings which, it was thought, could establish Nixon's guilt or innocence – he was given a rough time. As he spoke, cars outside could be heard responding to signs which demonstrators (one of them in a Nixon mask and prison garb) had been holding all weekend – 'Honk for Impeachment'. Haig accurately described the last few days as a 'firestorm'. At one stage, Haig said, 'We chose Senator Stennis to listen to the [Watergate] tapes first of all because he's . . . ' 'Deaf', shouted a reporter. After the President's return from Camp David, his press secretary announced that he had decided to cancel the promised broadcast. It was a situation in which even the most sober commentators began to express doubts about the President's grasp on reality.

This atmosphere of official defensiveness and public suspicion provided a backcloth to the test of will between the two super-powers. The timetable of the drama went roughly as follows:

8 PM WEDNESDAY: The Soviet Ambassador, Anatoly Dobrynin, arrived at the State Department in Foggy Bottom, to deliver to Kissinger a note from the Soviet party leader, Brezhnev, endorsing Egypt's call for a Soviet–American military presence in the Middle East. The two men had a brief discussion in which Kissinger made clear American objections (John Scali was publicly expressing the same views at the UN at about the same time). For American policy makers, the idea of sending troops was uniquely abhorrent. With an attitude coloured by 'peace-keeping' in Asia, they thought in terms of a commitment powerful enough to intervene in the fighting by main force. One American official later suggested that twenty to thirty thousand men was a minimum for such an operation. Whether the Russians ever meant any such thing is unclear – certainly they later settled for a 'police force' of merely deterrent of emollient proportions. The effect, in

any case, was to conjure up in Washington fears of an open-ended, Vietnam-style involvement on the ground.

10.45 PM: Dobrynin returned to see Kissinger with another message from Brezhnev. This note, which has been variously described as brutal, threatening and rough, triggered the crisis. Its threat was implied rather than actual. According to officials who read it, the content was: 'We strongly urge that we both send forces to enforce the ceasefire, and if you do not, we may be obliged to consider acting alone.' (Lord Cromer, the British ambassador in Washington, who subsequently had the note read over to him, remembers the language as being tougher; but the message was essentially the same.) Dobrynin left this second note with Kissinger without obtaining a reply.

10.50 PM: Kissinger telephoned President Nixon, who was then in his upper floor living quarters at the White House. Kissinger suggested that the US response to the latest Soviet communication should be military as well as political. Nixon agreed, asking Kissinger to work out the details and keep him informed.

11 PM: Kissinger convened a meeting in the Situation Room in the White House basement. This was later described as a National Security Council meeting; in fact only a committee of the NSC was present. Normally it is a five-man body but the chairman, the President, stayed upstairs. Another absentee was former Vice-President Spiro Agnew, who had recently resigned from office and been fined for income tax evasion in an uncontested suit. Those who attended *ex officio* were James R. Schlesinger, the Defence Secretary, and Kissinger himself, in his dual capacity as Secretary of State and the President's National Security Affairs Adviser. An NSC aide was later quoted as saying: 'Officially the meeting consisted of Kissinger, Kissinger and Schlesinger.'

The meeting was also attended in an advisory capacity by William E. Colby, the new director of the CIA, and Admiral Thomas Moorer, chairman of the Joint Chiefs of Staff.

The elements they had to consider were not simply the two Brezhnev notes. By this time there had been some feedback from John Scali about the 'ambiguous' position taken at the UN by his Soviet opposite number, Yakov Malik. There was also the electronic intelligence which had been passed on to Colby by the National Security Agency, which has access to satellite surveillance. This also was ambiguous. That day's information indicated the presence of seven Soviet landing craft and two ships with troop helicopters on their decks in Eastern Mediterranean waters. Signals had been monitored indicating that seven divisions of Soviet airborne troops weré on standby alert. One division had been put on a higher alert level: it was ready to move on call.

These factors in themselves were not specially alarming; there had been previous Soviet alerts during the war and even more landing craft in the area. The one new element was the evidence that the Soviet air force had pulled back most of the large transports, which had been used to airlift supplies to Egypt and Syria, to their home bases in the Soviet Union. The supplies had been flown from bases in Hungary. Just before the NSC meeting was convened, several Antonov-22s were reported heading for Cairo. Some Pentagon officials feared that these might be the vanguard of a massive airlift of Soviet troops. An alternative reading of the pullback of Soviet aircraft from Hungary could have been that the main job of resupply had already been accomplished and the Soviet Union – in accordance with the Kissinger–Brezhnev understanding of the previous Sunday– was running down its operation. When the AN-22s did land in Cairo, it was discovered that they were not carrying troops but supplies as usual. But by then, the United States had taken another step up the ladder.

11.30 PM: After sifting through the evidence, Kissinger and Schlesinger decided that a response was necessary to prevent any precipitate move by the Soviet Union. The one they chose was Defence Condition Three, one above normal, and one below that which obtained during the Cuban missile crisis. (There are five 'defence readiness conditions' in the American military lexicon: 5. Forces not in state of readiness, troops lack training. 4. Normal peacetime position as troops undergo training. 3. Troops placed on standby and awaiting orders. All leave cancelled. 2. Troops ready for combat. 1. Troops deployed for combat.) They also decided that it should be a world-wide alert, involving virtually all the 2.2 million US military men dotted around the globe. The argument later advanced for a global rather than a selective alert was the need to convince the Soviet Union totally of America's determination to avoid involvement on the ground.

11.35 PM: On receiving the necessary order from Schlesinger, Admiral Moorer transmitted it to the various service chiefs, who then passed it on to commands and sub-units throughout the world. 'All Commands' read the order, 'Assume Def Con Three.' The only significant exception to the general alert involved the Strategic Air Command (SAC) tanker planes along the US to Israel airlift route. These maintained their middle Atlantic patterns instead of being sent north for possible refuelling of long-range B-52 bombers.

MIDNIGHT : Bellevue, Nebraska, where the worldwide nerve centre of the SAC is located, was unusually animated. It had been a normal day at the base for most of the 11,653 military personnel and their 25,659 dependents. The base newspaper *Air Pulse* featured plans for Halloween celebrations on Thursday. Around midnight, as Admiral Moorer's alert order came through, hundreds of air force personnel – members of SAC's battle staff – were awakened and summoned to the command centre in a seven-storey building, four of the floors underground. Officers filed into balcony seats as computers began to churn out reams of data on weather at potential targets and information on the readiness of the 162,000 SAC personnel worldwide. Around the world, SAC bombers were drawn up on the tarmac, with crews waiting on board for orders to take off. Sixty B-52s were ordered to return from Guam to the United States.

I AM THURSDAY, OCTOBER 25 : Lord Cromer, the British ambassador, was informed of the contents of Brezhnev's note and the American alert decision. Cromer passed the information to Sir Alec Douglas-Home in London by breakfast time. He was the first foreign minister to be informed of America's action.

1.30 AM : Schlesinger returned to the Pentagon where he gave further orders to buttress the alert. The aircraft carrier *John F. Kennedy* with its Phantom squadrons was sent from the Atlantic to the Mediterranean. The 15,000-man 82nd Airborne Division at Fort Bragg, North Carolina, known as the 'quick reaction force', was told to be ready to move by 6.00 am.

2.00 AM : Other NATO members were informed of the alert through the Brussels office of the North Atlantic Council. Pentagon officials later claimed that the various European capitals were not informed until much later in the morning because of a failure in the Brussels communications machinery. (At the headquarters of NATO's Northern Europe Command in Oslo, senior officers were unaware of the alert as late as Thursday lunchtime – more than seven hours after it had been given.)

2.30 AM : Back at the State Department, Kissinger finished the draft of his reply to Brezhnev's note. He warned that the United States could not tolerate unilateral action by the Soviet Union in the Middle East, and that any attempt to introduce troops into the war zone would damage the cause of world peace. He also called for further joint action in the United Nations. Kissinger's reply apparently made no specific mention of the alert – it was assumed that the Russians had already found out about this through their own electronic intelligence. It is probable that

President Nixon, who later said that he was in direct contact with Brezhnev through the night, kept him informed.

3.00 AM: Schlesinger and Moorer completed details on the 'final package' of the alert. Kissinger went back to the White House and reported on the moves that had been made. President Nixon, in his capacity as Commander in Chief, formally ratified the initiatives of his Secretary of State and Defense Secretary.

3.30 AM: Kissinger went to bed.

The alert was on all the early morning news programmes in the United States, although there was no official Pentagon or White House announcement. A soldier from a missile base in Montana said, according to NBC, that it was the first time since 1962 that the silos had been put in such readiness. The news had 'leaked', much to Kissinger's chagrin. He later said privately that he had expected some of the individual alerts – like that of the 82nd Airborne – to become public but that he was unprepared for full revelation of the whole bag of tricks.

After the traumas of the weekend it all seemed too much. Initial reaction amongst the sceptical in Washington was either that the President had finally flipped or that it was all a fraud, to distract attention from Watergate. At that stage nobody outside the tiny group of decision-makers knew that it was Kissinger who had managed the details of the crisis and that Nixon had simply rubber-stamped his decisions.

Kissinger met the press on Thursday (the President postponing another scheduled conference on Watergate). Shortly after midday, he came into the big briefing room at the State Department to explain how, literally overnight, the policy of detente had been apparently turned into one of nuclear confrontation. He was bitterly dismissive of suggestions that the alert might have been prompted by domestic considerations – although in answer to one question about whether he suspected the Soviet Union of taking advantage of Nixon's Watergate problem, he gave the cryptic reply: 'One cannot have crises of authority in a society for a period of months without paying a price somewhere along the line'. (Later, Schlesinger and other Pentagon officials conceded that Watergate had played a part in the decision – not to distract domestic attention from Nixon's problems, but to show the world that despite the crisis at home America could still act firmly and decisively.)

Kissinger was at pains to minimise the confrontational aspects of the affair, nor did he level any specific charge at the Russians. 'It is,' he said, 'the ambiguity of some of the [Soviet] actions and communications, and certain readiness measures that were observed, that caused the President, at a special meeting of the National Security Council last night, at 3.00 am, to order certain precautionary measures to be taken by the United States.' He reminded listeners that both the Soviet Union and the United States had nuclear arsenals 'capable of annihilating humanity' and that they both had 'a special duty to see to it that confrontations are kept within bounds'. Indeed, Kissinger so smoothed over the crisis that it was difficult to appreciate that he had been primarily responsible for putting the superpower debate on a nuclear footing. One reason may have been that the Soviet threat – whether real or imagined – already seemed a thing of the past.

Within the Security Council a compromise had been evolved that would exclude the permanent members of the Council – and therefore the two superpowers – from the immediate peacekeeping operation. As one delegate put it: 'No-one within the UN had fully digested the problems until it seemed solved.' The crucial resolution, sponsored by eight non-permanent members of the Council – Guinea, India, Indonesia, Kenya, Panama, Peru, Sudan, and Yugoslavia – endorsed the use of a UN emergency force, excluding troops from the Big Five (the US, Russia, China, Britain and France). It has been hammered out in a series of discussions between John Scali, the US representative, and delegates from the nonaligned nations. The final piece slotted into place during the delay caused by Kissinger's press conference, when Malik called Moscow and obtained Soviet approval. The Secretary-General, Dr Waldheim, received unanimous approval to transfer forces of Austria, Finland and Sweden, then serving the UN in Cyprus, to the Middle East war zone.

Did the alert signify a real threat or was it, as Brezhnev later implied, a panic response to 'fantastic rumours'? After the event both superpowers peddled 'off the record' briefing stories about how each had been doublecrossed by the other. Neither seemed entirely credible. The American version had it that Sadat's October 24 call for US and Soviet troops had been a put-up job. Both Sadat and Brezhnev knew that the United States could never accede to such a request; it was simply a device to out-manœuvre the west at the UN and provide a cover which would enable the Soviet Union to establish a large presence in the Middle East.

The Soviet version of the doublecross was even more lurid. They claimed that they had been betrayed at two levels. First, Kissinger had deceived them, by flying from Moscow to Israel and hinting to Golda Meir that no harm would ensue if the Israeli armies pressed their military advantage after agreeing to the ceasefire. Second, they claimed that there had been an agreement to send American and Soviet troops to monitor the ceasefire; once formal UN Security Council permission was obtained.

The second allegation flatly contradicts the American assertion that the question of sending troops was never raised in Moscow. And if it had been, it seems hardly likely that Kissinger, who had spent over four years disentangling America from Vietnam, would have contemplated a similar involvement in the Middle East. Nor is there any evidence to suggest that Kissinger gave the Israelis any encouragement to break the ceasefire. On the contrary, Kissinger apparently received the news of the post-ceasefire encirclement of the Egyptian Third Army with great dismay. (So much for a limited Israeli defeat.)

It would be a remarkable comment on the nature of the East–West detente if either partner really tried to swindle the other in such dangerous circumstances. What is perhaps most likely is that a spectacular misunderstanding arose because the whole question of how the truce was to actually be organized was never properly discussed. Carving up the world between them, demonstrating that the United Nations were powerless without their prior agreement, confident that their proteges were utterly dependent on them, the two superpowers could not apparently permit themselves to think that Israeli and Egyptian soldiers and politicians might have wills of their own. For Kissinger's belief appears to have been that the ceasefire could simply be imposed by the two powers principally responsible for the supply of arms. From this simple miscalculation, the steps that led to the global confrontation were unnervingly logical.

There were those who thought all was well that ended comparatively well. 'He stirred. We growled. He heard it and backed down,' said a satisfied American official after a day on the brink. But it was only a fancy way of admitting that the superpowers could not arbitrate peace and war among their Middle Eastern client states without running themselves into the same, or even greater, risks of conflict.

With the establishment of the UN emergency force, the threat of confrontation between the superpowers ebbed away. Russian observers did arrive in Egypt before the weekend, but they numbered less than a hundred and were armed only with brief-cases. They reported demurely to the UNTSO headquarters in Cairo with offers of assistance. America announced its willingness to send similar civilian 'representatives', if these were requested by the UN; and by Friday the alert was already being phased down. In a belated press conference, President Nixon emphasized that the world had passed through its 'most difficult' crisis since 1962 but spoke up for the strength of the Soviet–American relationship. 'With all the criticism of detente,' he said, 'I would suggest that without detente we might have had a major conflict in the Mideast. With detente we avoided it.' He seemed less enthusiastic about 'our European friends' who, he felt, 'hadn't been as cooperative as they might have been in attempting to help us work out the Mideast settlement'.

While they refrained from public pronouncements, most European governments made it clear that they were finding the switchback of superpower diplomacy a little too hair-raising for their liking. At the same time, officials in the Pentagon and the State Department were putting on record their irritation at Europe's failure to rally round the American flag in the Middle East. Of all their NATO allies, only Portugal won marks for good behaviour – the granting of landing rights in the Azores to US planes resupplying Israel with war material.

All the other allies turned down requests for help with the airlift. America says that Heath rejected a personal request from Nixon for rights to land at Akrotiri in Cyprus; British sources maintain, with convincing relief, that the request was never made. West Germany cooperated in the early stages but subsequently withdrew its assistance when the US began to draw on strategic reserves of equipment stored on German soil. Greece and Turkey were deemed especially culpable by US officials – they not only barred American aircraft but raised no public objection to Soviet transport jets passing through their air space loaded with tanks and bombs en route for Egypt and Syria.

'We were struck,' said the State Department spokesman, Robert McCloskey, on October 26, 'by a number of our allies going to some lengths to separate themselves publicly from us. It raised questions as to how that action on their part can be squared with what the Europeans have often referred to as indivisibility on questions of security.' But perceptions of interest in the Middle East had long since ceased to be indivisible. In part, the reasons were political. Most European powers had become irritated by Israel's seeming recalcitrance in the face of 'world opinion' as expressed through the UN, and were inclined to blame Israel for the failure of previous attempts to negotiate a workable peace settlement. America, on the other hand, tended to see Israel in geopolitical terms as the only reliable ally in the Middle East, vital in the context of keeping Soviet power in the area in check.

But the more fundamental reason for transatlantic differences was economic: Europe imported seventy per cent of its oil from Arab countries whereas the United States was dependent on the Middle East for only eleven per cent of its consumption. An oil ban, of the kind that Arabs had just shown themselves capable of imposing, could literally bankrupt many European economies, while being no more than a mild embarrassment to Americans. Europe was finding that it simply could not· afford the consequences of total support for US policy in the Middle East.

4: The plight of the Third Army

The accommodation reached by the superpowers was not immediately reflected in the actions of their clients in the battle zone. On Thursday there was renewed fighting in the Suez area and once again the UN observers sent from Cairo failed to establish any satisfactory ceasefire line. A UN patrol, which had set out from the Israeli side, did make it to Port Suez but confessed, on arrival, that they had no very clear idea of where they should take up permanent positions.

The plight of the 20,000 men of the Egyptian Third Army was desperate. They had been cut off for four days and on the most generous estimate could not expect to hold out for another week. Some military experts thought that another three days would be their limit. On Thursday afternoon, the Israelis underlined the superiority of their position by announcing that they had agreed, on Cairo's request, to permit the shipment of blood plasma for the treatment of the wounded in the Third Army, but on condition that it came from the Red Cross headquarters in Tel Aviv. Earlier the Israelis had turned back three attempts – two by the Red Crescent (the Egyptian equivalent of the Red Cross) and one by the International Committee of the Red Cross – to send convoys with medical supplies down the Cairo–Suez road. No mention of the shipment from Tel Aviv was made on Cairo radio. Sadat's government, under pressure to show that it had not fought the war for nothing – or worse than nothing – was not about to tell its citizens that the succour of its wounded military heroes depended on the enemy's grace and favour.

Cairo was still claiming that a remarkable victory had been won. Egyptian spokesmen harked back to the triumph of the fall of the Bar-Lev defences – 'considered stronger than the Maginot and Siegfried lines' – denounced the US supply operation and remained studiously vague about Israeli 'infiltration' into Egyptian territory. Arab propaganda made the Israelis even more determined to press home their advantage around Suez. The

An Israeli rabbi tags the dead. The rate of deaths was even heavier than in the War of Independence of 1948–1949

influential commentator, Zeev Schiff, put the official line very precisely in Thursday's *Ha'aretz*: 'The Egyptians are going to try, with the aid of the Russians, to turn the resounding defeat of their Third Army into a victory. This should not fluster us. We must not make a false step and lose this card from our hand. We have no obligation to permit supplies to reach this army. We must remember that it is an enemy army which has shed much of our blood and killed many of our sons, and that any minute may bring a renewal of the fighting.

'This is not the same as the Six-Day War, when Egyptian soldiers retreating in the desert were given drinking water after their defeat. Providing the Third Army with water at this point would mean strengthening it and helping to turn it into a well-consolidated base from which future aggression could threaten us. What we should do is to allow the Third Army men to return to Egypt, after leaving their arms in Sinai.

'If they want to drink water, let them go home and drink.'

But the Arabs held two cards of their own. Neither was of great military significance, but both had a strong emotional content. The first was the maintenance of a naval blockade on the Bab-el-Mandeb Straits at the southern entrance to the Red Sea which the Israelis viewed as an act of war and a violation of the ceasefire. The second, and much more explosive, was the question of prisoners of war.

In accordance with the Geneva Convention of 1949, the Israelis had regularly forwarded to the Red Cross details of Arab prisoners captured. These showed that by the morning of October 24 the Israelis held 1,300 POWs – 988 Egyptians, 295 Syrians, 12 Iraqis and 5 Moroccans. The reporting procedure on the Arab side had been notably more negligent. Egypt had reported only 48 Israelis captured, and Syria, which had exhibited captured Israeli soldiers on television, had reported none. Israel's estimate of its missing presumed captured numbered almost 400 and the first atrocity stories had already appeared in the Israeli press.

There were well authenticated reports from the Syrian front of graves being found in which Israeli soldiers, blindfolded and with their hands manacled, had been buried after being shot. Israel had the disagreeable impression that the two Arab countries were deliberately avoiding their obligations under the Geneva Convention in order to create uncertainty about the fate of their POWs while Egypt was uncertain about the fate of its Third Army.

Friday, October 26, was the first day of the Qorban Bairam holiday, which marks the end of Ramadan. It is normally a festive occasion, but the celebrations in Cairo were unusually subdued as government offices and factories were told to continue working as usual. The tone of the Egyptian media on the subject of the war was reassuring rather than euphoric. *Al Gomhouria* warned against the hope of quick solutions, noting that 'the popular war of liberation is a continuous one'. Mohamed Heikal now urged the clearly reluctant readers of *Al Ahram* to 'rally round the flag and at the side of the decision maker'. Sadat, he explained, had to agree a ceasefire because Egypt found itself 'up against direct American intervention. . . . The United States gave Israel weapons which she herself has not used in action.' Heikal also sought to allay popular suspicions of superpower collusion at Egypt's expense. In reality, a new phase of superpower collusion had just begun – but it was to be at Israel's expense.

While the other fronts stayed quiet, the encircled Third Army made a last desperate attempt to improve its position. Under cover of tank and artillery fire, the Egyptians attempted to take control of the pontoon bridges south of the Little Bitter Lake and to lay a new one across the canal south of Port Suez. After a battle lasting three hours, in which the Israeli air force played a prominent part, the attempt to establish an east-west linkup between the Egyptian forces was foiled and the Arabs' new bridge lay in ruins. The day also brought more positive evidence of the disintegration of Third Army morale as the Israelis rounded up numerous small bands of soldiers – often without a fight – who had detached themselves from the main force and were trying to make their own way back to the Egyptian heartland. Some of the

Egyptians carried leaflets advising them to surrender which had been dropped by Israeli planes over Third Army positions earlier in the week.

Again, the interests of the United States and the Soviet Union coincided. With one eye on the possibilities for a longterm settlement in the Middle East, Kissinger no more welcomed the prospect of the Third Army's collapse than the men in the Kremlin. ('Let me tell you something about my view of solving disputes.' Kissinger later told Heikal in a revealing interview. 'If we wish to solve a critical dispute the point from which we should start should be one at which each party will feel that it has got something'.) If the Third Army went under, any chance of negotiation would be dead – the humiliation for Egypt, and the sense of betrayal among the Arabs generally, would be too great. On Friday evening, Kissinger initiated an intensive round of diplomatic negotiations to prevent this.

He contacted Israel, Egypt and the Soviet Union directly, although Waldheim was kept informed. Shortly after midnight a formula was evolved to which all parties could agree, though Israel's consent was given with extreme reluctance. The State Department was able to announce that as a result of its 'good offices' agreement had been reached between Egypt and Israel that 'would permit a convoy of men and supplies' to go through to the Egyptian Third Army, under the aegis of the UN and the Red Cross. The term 'good offices' apparently masked some very tough talking between Kissinger and the Israeli ambassador in Washington, Simcha Dimitz. According to Israeli sources, its government was informed by America that the Soviet Union was still fundamentally committed to saving the beleaguered Egyptian force. It was implied that Israeli intransigence in the Suez area was a danger to international stability, as the United States could not back down from its publicly expressed opposition to Soviet troop involvement. As a result of the brink-manship of the preceding days, the Israeli government found itself unsubtly landed with the custody of world peace. Speaking bluntly, and more than a little angrily, about how the arrangement to resupply the Egyptians came about, Lieutenant-General David Elazar, Israel's Chief of Staff, said: 'We were compelled to agree. It was imposed on us to arrange the convoy.'

The guns fell silent on both fronts on Saturday, October 27 – twenty-four days after the outbreak of hostilities. Even then, the portents were not wholly encouraging: fifty-six Finnish soldiers, members of the UN emergency force who had been flown from Cyprus to Cairo on Friday evening, spent an ill-tempered day held up at an Israeli roadblock on their way to Suez. The local Israeli commanders in Suez itself were openly incredulous at the

Egyptian prisoners of war packed 140 to a truck after the fighting around
Suez town on 'ceasefire' day

idea of a reprieve for the Third Army. It was well after midnight
before details of the supply operation were finally ironed out by
Israeli and Egyptian military chiefs; they met at a milestone on
the Suez–Cairo highway sixty-three miles from the Egyptian
capital – Kilometre 101. On Sunday morning, the first vehicles in
a hundred-truck convoy, moving in groups of ten and operated
by UN personnel, were directed on to the Egyptian lines after
inspection by Israeli troops. The Third Army – and Egypt's face
– had been saved.

The Israeli leadership did not feel inclined to disguise its
irritation with this anti-climactic end to its Egyptian campaign.
Interviewed on Sunday by the American CBS team, Mrs Meir
ended up by taking charge. 'I want to tell you something', said
the Israeli Premier. 'Sadat must, I think, be given time to enjoy
his defeat. And not immediately, by political manipulations, turn
that into a victory. Not because I want him defeated or humili-
ated. But for God's sake, he started a war, our people are killed,
his in the many thousands are killed, and he has been defeated.
And then by political arrangements, he is handed a victory and
has become or thinks he has become a hero in the eyes of the
Egyptian people.'

The brute statistics of war indicated that the Israelis had won.
According to estimates made by the Defense Department in

217

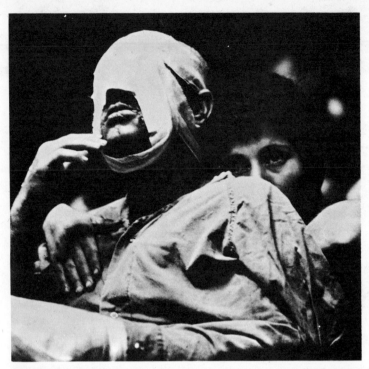

Bandaged soldier is visited by his wife in a Tel Aviv hospital. The heavy casualty rate prompted angry questions in Israel

Washington, which tended to be more reliable than those published by the combatants during the conflict, Israel's casualty figures were less than a third of those sustained by their Arab opponents – 5,000, compared with 7,700 for Egypt and 7,700 Syrians. The number of prisoners of war held by Israel was almost embarrassingly large. In the last week of the fighting it had swollen to almost 9,000, of whom over 8,000 were Egyptians. The number of Israeli POW's held by Egypt and Syria was less than 400. The combined Arab forces were estimated to have lost about 2,000 tanks and some 450 planes; compared with Israel's loss of 800 tanks and 115 aircraft. In terms of territory controlled, Israel also had an advantage; in Syria it occupied positions well in advance of the 1967 line, and its west bank holding in Egypt more than made up for the Egyptian gains on the east. Yet it was a victory that had little savour for a nation grown accustomed to clear-cut military achievement.

The cost to Israel in lives had been greater than in any conflict since 1948. The figures subsequently released revealed that 2,412 Israelis had been killed in the fighting, more than twice the number killed in the Six-Day War. But the Six-Day War had been one of rapid and triumphant advance, at the end of which Israel had made huge territorial gains – including Jerusalem, which had an emotional value greater than any territory.

The real comparison is with the War of Independence, in which 6,200 Israelis were killed. On the face of it, those losses were much higher. But they were spread over a much longer period. Allowing for the ceasefires which interrupted hostilities, there were probably some 240 days of fighting in the War of Independence. In crude terms, then, Israel lost on average twenty-five killed for each day of fighting.

In 1973, losses ran at the rate of 105 killed per day up to October 27, when fighting stopped on both fronts. Allowing for the fact that the Jewish population is now five times larger, this suggests that the cost in lives was roughly comparable. Certainly the Yom Kippur War was more like the War of Independence than the campaigns of the fifties and sixties.

Moreover, there was little hope of early demobilization for Israel's citizen soldiers, as their leaders talked an uneasy truce around Kilometre 101. Major General Aharon Yariv, leader of Israel's negotiating team, was greeted by his soldiers each time he emerged from the UN tent with shouts of 'Can we go home?' He could only shake his head. Egypt might have failed to impose a war of attrition on Israel, but the attrition on nerves of the peace was only faintly more bearable. To assist young mothers, the Israeli education service set up seminars in the elementary schools to help explain to their children why their fathers were so long at the war. A child psychologist advising one such group in Jerusalem said: 'Make it simple. Even if it isn't.'

Section V

Below left: Captured Syrians, and (right) captured Israelis, after the Golan fighting. Syria ignored the Geneva convention, and many Israeli prisoners of war were reported tortured or killed.

'A question which has nothing to do with you'

1: The forgotten Palestinians

October 25, 1973, was the day of America's nuclear alert; and the day when the United Nations decided to send a peacekeeping force to the Middle East to supervise the ceasefire. It was also the day when a disturbing UN report on the refugee camps which care for more than 600,000 Palestinians was published. The report made little impact; by now, the war had pushed the problems of the Palestinians right off-stage.

The Palestinian commandos understood this perfectly. One day during the war, in the southern Lebanese town of Tyre, the funeral of a dead commando was taking place. A cheap American saloon carried the body; armed men in camouflage somewhat unsteadily rode shotgun on the boot of the makeshift hearse. Files of commandos marched behind, carrying automatic rifles, reversed at odd angles. An incessant chant against the Israelis crackled through a converted Japanese stereo set from a loudspeaker van.

Suddenly, the double sonic boom of two Israeli fighters was heard. The cortège stopped. The commandos looked up, to see the smoke trails of two SAM rockets which had been fired at the aircraft, above the Golan Heights. The rockets exploded, missing the fighters. Three minutes later, the aircraft turned, and passed Tyre, flying out to sea beyond the harbour wall. The funeral moved on again.

'We're irrelevant in all this', said one commando, 'but it's supposed to be for us.'

The feeling was shared by many of the Palestinians living in the sixty-three refugee camps run by the UN Relief and Works Agency (UNRWA). But even though the Palestinians were left out of the 1973 war, they could not be left out by the subsequent peace. Any settlement that did not involve them would result in a continuance of the guerrilla war. And the UNRWA report, published on October 25, described a situation where Palestinian support for guerrilla warfare was certain to increase.

UNRWA, it said, faced 'a cash crisis' at the beginning of 1974. The projected deficit for 1974 – $10 million – is roughly what the war was using up every half-hour of its twenty-day duration. But it is enough for a cut-back in UNRWA's work which, the report concluded, 'would cause more hardship, frustration and bitterness among the Palestine refugees ... and would heighten tension and encourage further violence in the region.'

There are about two-and-a-half million Palestinian Arabs living outside Israel. A million live under Israeli occupation in the Gaza Strip or the West Bank of the Jordan; 900,000 live on the East Bank of the Jordan, and another half million live in Syria and the Lebanon. The rest are scattered around the world: 15,000 are estimated to live in West Germany, and 7,000 in the United States. Altogether, three out of five Palestinian Arabs (that is, one-and-a-half million) have been given refugee status by the UN, though by no means all refugees live in UN camps. Most refugees left their homes during the 1948–9 war; the rest left in 1967.

In one sense the Palestinians did have a choice: the Jordan government had offered full citizenship to Palestinians who wished to settle in Jordan. But more than one third of the refugees in UNRWA's care live in camps in Jordan, and very few ever decide to give up their refugee status. Partly this is because the camps inculcate a rigid sense of national identity. Until the 1973 war, the demand of all Palestinian leaders – whatever their tactical differences – was the establishment of a Palestinian state with the same borders as the old mandate territory.

Inside the camps the children are brought up to share their parents' bitterness. UNRWA's largest refugee camp is Baka'a, twelve miles north of Amman. It cares for 50,000 Palestinians. Eight-year-old Rashid is typical of the children growing up in the camp. During the recent war, he told a *Sunday Times* correspondent: 'I am from Haifa. My home is in Haifa. I live in a white house by the sea. We have orange groves behind my home.' Rashid, however, has never seen Haifa: his family left in 1948.

After the war, it seemed that for a permanent peace settlement to be successful, it must embody two symmetrical concessions: Israeli acceptance of a Palestinian Arab state, and Palestinian acceptance of a Jewish state. But the only parts of Palestine which Israel was conceivably likely to relinquish were the occupied Gaza Strip and West Bank. Compared with the dream of returning to orange groves in Haifa, it was bound to seem to Palestinians a meagre reward.

The 1973 war, although not directly involving the Palestinians, led to the first signs that some of their exiled leaders would accept just this. An article appeared in *The Times* on November 16, by Said Hammami, the London representative of the Palestine Liberation Organization (PLO). He accepted the possibility of a negotiated settlement with Israel, with a Palestinian state consisting of Gaza and the Jordan West Bank. Such a state, he wrote, 'would lead to the emptying and closing down of the refugee camps, thereby drawing out the poison at the heart of the Arab–Israeli enmity.'

The article, though carefully presented as a personal view, was written after close consultation with other PLO leaders. It represented the views of many PLO officials who wanted to exploit the new opportunities which the war opened up. Before 1973, there was no immediate prospect of Palestinian Arab control over any part of Palestine – so there was no incentive to offer territorial compromises. But after the 1973 war, Egypt and the Soviet Union both held out the hope of a Gaza-West Bank state, following Israeli withdrawal – and made their support for the idea conditional on Palestinian acceptance of the compromise.

The immediate imperative for the PLO leaders was to exclude Jordan from the opening moves towards the creation of an independent Palestinian state. King Hussein had traditionally been as reluctant as Israeli leaders to accept the idea. Although he had been the only Arab leader to come up with any concrete proposals on the Palestinian issue, his 1971 offer significantly had envisaged a Palestine–Jordan federation, with the federal capital in Amman. For Hussein there would be immense practical advantages in such a solution: it would link the east bank of the Jordan to the more prosperous west bank; it would also re-establish Hussein's leadership over the Palestinians.

But few West Bank Palestinians seemed to like the idea. A survey conducted shortly before the 1973 war by the Israel Institute of Applied Social Research (with field work done by West Bank Arabs) found that only 8 per cent supported Hussein's idea. A larger minority – 19 per cent – preferred a return to direct rule by Jordan; 44 per cent wanted an Independent Palestinian State; most of the others thought the West Bank should be placed under international control. These figures – even more than most opinion polls – must be treated with great caution; but the survey is the best guide we have to West Bank opinion.

In the aftermath of the war, Jordanian officials were anxious to defer as long as possible the embarrassing problem of facing the demands of the Palestinians. 'We must first secure the end to the occupation by the Israelis', a government minister told the *Sunday Times*. If Jordan succeeded in recovering the West Bank without first reaching an agreement with the Palestinians, Hussein would obviously be in a strong position: the future of the West Bank would then have to be negotiated directly with him, rather than in the wider context of an international peace conference. The point was not lost on the Palestinians.

It was partly for this reason that after the war many Palestinians suddenly espoused the idea of an international peace conference:

Kissinger with Morocco's King Hassan in Rabat – first stop on his November peacemaking tour of the Middle East.

if they could participate at some stage as an independent delegation, they would have their best chance in years of out-flanking Hussein. At Algiers in late November, a meeting of Arab leaders (with the notable absence of King Hussein and Colonel Gadaffi) recognized the PLO as the sole voice of the Palestinians. Amman was virtually removed from the Palestinian equation. But behind the scenes, there were strong pressures – especially from Moscow – for the PLO to become a more broadly based movement.

Whatever happened, it would take time to bring about a Palestinian settlement. But meanwhile, there were immediate problems which could not wait for a peace conference.

The end of the fighting had left Israeli troops on the west bank of the Suez Canal, the 20,000 troops of Egypt's Third Army cut off on the east bank, and both Israel and Egypt holding prisoners of war. It was an unstable situation, as President Sadat warned on October 31, in his first press conference since the beginning of the war: 'I cannot afford to stand with my hands tied', he said; Egypt's military leaders were pressing him to resume fighting, and he needed quick political dividends from his decision to accept the UN ceasefire resolutions of the previous week. Above all, he wanted to get supplies through to the stranded

Third Army. Quick action, however, was precisely what Golda Meir did not want. As she had said in her CBS television interview three days earlier, 'Sadat must be given time to enjoy his defeat'.

Although there is no evidence that either Egypt or Israel then intended to resume fighting, it took no great foresight to realize that unless some deal could be made concerning Egypt's Third Army, and also the prisoners of war, the ceasefire could break down almost of its own accord: the dangers of a skirmish escalating into general fighting were considerable. Once again, it was the peripatetic Henry Kissinger who knitted the deal together.

On the evening of Tuesday, November 6, he arrived in Cairo. The fact of the visit was itself significant, for Egypt had severed diplomatic relations with the United States in the wake of the 1967 war, and few people expected a swift reconciliation between Egypt and her enemy's main arms supplier. But the next morning the surprise happened: Kissinger and Sadat appeared together for an impromptu press conference, looking for all the world as if they were long lost friends. Egypt and the US were to resume diplomatic relations. Sadat said he would like Kissinger to remain a mediator in the Middle East conflict. And when Kissinger said 'I think we are moving towards peace', Sadat immediately chimed in: 'I think I agree with him.'

Sadat was fascinated by Kissinger – the insecure, mercurial man apparently responding to the confidence and certainty of the other. Sadat saw Kissinger without his advisers – and agreed to Kissinger's plan almost without demur. Sadat was later criticized for this by his staff. But he explained: 'I liked Kissinger very much. I regard him as a friend. And I don't like to haggle with my friends. Besides, I wanted to show him that I am a very very reasonable man – unlike Mrs Meir. She will haggle over every point. So now I have nothing more to give Kissinger. I have given him everything I have. Now I want something in return.'

For the moment, the best thing Kissinger could offer was a more stable ceasefire: Assistant Secretary of State Joseph Sisco flew to Israel to win Israel's support for a plan which Kissinger had hammered out with Sadat. On Friday, November 9, the day before Israel finally accepted the plan, the terms were published. Israel was to allow non-military supplies through to Egypt's Third Army; UN troops would take over the Israeli checkpoints on the Cairo–Suez road; there would be a full exchange of prisoners between Israel and Egypt; and direct talks between Israeli and Egyptian officials would begin 'to settle the question of the return to the October 22 positions'.

On Sunday, November 11, Israel's General Yariv and Egypt's General Gamasy met at the Kilometre 101 checkpoint to discuss how to implement the Kissinger plan. At first, they were deadlocked. Israel insisted on inspecting the supplies going to Suez town to make sure no arms were smuggled through. But by the following Wednesday agreement was reached: the Israelis could not have a checkpoint at the entrance to the town, but they could inspect the supplies at a nearby UN-controlled parking lot. On Thursday, November 15, the exchange of prisoners began, and the UN took over the Israeli checkpoints on the Cairo-Suez road. By November 22 the last of the 8,301 Egyptian and 241 Israeli prisoners were home.

The problem of the Israeli prisoners held by Syria was not so easily solved. As Israel was unsuccessfully trying to obtain from Damascus a list of POWs in accordance with the Geneva Convention, the bodies of twenty-eight captured soldiers were discovered in four places on Golan. The government at first, fearful of Syrian retaliation on surviving POWs, said nothing. Then on November 10, Israel officially complained to the International Red Cross. The photographs and circumstantial evidence Israel supplied clearly indicated that the soldiers had been murdered. The news led to riots in Israel by families of the 113 still listed as missing on the Syrian front.

Much of the pressure for a peace settlement between Israel and the Arabs came from outside the Middle East. There were powerful diplomatic reasons for the anxiety of the superpowers: the nuclear alert had rendered their detente distinctly fragile; and the tension between the United States and Europe had come close to undermining NATO. But what gave the need to arrange a peace agreement its peculiar urgency was the cut-back in Arab oil production, which immediately raised the alarming possibility of a major economic recession in Western Europe.

The key country in setting up the oil embargo was Saudi Arabia, which had been producing almost half of all Arab oil. King Feisal had traditionally been a pro-western emphatically anti-communist leader; but during the war, he acted in the light of the old Arab proverb: 'The enemy of my enemy is my friend; the friend of my enemy is my enemy.' Henry Kissinger received a far cooler reception from Feisal after the war than he had from Sadat. Feisal made it clear that he would prefer to stop production altogether than see any of the occupied land ceded to Israel. In particular, he said, Israel must give east Jerusalem back: he was, as defender of the Holy Places of Mecca and Medina, determined to pray in Jerusalem's Aksar Mosque before he died. In purely temporal terms, Feisal could afford to take a strong line: Saudi Arabia could live off its accumulated oil revenue reserves for more than three years without receiving another cent in royalties.

The relative economic importance to the West of the war itself, and of the oil embargo which only started to have a serious effect after the fighting stopped, can be gauged by those sensitive barometers of capitalism, stock exchange prices. The main indices in London, New York and Tokyo were all marginally higher at the end of the war than at the beginning. But in the following month, all three dropped sharply – New York and London by over 15%, Tokyo by 10% – and dropped again in December. The markets had taken little notice of the fluctuating fortunes on the battlefield; but they winced at each change, or hint of change, in Arab oil policy. So long as the new-found unity between President Sadat and King Feisal could be made to last, the Arabs had a potent weapon for aiming at the West.

The man who launched the fourth Arab–Israeli war, Egypt's General Ahmed Ismail, had few doubts about what the war had achieved. 'We have changed our whole image before the entire world', he told *Al Ahram*. 'Once it thought we were a motionless dead body. Now the world has awoken to the fact that we can move, can fight, and can achieve victory.' Ismail went on to argue that Israel's theory of secure borders was 'false and un-tenable: the Suez Canal was not a forbidding barrier; nor was the Bar-Lev line an adequate obstacle in the face of readiness to sacrifice.' The Arab blockade of the Bab-el-Mandeb straits at the southern entrance to the Red Sea had 'categorically proved that Sharm el Sheikh does not have the great importance Israel had thought, and on the basis of which it had built its ambitions in Sinai'.

Such words seemed almost perversely optimistic to Israeli diplomats, who pointed out that Egypt and Syria, setting out to to recover occupied territory by military means, had actually suffered a net loss by the time of the October ceasefire. Ismail, however, was talking about the recovery of credibility as much as of territory. There was no doubt that, by comparison with the debacle of 1967, the Arab armies – and more particularly Egypt's – had made a radically better showing. It was Arik Sharon who acknowledged it as succinctly as anyone: 'I have been fighting for twenty-five years', he said, 'and all the rest were just battles. This was a real war.'

In Ismail's view, 'the important thing in the administration of restricted wars is that any fighting army should be able to fulfil its calculated political objective while maintaining the largest bulk of its forces.' The Egyptian objective had been to create a new political situation by means of a limited military campaign, and that had certainly been achieved. Explaining in March 1973 why war was inevitable, Sadat had said the world had 'fallen asleep over the Mideast crisis'. In October, without doubt, there was an awakening. Exaggerating only slightly, Henry Kissinger told Mohammed Heikal of *Al Ahram* that he had not opened the Middle East file before October 6. 'I had imagined it could wait its turn.' By breaking through the Bar-Lev line, Ismail's army had remodelled the order of precedence in international affairs.

Of course, if General Sharon had managed to get the Israeli bridge across the canal on schedule, Egypt would have had difficulty in 'maintaining the largest bulk of its forces': given another thirty-six hours Bren Adan's tanks might have consummated the destruction of the Third Army. One strictly military lesson of the war was that the cumbrous Egyptian military machine was still inadequate in a fluid situation. Ismail believed he saw other points as well.

'I can almost state that the tanks have lost their mastery – not their value, but as I said their mastery – as a result of the development of anti-tank missiles.' The same, he thought, applied to manned aircraft, as a result of the development of anti-aircraft missiles. A good many military commentators extended Ismail's cautious assessment into declarations about the 'death of the tank' and the 'end of the manned aircraft'.

On this basis, the end of Israel's military advantage was foretold. But although the war did suggest that reassessment and re-equipment by both sides would be needed on a huge and costly scale, the balance sheet at the end was in reality a complex one.

Given time to deploy, infantry armed with large numbers of personal wire-guided missiles showed that they could effectively deny territory to a tank force. Equally, the battle on October 14 suggested that the Egyptian infantry had to have time to get themselves established before they could hope to stand up to tanks in a fast-moving daylight action. Speed of tactical response remained so much the key to battle situations as to suggest that the death of the tank had been prematurely announced.

Missiles powerful enough to inflict serious damage against the present generation of tanks have been pushed a long way in the direction of lightness and simplicity of handling (while going up, naturally, in cost). But the mathematics that govern the penetrating power of a HEAT charge, – used in slow-moving antitank missiles – mean that only a small increase in the tank's armour thickness would lead to a disproportionate increase in the weight of the missile and its launcher. A heavier missile would mean a vehicle launcher. And the battle of vehicle against vehicle inevitably becomes the battle of tank against tank.

The Israeli army will therefore need to strengthen its existing tank force with a substantial number of new tanks. There is clearly no possibility of buying the new Anglo-German main battle tank which is under development, and there could be problems even with the American xm-1. Israel may in that case be forced to design and build her next generation of tanks at home: the technical expertise is available, but the cost could be staggering.

At the same time, the Arab armies have to face the fact that the war demonstrated the almost total obsolescence of the t-54/55 which still makes up far the largest part of their armoured detachments. Even the few t-62s they were able to deploy suffered severely through the lack of any effective fire-control system. And neither t-55 nor t-62 could stand against the American tow missile which the Israeli infantry received part-way through the war. (The Israelis claimed virtually 100% success with it.)

Failing a peace agreement which really does establish something like normal relationships between Israel and Egypt, both sides will have to rebuild their armoured forces. Whichever suffers the more, both the Egyptian economy and the Israeli economy will suffer enormous distortions in the process. And the cost of the air war, too, will increase yet again. Manned aircraft were not rendered useless by anti-aircraft missiles – on the contrary, their infinitely flexible destructive capacity was demonstrated yet again. What did emerge was that manned aircraft needed the protection of complex electronic equipment in order to survive. And the rate of obsolescence of each generation of equipment seemed to be accelerating. The Israelis had broken off the aerial side of the 'War of Attrition' in 1970 with a clear lead in electronic counter-measures against missiles. On October 6, the Egyptians and Syrians went to war with new missiles that the Israelis could not counter effectively. Within ten days, by a combination of ground jamming, airborne ecm equipment, and attacks against missile sites, the Israelis had partially regained the initiative. But for how long?

2: The problems of peace

Israelis emerged from the sixteen-day war shocked by its cost in dead, wounded and missing, disillusioned and frightened by the early military setbacks, and with their suspicions of Arab intentions confirmed. But the realization that the war had brought about a complete change in Israel's way of life came slowly, and was shot through with paradox.

At the outset of the Arab attacks, there had been anger and a determination to 'get it over in a few days'. When this did not happen, there was bewildered acceptance of the Arab success but stubborn confidence that Israel's total victory was merely deferred. The Golan advance, followed by Sharon's crossing of the canal, precipitated a mood of euphoria, but it was short-lived. Israelis' fury, when the superpowers stepped in to prevent their army from routing the Egyptian forces, was the greater for their dawning awareness that the six years of apparently total supremacy in the battlefield were over. There would, from now on, be no clean victories.

The gloomy consensus in Israel was that, for all the pieties uttered by Henry Kissinger and the UN, the Arab states did not want to make a permanent peace – above all, now that they had discovered the oil weapon. There were reports, widely credited, that Sadat still maintained that Security Council Resolution 242 did not call upon Egypt to recognize Israel, but only its borders. On November 12–13, a poll by the Israel Institute of Social Research of Israel's urban Jews (about seventy per cent of the population) found that over four-fifths believed that the Arab goal had been the destruction of Israel, and that they would return to the attack in a year or two with the same purpose.

During the war, Israeli opinion inevitably had hardened against compromise. The Arab attack had strengthened the argument that Israel's security was dependent on the retention of some occupied territory – the expanse of Sinai had enabled the army to buy time with space. But with the publication of the casualty figures, anger focussed with unprecedented sharpness on the military leadership, which itself was indulging in mutual recrimination in the western press. The main target for popular criticism became Defence Minister Moshe Dayan – before the war, the Labour party's greatest electoral asset – who was blamed for complacency about Arab intentions. His 'maximalist' approach to the territorial issue also came in for reproach from those who argued that it was Israel's obduracy in the face of Arab demands for the return of their land which had made war inevitable.

The question of Israel's borders was already, before the war, central to the impending general election, which was postponed from October to December 31 as a result of the emergency. Then, the Labour coalition's compromise platform had favoured Moshe Dayan's policies. (The document enshrining this compromise, drawn up by the influential Minister without Portfolio, Israel Galili, envisaged a limited expansion of Israeli settlements in the occupied territories.) On September 10, Dayan had set out out his 'five no's' for *Ha'aretz*: Gaza must not be Egyptian or Golan Syrian; there must be no Palestinian state, and no Arab Jerusalem; and Israel would not desert the settlements it had founded in the occupied territories.

The territorial issue had perennially been linked to two arguments – often voiced by the same persons, but essentially separate. 'Greater Israel' implied both the size and the nature of the country. Even if Israel could afford, militarily and diplomatically, to retain control of all the territories captured in the 1967 war, it would mean creating a predominantly Arab Israel. Acceptance of this demographic fact was implied in the 'not one inch' platform of Arik Sharon's rightwing Likud coalition. But most Israelis, and their leaders, wished to maintain a Jewish state – and this very concept excluded the expansion of borders to their post-June 1967 ceasefire limits.

In some respects, the interim arrangements after 1967 had worked: the Arabs in Israel and the occupied territories were better off in economic terms; jobs were available, and they were relatively well-paid. And the labour pool provided in particular by the refugees in the Gaza Strip had proved invaluable to the Israeli economy. For all the fury that Israel's policy of creating Jewish settlements in the administered territories had aroused in the Arab world, some kind of working arrangement had been achieved by 1973.

During the fighting, two things had emerged from regular opinion surveys. One was that consistently while the war was going on, more than half the Israeli Jews who were polled said that they did not hate the Arabs at all (only eleven per cent hated 'all of them'). The other was that Arabs on the West Bank responded to the war in a pacific way. The bridges across the River Jordan remained open and commerce continued; and guerrilla appeals for industrial sabotage by Arab workers in Israeli-held territory were notably ineffective. The Social Research survey of November 13 recorded that forty per cent of Israeli Jews believed that the loyalty of Arabs in Israel, and their 'identification with the state', had increased during the war. To some extent, this degree of Arab acquiescence was due to the fact that Israel is not an apartheid state; and Arabs had benefited from Israeli government in ways which, politics aside, they had clearly come to recognize.

But the realities after the 1973 war of the oil boycott, Russo-American detente and Kissinger's determination to achieve a compromise solution, ruled out any possibility of holding on to the pre-October ceasefire lines and threw Israel back on the definition of 'secure and recognized boundaries'. Mrs Meir's speech to the Knesset on November 13 – her first since October 23 – reflected this. Predicting a 'struggle over future frontiers and over the conditions of peace', she served warning that Israel

1973

■ Pré-1967

······ 1967 Cease-fire Lines

□ Occupied Territories

▲▲▲▲▲ October 25 1973 Cease-fire Lines

▨ 1973 Egyptian gains

▤ 1973 Israeli gains

Beirut

LEBANON   SYRIA

Damascus

GOLAN HEIGHTS

Haifa   Nazareth

Mediterranean Sea

Tel Aviv

WEST BANK

R. Jordan

Jerusalem

Amman

Gaza

DEAD SEA

Port Said

SUEZ CANAL

Beersheba

ISRAEL

Ismailia

Bitter Lakes

CAIRO

Suez

SINAI

JORDAN

Eilat Aqaba

EGYPT

Gulf of Suez

Gulf of Aqaba

SAUDI ARABIA

Sharm el Sheikh

The shape of Israel as the fighting ceased

At a cost of 2,400 dead, Israel had broken the Arab assault and even gained territory – though with vulnerable defence lines could respond to US pressure only up to a point: 'Anybody who thinks this war taught us that deep and defensible borders have no value in conditions of modern warfare is in error. We did not learn that we must return to the borders of June 4, 1967, which tempt our neighbours to aggression.'

Yet on the same day, the Social Research Institute's poll found that three-quarters of urban Jews were prepared to give up all or nearly all of the land occupied in both wars in exchange for peace – a return, after the wartime drop to fifty per cent, to the pre-October response to the same question. And despite their doubts about Arab sincerity, seventy-three per cent supported the government's decision to sign the ceasefire pact; over half those polled also believed that the Arabs might now be willing at least to enter negotiations. There was a strong feeling that peace-talks, however impermanent the results, were the only option. As one bereaved father told a *Newsweek* reporter: 'We have been living in a fool's paradise since the Six-Day War. . . . We couldn't afford all that boasting and self-confidence. If we have to give up some occupied territory, and come to our senses in other ways, then some good may yet come of all this.'

Diplomatic pressure upon Israel was also becoming more and more intense. During November, eleven African states broke off diplomatic relations, bringing the total number of hostile African states to twenty-eight. Immediately after the war, as General Sharon began giving politically slanted interviews from his active service HQ on the western side of the canal, a joke began to circulate in Tel Aviv: Question: 'Who is the only political leader in Africa sympathetic to the Israeli government?' Answer: 'Arik Sharon – and he's not all that sympathetic.'

Relations with western European states had cooled as their oil reserves diminished, despite strong public support for Israel at non-governmental levels. On the home front, Israel's economy – already beset by inflation before the war – was placed under acute strain by manpower shortages, although the effects were not immediately assessable. Mobilization, affecting the bulk of the Israeli labour force, was cutting building programmes and industrial output. Casualties had disproportionately hit the skilled sector; and side-effects of the war included shortages of civilian transport, sharp reductions in tourism (a major foreign exchange earner) and shortages in the shops.

The inconclusive ending to the war necessarily sharpened debate in Israel on the questions of the likelihood of peace, and the sacrifices its leaders should be prepared to make to obtain it. A captain interviewed on the Syrian ceasefire line shrugged off the impact of the war on his men: I believe that everyone is more convinced now of what he thought before.' But confidence in the political leadership – in Golda Meir as well as Moshe Dayan – was seriously eroded. And an increasing number of people argued that the costs of Israel's present relations with the Arab world were exorbitant. The difficulty was to transmit these feelings into political reality.

Israel is an open democracy, whose citizens express their opinions with striking volatility. But its electoral system is very complex, based on a mixture of corporate institutions and proportional representation. The political set-up is stable to the point of stagnation. Everything militates against change and, as in France, favours the political median. This makes it very hard to articulate new or radical thought in the international field. Any deal with the Arabs would demand a fresh line of approach; and even the task of drawing up a political list of candidates ready to endorse a peace package might prove almost impossible. There was much flexibility among the electorate at the end of the war. But this would not necessarily transmit itself into a working formula for flexible policies.

There were still those who echoed the Likud in its call for 'no concessions'. For all the beating Dayan's reputation had taken, uncertainty about the future exacerbated the desire for territorial security at almost any diplomatic price. One hardline solution advocated during the war had been to administer such a blow to the Arabs that their 'entire military and economic infrastructure', as one contributor to *Davar* put it on October 16, would be permanently crushed. But if there was one thing the October war had made clear, it was that the United States was not prepared to tolerate the possibility of any action of that kind.

The assumption behind such proposals was that 'the real issue today, as it was in 1967, is the determination by Egypt and Syria to destroy Israel'. It was so expressed, in the context of a plea for an 'end to the language of hate and vilification', in a letter published by the *New York Review of Books* on November 15. Signed by the distinguished historian Jacob Talmon and twenty of his colleagues at the Hebrew University, the letter recalled the Arab refusal to negotiate in 1967, and their continuing demand that Israel should make a prior commitment to withdraw from all the occupied territories – a 'gesture' which they did not see as 'morally acceptable or practically feasible'. They appealed for 'a peace process' and 'free negotiation'; but their tone did not suggest strong optimism that these would materialize. The letter probably reflected majority opinion in Israel.

If this argument presupposed perpetual Arab enmity, the other side's was based on something equally difficult to prove. Another of Israel's leading academics, Professor Daniel Amit, published his response a week later. Acknowledging that there had at first been an Arab 'desire for the annihilation of the Jewish state', he asked: 'Is it possible to force such a straitjacket on the interpretation of events for all time to come?' Amit argued that for some years, Arab foreign policy (apart from Syria) had 'related to Israel as Israel' and that 'almost without exception all the aggressive declarations of the Arab states in the past few years have concerned their occupied territories'. Would the war have broken out, 'had the government of Israel declared, before fighting began, that she accepted as a basic element in any agreement the right of the Egyptians and the Syrians to all the territories captured in 1967, and that she recognized the existence of the Palestinians as a party in the Israeli–Arab conflict?' Israel might have 'many reasons for distrusting the Arabs', but what were they in turn to make of Dayan's 'five no's'? Amit closed with a warning. 'There are now clear signs of possible escalation in which the local balance of power will become irrelevant . . . with all the attendant dangers this poses to the very existence of Israel.'

If the Arabs were genuinely willing to coexist with Israel, there was point in the criticism made by a reserve officer back from the front line in an open letter to Mrs Meir published by *Ha'aretz* on November 12. Israel had been wrong, he said, to trust to its strength, within borders 'whose physical solidity is shattered by their doubtful legitimacy'. Dayan's confidence that the *status quo* might last for ten or twenty years had proved unfounded and now, it was argued, that 'the Arabs have overcome the barrier of fear, the Jews must overcome the barrier of trust.'

In certain ways, the Labour party's electoral platform, published after heated argument on November 28, almost explicitly put its trust in the sincerity of Anwar Sadat's desire for peace. It undertook to seek at Geneva 'defensible borders that will ensure Israel's ability to protect herself effectively . . . and which will be based on territorial compromise'. The government had probably not moved far enough to satisfy the Arabs; and the manifesto reaffirmed that Israel could not return to the pre-June 1967 borders which 'invited Arab aggression', nor agree to the creation of a Palestinian state on the West Bank.

The crucial point, however, was that it emphasized its readiness for territorial concessions, in vague terms which allowed as much leeway as possible for untrammelled negotiations, at a moment when opinion in Israel was again beginning to harden. The risk was that if the concessions required of Israel appeared likely before the elections to be too stiff for Israelis to accept, the Labour party's platform would be extremely vulnerable to a Likud attack which played on popular anxieties.

The Arab summit at Algiers published the agreed communique the same day. The summit had given Sadat a mandate to embark on negotiations at Geneva; but it did not give him a free hand when he got there. The communique announced two 'paramount and unchangeable' conditions for any peace agreement. First: 'Evacuation by Israel of the occupied Arab territories and first of all Jerusalem.' Second: 'Re-establishment of full national rights for the Palestinian people.'

The communique strengthened the influence of those in Israel who argued that any agreement was likely to carry almost unacceptable risks – that it would only be a first, sly step towards annihilating the Jewish state. The specific reference to Jerusalem was calculated to evoke a xenophobic response; and the term 're-establishment of full national rights' could be taken as implying full backing for the maximum demands by the Palestinians – particularly as the summit had also endorsed in extravagant terms the creation of a Palestinian government-in-exile.

Israel's choices at the close of the October war were, however formulated, unenviable. Peace negotiations would be slow and complicated. And if the Arabs had felt, in 1967, that they could not negotiate because any agreement would be made under duress, it was now Israel's turn to fear coercion. But the alternative was to continue living in a state of semi-mobilization, awaiting the next round of fighting. And even then, as the war had amply demonstrated, the conduct and outcome of any further fighting would be influenced by factors outside Israeli control – the arms and support of the superpowers.

The first war between Israel and the Arab nations, in 1948, was an almost entirely local conflict. The concept of superpower diplomacy had not yet arisen. The Soviet Union had not yet emerged from the pro-Zionist phase of its Middle Eastern policy, and in any case Russian influence in the area was almost non-existent. In 1956, after many border skirmishes, the Israelis and the Arabs played out a sub-plot in the grotesque drama of Suez: the last attempt by Britain and France to assert the validity of an imperial role which nobody believed in any more.

In 1967, largely by virtue of a pre-emptive strike, Israel maintained the illusion of independence. And indeed in those days, when the technological and economic burdens of war were just that little bit lighter – and when Israel still had other friends and suppliers in the world – the Israeli government could afford to treat its own superpower backer with considerable brashness from time to time. (When an American intelligence ship sailed slightly too near the fighting, and got shot up by the Israeli air force, apologies from Tel Aviv were quite without humility.) But a pre-emptive strike, as Israel discovered, is a difficult weapon to use more than once.

This time, the Arabs gave themselves the illusion of independence by striking first. But then the Soviet Union found that other aspects of its foreign policy, notably the detente with America, were seriously inconvenienced by the intransigence of Arab leaders who refused to accept an early ceasefire. And, as the ability of Egypt and Syria to rearm for a further conflict was very largely dependent upon the acquiescence of the Soviet Union, it was probable that the strings attached to any future arms deliveries would in future be still shorter and more tightly drawn.

Of course, certain and permanent control still eludes the superpowers. None the less, they are the ones who make the conflict possible, who draw up the rules of the game – and whose interests, at the end of the day, are the decisive interests. Logically, of course, this is clear to most of the people in the Middle East. Emotionally, it is perhaps the hardest point of all to accept and act upon. It is not easy to think of one's own compatriots – one's own friends and children – living and dying according to the rules of an international power struggle which is not fully controlled by one's own government. The point was put by Henry Kissinger shortly after the ceasefire, using perhaps more clarity than a professional diplomat would allow himself.

'There is another consideration which I would wish you to take into account', he said, after a long discussion with Mohammed Heikal of *Al Ahram* about the various problems standing in issue between Israel and the Arab nations. 'The consideration is simply this: the United States cannot, either today or tomorrow, allow Soviet arms to achieve a great victory – though it may not be a decisive victory – over American arms. This is a question which has nothing to do with you, nor with Israel either. This is a question which is directly related to the balance of power between the two superpowers.'

In the end the superpowers cannot guarantee a Middle Eastern peace – all they can really guarantee is that each side has, up to a certain point, the capacity to fight. And they do this, as Dr Kissinger frankly said, for reasons which ultimately depend upon the state of their own international rivalry. Clearly, neither of the two superpowers desires a nuclear exchange. Both may be sincere in desiring an end to the 'brushfire' wars around the world – if only because any one of them could, as October 1973 showed, lead perilously near to superpower confrontation.

But the evidence suggests that the superpowers, whatever their desire for peace, will continue to underwrite even the most extensive of conflicts by proxy, rather than suffer damage to their own international prestige and influence – so long as minor nations continue to play their part in the system. The question, in the aftermath of the war of October 1973, is whether the stakes still seem worthwhile to Israel and the Arab states.

Two features characterised the war: massive conventional tank battles, the biggest since World War II, and the use of missiles, the first time they have played a dominant part in a major conflict. There is no doubt that in tank-to-tank confrontations, the Israelis more than held their own, despite being outnumbered, and the next few pages analyse why. Yet, for a long time, Israel's traditional virtuosity with armour and air support was severely limited by the Arab missile arsenal, described in the second appendix.

THE TANK BATTLE: The numerical balance as the fighting began

According to estimates published shortly before the war, the Egyptians began with 1,650 Russian T-54 and T-55 tanks (the two marques differ only in small details) designed in the mid-Fifties, plus about 100 of the main modern Russian battle tank, the T-62. The Syrians had about 1,100 T-54/55s and an unknown number of T-62s. (Between them they also had some 300 Second World War vintage T-34s,

though these seem mostly to have been dug into static positions as supplementary artillery). As the war progressed, Iraq committed up to 250 of its T-54/55s, and Jordan about 100 British-made Centurions. So the total effective Arab commitment was well over 3,000 tanks.

The Israelis had about 1,700 tanks at the start of the war, about half of them Centurions and the remainder mostly American Patton M48s (fifties vintage, but mostly late models with 105mm guns) with some up-to-date M-60s. They also used in a battle-tank role about 150 Super Shermans (a World War II American veteran which the Israelis themselves had upgraded by adding a large 105mm French gun) and some remodelled Russian T-54/55s which they had captured from the Egyptians in the Six-Day War and equipped with British-made 105mm guns.

These figures, based on estimates by the London-based Institute of Strategic studies, dated September 1973 and updated by US Pentagon estimates, do not include tanks delivered from the US and the Soviet Union during the war. These deliveries are believed to have further increased the numerical balance in favour of the Arab countries, particularly Syria. But how effective the additional arms shipments were depended to some extent on the availability of highly-trained crews and maintenance teams, which were in short supply on both sides, but particularly so in the Arab armies.

The Arabs' numerical advantage must also be weighed — as we shall see on the following pages — by examining the relative effectiveness of the tanks' armaments, and exploring how well the different types of tanks are adapted to fighting in hot desert terrain.

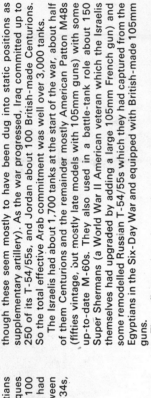

ISRAELI

American
Sherman
(M4A3E8)
with French
105 mm gun
Total : 150

ARAB

British
Centurion
with
standard
105 mm gun
Total : 850

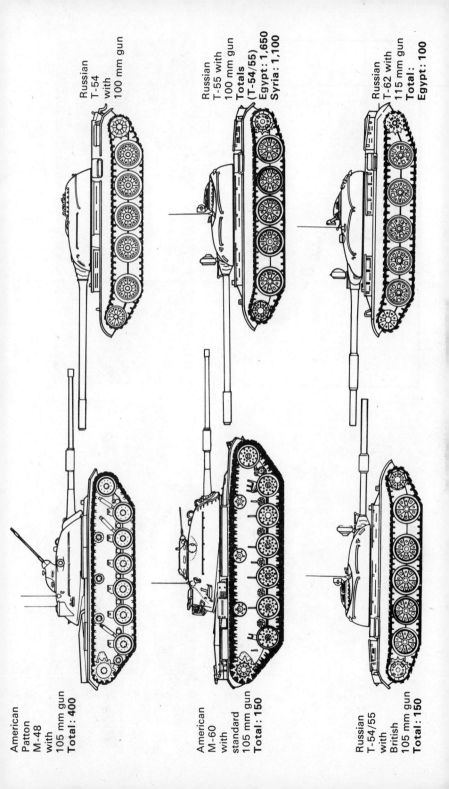

American
Patton
M-48
with
105 mm gun
Total: 400

Russian
T-54
with
100 mm gun

American
M-60
with
standard
105 mm gun
Total: 150

Russian
T-55 with
100 mm gun
Totals
(T-54/55)
Egypt: 1,650
Syria: 1,100

Russian
T-54/55
with
British
105 mm gun
Total: 150

Russian
T-62 with
115 mm gun
Total:
Egypt: 100

THE TANK BATTLE: The ammunition

Loading up a Centurion tank in Golan. The ammunition is 105 mm APDS (armour-piercing discarding-sabot). The pointed tip of its thin penetrating bolt of hard heavy metal is clearly visible.

First published picture of the latest Russian 115 mm ammunition inside a captured Syrian T-62. The long thin rounds are APFSDS (see below) which fly and penetrate like a massive arrow.

During a brief pause from battle near the Golan front: a crew member of an Israeli M-48 sits on his tank holding a 105 mm HEAT (high-explosive anti-tank) shell, as used in NATO tanks.

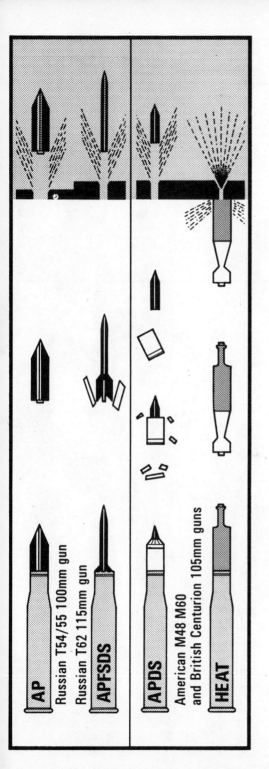

AP
Russian T54/55 100mm gun

APFSDS
Russian T62 115mm gun

APDS
American M48 M60
and British Centurion 105mm guns

HEAT

The diagram shows how different types of ammunition work. The vast majority of Arab tanks (Russian T-54/55s) have only simple AP (armour-piercing) ammunition – a solid, full-calibre shot of steel. Because there is no way of concentrating its energy, the penetration through armour plate is only half that of other types. However, the few modern Russian T-62s used by the Arabs did have the more sophisticated APFSDS (armour-piercing fin-stabilized discarding-sabot) ammunition. As this leaves the smooth 115 mm barrel, the 'sabot' (a sort of light-weight packing) is stripped off by air resistance to reveal a long thin 'arrow' of hard, heavy metal. Almost all the energy from the gun is thus concentrated on to a smaller diameter, greatly increasing penetration. APDS (armour-piercing discarding-sabot) used by the Israelis, works

on a similar principle. Stability in flight, however, depends on the spin imparted by the gun's rifled barrel, rather than on fins, so the central bolt cannot be quite so thin. At long range there is little to choose between the two kinds of stabilization, since the drag from fins slows down the Russian shot.

The Israelis' American tanks also use HEAT (high-explosive anti-tank) shells, which employ a quite different idea. The shells are hollow and contain high explosive. When this detonates at first contact with the target, it 'implodes' on to a cone of copper inside the shell. The cone is shaped in such a way that it turns into a thin jet of molten copper, moving at huge velocity, which literally hoses its way through the armour plate. HEAT charges are also used in slow-moving anti-tank missiles.

THE TANK BATTLE: Which tanks were best suited to the desert terrain?

Above is a tank commander's eye view of the classic desert terrain of the big Sinai armoured battles (the smoke rising on the horizon is from the barrage on the canal). Fighting on these rolling sand dunes requires tanks with special characteristics, illustrated on this and the next two pages. There is no doubt that the British and American tanks – bred partly from the experience of the North African campaigns in World War II – are better adapted to desert fighting than Russian tanks, conceived for the different vistas, climate and types of cover of Europe.

Range (see right) is crucially important in desert fighting. Apart from the characteristics of their different types of ammunition, the Russian tanks rely purely on visual judgment for range-finding. The American tanks, by contrast, have a sophisticated device of optical prisms for estimating range, while the British Centurions have a neat and simple system of zeroing-in with tracer bullets from a range-finding machine-gun before the big round is fired (this system also corrects for side-winds). The net result is a gain of up to half a mile at long range, for comparable accuracy.

Desert heat is another factor. Russian tanks tend to overheat in the desert, and are often used with their engine louvres vulnerably open. But the main effect is the subjective one on the crew, who are cramped into a smaller, hotter space in Russian tanks (see scale drawing below). The consequent fatigue can critically affect firing accuracy and other technical functions.

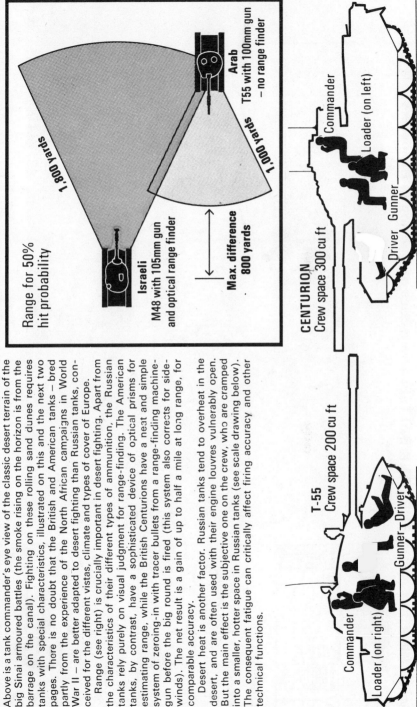

Range for 50% hit probability

1,800 yards

1,000 yards

Israeli
M48 with 105mm gun
and optical range finder

Arab
T55 with 100mm gun
– no range finder

Max. difference
800 yards

CENTURION
Crew space 300 cu ft

Commander

Loader (on left)

Driver   Gunner

T-55
Crew space 200 cu ft

Gunner—Driver

Commander

Loader (on right)

THE TANK BATTLE: The tactics of fighting in the desert

In a fold in the Sinai sand dunes: an Israeli Super-Sherman in 'hull-down' position.

American M48

8' 7"

Russian T55

7' 11"

British Centurion

8' 7"

Russian tanks are designed with low, rounded profiles to present the minimum target to enemy guns. The scale drawings (above left) show the contrast in height between the T-54/55 and the larger Western tanks. This Russian geometry involves a crucial disadvantage, particularly in desert terrain.

Because of its low turret, the Russian gun can depress only four degrees compared with ten degrees in its Western counterparts. The diagrams (left) show the result. Tank commanders like to keep 'hull-down' as long as possible (ie with the tank hull out of enemy view). As can be seen, a Russian tank with its limited gun depression becomes much more exposed when it moves up a sand dune to firing position.

Such considerations gave the Israelis a marked advantage in tank-to-tank confrontations. But the Arabs nearly tilted the tank battle – and the air battle – the other way with their Russian missiles. The anti-tank weapons are illustrated at the end of the next section on the missile war.

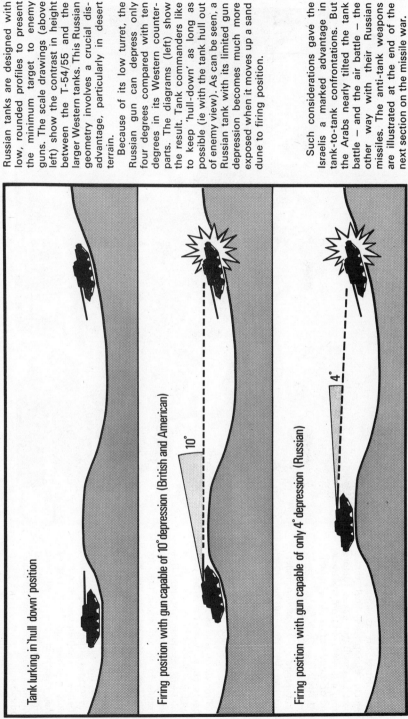

Tank lurking in 'hull down' position

Firing position with gun capable of 10° depression (British and American)

10°

Firing position with gun capable of only 4° depression (Russian)

4°

THE MISSILE WAR: The Arabs' arsenal of Russian surface-to-air missiles

On the right is a SAM-3 missile (NATO code-name Goa) captured intact on its transporting vehicle during the final thrust west of the Bitter Lakes (before firing it is removed from the truck and operated from a fixed launching site).

SAM-3 is 22 feet long, has a slant range of seventeen miles, and can be used against low-flying aircraft. It is controlled from the ground by a radar system which tracks both missile and target and calculates the missile's path.

Propulsion is in two stages. The rear section, with its large rectangular stabilization fins, is a solid-fuel booster rocket. This separates after launch, leaving the missile to fly on liquid fuel, its direction controlled by the forward 'canard' fins and by the small rear fins just behind the V-shaped main wings.

For the Arabs, the main disadvantages of SAM-3 and SAM-2 (below) were their relative immobility and the fact that most of their electronic secrets had been cracked by the Americans in Vietnam, making counter-measures possible.

Above is a SAM-2 launching site overrun by the Israeli attack north of Suez city. SAM-2 (NATO code-name Guideline) is used mainly against high-flying aircraft (up to 50,000 feet). Its propulsion and control are similar to the SAM-3 (above) but it is readily distinguishable by its greater length (35 feet 6 inches) and by the tapered stabilization fins on its solid-fuel booster stage. Like SAM-3 it has ground-command radar guidance, making it easier to devise electronic countermeasures to protect over-flying aircraft.

SAM-6 (left), used in combat for the first time, was the missile that gave the Israeli pilots most trouble. It is mounted on a mobile launcher, with an accompanying radar vehicle, making fixing sites unnecessary. Its length has been kept to only 19 feet by the ingenious device of using the casing of its solid fuel booster rocket to act as the combustion chamber for its ram-jet second stage. Its guidance system (see next page) is more difficult to counter than SAM-2 and SAM-3.

THE MISSILE WAR: SAM-6 in operation, and how it extended the missile screen

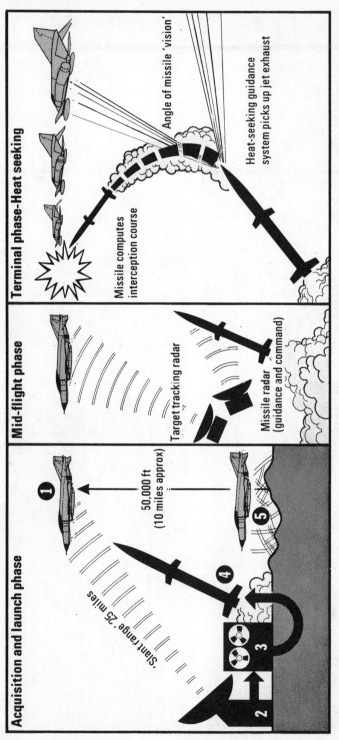

Acquisition and launch phase

50,000 ft (10 miles approx)

'Slant range' 25 miles

Mid-flight phase

Target tracking radar

Missile radar (guidance and command)

Terminal phase-Heat seeking

Missile computes interception course

Angle of missile 'vision'

Heat-seeking guidance system picks up jet exhaust

Above is a schematic diagram of the two-phase guidance system of SAM-6. The aircraft (1) is detected by the targeting radar (2) with its associated computer (3) which calculates the launching instructions for the missile (4). Another ground radar tracks the missile in mid-flight and guides it towards target. In the terminal phase, the missile takes over the guidance itself, using a heat-seeking device which directs it towards the infra-red radiation from the plane's jet exhaust. SAM-6 is also used against low-flying aircraft (5), though its range is then reduced to 15 miles and acquisition is more difficult because of radar 'clutter' from the ground.

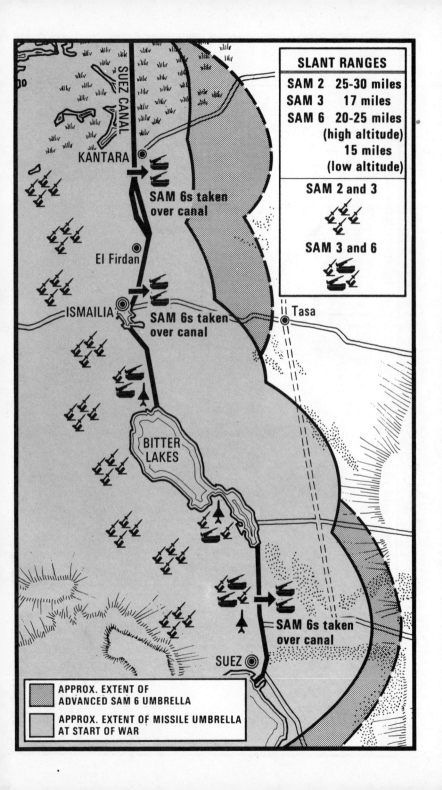

SLANT RANGES

SAM 2   25-30 miles
SAM 3   17 miles
SAM 6   20-25 miles
         (high altitude)
         15 miles
         (low altitude)

SAM 2 and 3

SAM 3 and 6

SUEZ CANAL

KANTARA

SAM 6s taken
over canal

El Firdan

ISMAILIA

SAM 6s taken
over canal

Tasa

BITTER
LAKES

SAM 6s taken
over canal

SUEZ

APPROX. EXTENT OF
ADVANCED SAM 6 UMBRELLA

APPROX. EXTENT OF MISSILE UMBRELLA
AT START OF WAR

THE MISSILE WAR: The counter-measures tried by Israeli pilots . . .

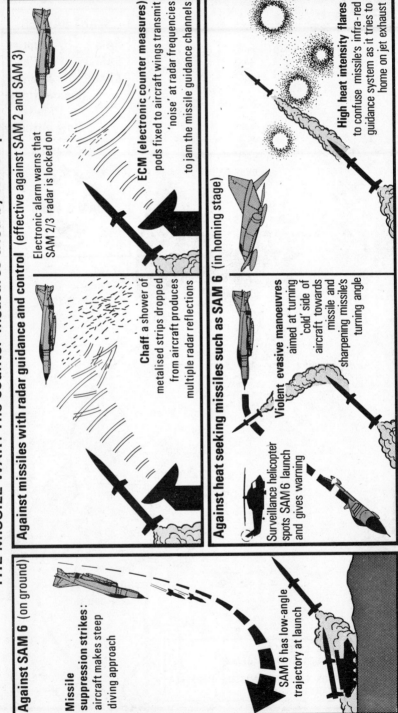

Against SAM 6 (on ground)

Missile suppression strikes: aircraft makes steep diving approach

SAM 6 has low-angle trajectory at launch

Against missiles with radar guidance and control (effective against SAM 2 and SAM 3)

Electronic alarm warns that SAM 2/3 radar is locked on

ECM (electronic counter measures) pods fixed to aircraft wings transmit 'noise' at radar frequencies to jam the missile guidance channels

Chaff a shower of metalised strips dropped from aircraft produces multiple radar reflections

Against heat seeking missiles such as SAM 6 (in homing stage)

High heat intensity flares to confuse missile's infra-red guidance system as it tries to home on jet exhaust

Violent evasive manoeuvres aimed at turning 'cold' side of aircraft towards missile and sharpening missile's turning angle

Surveillance helicopter spots SAM 6 launch and gives warning

Most of the electronic secrets of SAM-2 and SAM-3 were known before the war. In Vietnam, the Americans had developed ECMs (electronic counter-measures) consisting of a cockpit alarm (nicknamed 'Sam-song') to warn when missile radar is locked on, and underwing pods which transmit rival signals to jam the radar guidance. Both these were of little effect against the new SAM-6, even in its mid-flight radar-guided phase, because its guidance frequencies were unknown (the problem was complicated because SAM-6 uses at least four different frequency bands). The Israelis were reduced to using the World War II device of dropping showers of 'chaff' to blur radar acquisition – although for maximum effect even this method requires knowledge of the frequencies, since the length of the pieces of chaff should ideally be a multiple of the radar wavelength.

In SAM-6's heat-seeking homing phase, no such electronic response was possible. There were Israeli attempts to confuse infra-red sensing by dropping decoy flares. Otherwise all that could be done was to try violent evasive tactics. One high-g manoeuvre, which pilots have labelled the 'split-S' involves two aircraft. The lead plane dives sharply into and across the missile's approach, as in the diagram, while the following plane dives across the first plane's vapour trail. It sometimes worked: but very often the dive took the planes into range of the Arabs' highly efficient Russian ZSU-23 radar controlled anti-aircraft guns, where they got chewed up by flak. There were many attempts at direct suppression strikes against the mobile SAM-6 launchers (see diagram) though these were obviously highly risky.

There is some evidence that towards the end of the war, the Russian technicians were producing a new generation of counter-counter-measures (see right). The use of decoy flares was fairly easily nullified by fitting filters to distinguish between the flares and the jet engines. And although satellite surveillance may have produced some knowledge of SAM-6's operating frequencies, there was the possibility of using increased radar power and switching from frequency to frequency to confuse jamming devices.

. . . and Arab counter-counter-measures

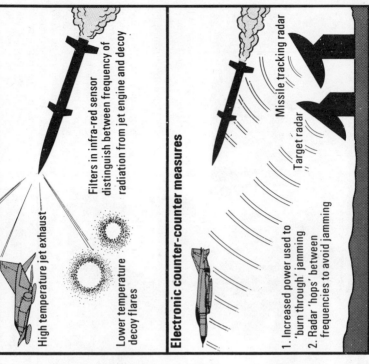

Heat seeking counter-counter measures

High temperature jet exhaust

Filters in infra-red sensor distinguish between frequency of radiation from jet engine and decoy

Lower temperature decoy flares

Electronic counter-counter measures

Missile tracking radar

Target radar

1. Increased power used to 'burn through' jamming
2. Radar 'hops' between frequencies to avoid jamming

THE MISSILE WAR: The infantry missiles that tilted the tank battles

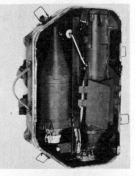

Sagger, the Russian wire-guided 'suitcase missile' that greatly embarrassed Israeli tanks. It can be carried by a single infantryman in a case that converts into a launching platform. On firing (left) the missile flies like a fast model aircraft paying out fine electrical wires behind attached to the joystick guidance assembly (above right). It has a bright tail light for identification, which the operator tracks visually on to target with his joystick. Its armour-piercing charge works on the HEAT principle. As well as its infantry use Sagger can also be fired from a special armoured vehicle. The one in the picture (below left) was captured intact by the Israelis.

Right: the main problem of controlling Sagger is in 'gathering' it on to the line of the target after launching it from a remote position. This usually takes a quarter of a mile. Once on target, nerve rather than skill is needed.

Approx ¼ mile to 'gather' missile on line of target

Joystick with simple sight

Bright tail light for keeping visual track of missile

Launcher

SAGGER – maximum range 1 mile

Below: the American 'second generation' wire-guided missile, Tow, which the Israelis put into action later in the war. It is more sophisticated than Sagger, with automated gathering and steering, but more cumbersome and expensive. The operator merely has to hold the cross-wires of his sight on the target, and the computer does the rest. Because less skill is required it is likely to be more effective in the heat of battle. Wire-guided missiles typically take 10 seconds to reach target, which can seem a long time when the operator is exposed to fire.

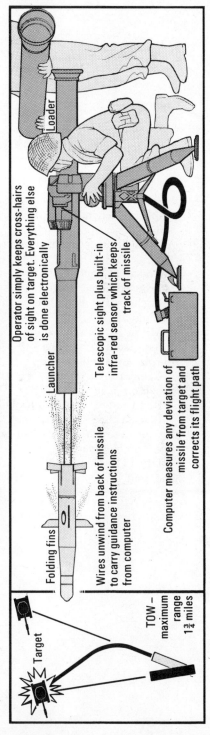

Operator simply keeps cross-hairs of sight on target. Everything else is done electronically

Telescopic sight plus built-in infra-red sensor which keeps track of missile

Loader

Launcher

Folding fins

Wires unwind from back of missile to carry guidance instructions from computer

Computer measures any deviation of missile from target and corrects its flight path

Target

TOW – maximum range 1¼ miles

Picture Acknowledgments

Most of the photographs in this book are by *Sunday Times* photographers, Kelvin Brodie, Frank Herrmann, Bryan Wharton and Sally Soames.
Additional photographs were provided by:

Romano Cagnoni (Pages 90–1, 138–9 and 218)
Leonard Freed (Page 144)
Michel Astel Bamahane (The pictures of Sagger on pages 254 and 255)
Micha Bar-Am, Magnum (Pages 107, 172 and 175)
Associated Press (Pages 18–19, 119 and the picture of General Elazar on page 96)
Camera Press (Pages 4, 41, 71, 169 and the picture of General Shazli on page 96)
Rex Features and Jacques Bulor (Page 1)
Rex Features and Sipapress, Paris (Pages 110, 221, 225, 248, the picture of Moshe Dayan on page 96, and the picture of a SAM-2 on page 249)
UPI (The photograph on the title page and pages 56, 57, 60–1 and 106)